Praise for *Gym Launch Secrets*

Thanks to Gym Launch Secrets, we went from losing money (making $3K monthly and spending $8K) and were 3 weeks from closing our doors to grossing over $600K within 18 months and have built a team of 8. In turn, saving our entire livelihood and renewing our passion to help people again! Thank you, Alex!

— **Chris Barnett | Dream Body Fitness | Boise, Idaho**

If you read long enough, you will find my story in this book. When I met Alex, I was less than a month away from going out of business and buying food for my kids with the change from my car. Gym Launch isn't a marketing company, it's not a coaching program, it's not even motivation. It's a freaking lottery ticket that you can continue to cash in over and over again with the skills that Alex and his team teach you.

— **Josh Ponton | Renegade Boot Camps | Plano, Texas**

The information in this book has helped us double our revenue, make a second location profitable the very first month we opened, and most important, build a business not a job! It is priceless information.

— **Mike and Dori Berean | Krav Maga Great Lakes | Brighton, Michigan**

Thanks to the marketing and retention information Alex wrote here, we more than doubled our membership and nearly tripled our revenue in the first 6 months using his systems! This is seriously the most comprehensive guide to running a gym I've ever seen!

— Ryan Carow |
Vinco Fitness Systems LLC |
Little Chute, Wisconsin

This is the most informative and applicable text I've read in the last 15 years. If you operate in the fitness space, then you need to read this book.

— Trevor Kashey | TKN |
Hilliard, Ohio

Alex Hormozi's systems are like a money-making machine. Use them to make 10X profit.

— Monika Arora |
Women Rock Center |
Calgary, Alberta, Canada

Since working with Alex, I was able to cut my attrition in half by just implementing a few of his tactics. Gym Launch and his team are simply the best and actually care about your success. If you want to save thousands and make thousands, read this book.

— Billy Whitehead |
Quakertown Fitbody Boot Camp |
Quakertown, Pennsylvania

With the simple step-by-step action plan Alex has laid out here in his manifesto, even a complete numbskull with zero business experience couldn't screw it up. These are the cheat codes to building an insanely profitable 7-figure-producing gym in months, not decades.

— **Dallas James Wicker |
The Transformation Center |
Santa Rosa, California**

Thanks to Gym Launch Secrets from taking me from being $45K in debt and not knowing how to pay my bills as a personal training studio to making a quarter million dollars in 11 months by using these step-by-step processes! Blessed.

— **Mel Batterman |
AMP Personal Fitness LLC |
Las Vegas, Nevada**

Because of Gym Launch Secrets and Alex Hormozi, I was able to save my gym from eviction. I followed his plan, gained 53 new clients, and generated $34,277 in revenue in just 9 days!!! I paid my landlord in full and have retained 38 of those clients on recurring EFT to this day !! My gym would be closed today if not for his help! It is life-changing.

— **Robyn Thrasher |
Robyn Thrasher Fitness |
Tampa, Florida**

I found Gym Launch the week after I lost 50 members to one of my trainers that opened a gym a mile away. I had 75 members, and my EFT didn't even cover rent. I got on my call [with

Alex] and I was skeptical but signed up, because I needed this to work. That was October 1, 2017. By January 1, 2018, our EFT was at 170 members. Built the systems, trusted the process, and worked our butts off, but we did it. We replaced all the list members and added 25 more on top of it. Saved my gym.

— Robert Walter |
Probodies Fitness Pearland |
Pearland, Texas

Before Gym Launch, I was struggling to manage two locations and a team of 8. Alex helped me to structure my business the way it should be and helped me to win my freedom back! The added revenue made from this program has been a game-changer for not only myself but also my family, my staff, and my clients!

— Matt Priess |
North Lincoln Fitbody Bootcamp |
North Lincoln, Nebraska

Inside these pages is my story and countless others. I'll even bet that within a few pages you see yourself too. The fitness industry is full of impassioned and selfless devotees to help all who are just as hungry and broke. Gym Launch won't just save your company, it will save you. Like it did for me. And that's how your legacy is built. This isn't a marketing book—it will teach you how to get your fire back so you can stay in this game longer and leave a bigger impact. It doesn't hurt that it took us from a $15K company to a profitable 6-figure company either.

— Anthony Ronchi |
Crossfit Paradigm Performance |
Rochester, New York

Alex Hormozi taught me how break my personal beliefs about how successful a microgym can be and how quickly it can be achieved, given the proper systems. Those systems—like client-financed acquisition, high-level sales training, and rock-solid retention strategies—were my secret weapons to scaling quickly, which has taken my gym from $626K to $1.3 million (doubling our size) in only 12 months. Thank you, Alex.

— **Joey Huber | Body By Design | Waukesha, Wisconsin**

I had no clue how to run a gym. When I started with Alex, I was training a few people in my garage gym, and two weeks later, we were overwhelmed and had to move into a bigger location. I've learned so much, from how to run ads on social media to increasing cash flow. But one of the best strategies, which made a huge difference, is client retention—the psychology he teaches on creating value in your program, which develops a culture where clients never want to go anywhere else. That information alone was priceless. There's no way I would have figured this stuff out on my own.

— **Vickie Lencrerot Clark | The Weight Loss Connection Transformation Center | Stone Mountain, Georgia**

Thanks to Gym Launch, Alex and Leila's team, I have become a SUCCESSFUL gym owner. With all the successful, tested systems in Gym Launch, I now have what every business owner dreams of—FREEDOM. I now have the freedom to spend time with my wife and kids. I have financial stability for the first time with my business, my family, and their future.

Thank you, Alex Hormozi, Leila Hormozi, and the entire Gym Launch Staff.

— **Mikey Shields | Get Fit NM | Albuquerque, New Mexico**

Thanks to Gym Launch Secrets, we went from losing money on marketing and being in the red for 3 months straight. Everything we threw at Facebook never gave us a return. Our team was running the show. Every day we felt exhausted, desperate, and hopeless. I considered getting a [second] job in order to support the gym. Since working with Alex, we went from making $39K a month to doing our best month at $100K. We focus 100% on building our systems, training our team, and finding ways to optimize our incredible facility. We are no longer business operators, we are business owners. Thank you, Alex, for showing us what is possible and helping us change lives in our community.

— **Trami Thi | Twice Bitten CrossFit | Oklahoma City, Oklahoma**

Gym Launch Secrets saved our gym. Before Gym Launch, we were overworked, underpaid, and had no vision of how the gym was going to support our future. But Gym Launch Secrets enabled us to compete head-to-head with franchise gyms that have deep marketing pockets.

We went from barely paying the bills to doubling our revenue in less than a calendar year. We now have a thriving gym, a thriving gym community, and a business that fully supports our family. Alex and his business strategies have completely shaken up the microgym industry. The business tactics in this book will create a future that puts you in control of a prosperous and thriving gym.

— Brian Sweeney | Raise The Bar Strength & Conditioning | Manassas, Virginia

Alex helped me triple my EFT in less than 9 months, after I couldn't break the $10K mark for over a year. I also went from hating my business to loving what I do again.

— Chris Schenck | Tribird Personal Training | Mesa, Arizona

Using Alex's mastermind strategies, I went from an eviction notice on my door to trying to buy my building! I quadrupled my EFT in 4 months and now sleep, spend time with my kids, and manage a team of 5 while working *on* my business and not *in* it!

— Claire Pearson Raw | Raw Fitness | Lafayette, Colorado

Thanks to Gym Launch, we went from not knowing if we were going to be able to afford our next month's lease payment to making $16K in 3 weeks! Simply amazing. All you have to do is follow the steps and put in the work, and it works for you!! Thank you so much, Alex. You are truly a lifesaver.

— Alexis Mokuahi-Reyes | Fusion Health & Fit Training Center | Atascadero, California

Thanks to Gym Launch Secrets, I was able to give every client amazing results, and paid myself for the first time after owning a gym for 5 years. Now my business runs like clockwork. I can go away and come back and my revenue has gone up! Joining Gym Launch was the best decision I ever made!

— Saul Carter | Turlock Fit Body Boot Camp |
Turlock, California

Alex and Gym Launch have completely transformed my business from good to top-notch! Huge thanks to them for the step-by-step process!

— Taylor Nelson |
Train Smart Health And Fitness Center |
Pocatello, Idaho

Thanks to Gym Launch, I was able to take my gym from $3K a month in revenue and failing to $25K–$30K per month, profiting and growing every month, in just 12 months. Not to mention, I went from working 16-hour days and taking multiple part-time jobs to pay my bills to training zero classes, hiring a team of 4, and paying myself more than I could have imagined making as a gym owner.

— Jay Duquette | MVNU Training |
Shrewsbury, Massachusetts

When I reached out to Gym Launch, I was desperate. I had a $9,500 bill I couldn't pay, with only $500 left in my business bank account. I told the Gym Launch guy that they could debit payment one, but if he didn't help me get new business in the next 7 days, there wouldn't be any money to take payment two. Two months later, I had sold 82 challenges at $499 each and doubled my weekly EFT. Saved my business, saved my home from being sold. Forever grateful.

— Ben Hawksworth | TNT Group Training | Perth, West Australia

I'm a single mom of two boys who wasn't sure we would be able to keep the roof over our heads. Enter Gym Launch, where I went from borrowing money to paying rent and payroll, to 10x my ROI in literally 6 months, and now stacking cash in the bank! If Alex is talking, my credit card is out and ready to buy it! Applying everything he and this group have taught me has bought me freedom I would not have had, and I have barely touched the surface. It's amazing to find a coaching program that promises to overdeliver and then overdelivers on overdelivering. If you don't buy this book, you hate money. It's that simple.

— Kathe Shandera Downs | Gretna Fit Body Boot Camp | Gretna, Nebraska

Being a great trainer doesn't mean that you're going to have a great fitness business. I could go on and on about the systems, sales tactics, marketing plays, and other key areas Alex taught me, but how about I tell you what you need to hear. Before working with Alex, I was the sole employee at my gym, working 16 hours a day, never spent time with my son, had NO leads, no idea how to actually market successfully, and as a result, hadn't made rent in the gym in 2 months AND was on the brink of bankruptcy. After just 1 month of working with Alex, monthly recurring revenue jumped to $25K.

Now we have 3 full-time employees and systems are in place so the gym RUNS ITSELF. I work 10 hours a week tops, and I have all the time in the world to spend with my son, AND WE'RE STILL GROWING!!

— Dan Drynan | Orchard City Athletics | Kelowna, British Columbia, Canada

We were hobbyist gym owners looking for a way to get out of our "real jobs" and do what we loved for a living. Within 4 months of working with Alex, Leila, and their staff, we were both out of the rat race and had two gyms, and we haven't really looked back since. If you already own a gym, this will revolutionize how you run it and how much money you make, which will let you help the most people. If you don't own a gym yet, do what we did for our second location and start from scratch using everything they provide.

— Dominic Parker | Impact Athletics | Uncasville, Connecticut

Before Gym Launch, I was losing money, relying on marketing companies to acquire leads (poorly), and I was barely paying my expenses. In less than 2 months with Gym Launch, I had increased my revenue by 4x. I now know how to run my own marketing and acquire leads profitably.

— Jen Shifflett | Myrtle Beach Fit Body Boot Camp | Myrtle Beach, South Carolina

Using the tools that Gym Launch provided, we have grown our recurring memberships, learned to provide a better experience to our customers, and learned how to profitably acquire clients. Added bonus: our new clients are much higher quality! They see more value in what we offer and are far less demanding than many of our original clients.

— Jason Caryl | Elite Functional Fitness | Yakima, Washington

When we found Gym Launch, we were about to close our doors. Within 2 months, we made $40K in a town of 1,800 people. But most importantly, my husband and I went from working 15-hour days to hiring a full staff and pulling ourselves out of the day-to-day. This is absolute GOLD, even in the smallest areas.

— Shelby Snodgrass | 719 Fitness Center | Neligh, Nebraska

I had what I thought was a pretty successful fitness business with 350 members and 5 employees, but when I joined Gym Launch, I started to realize I was actually on a sinking ship. My attrition was high, my revenue was relatively low, and I wasn't setting the bar high enough for my team. Alex gave me specific systems to drop my attrition in half, increase my prices dramatically, adding an instant $20K a month to my revenue, and leadership strategies as well as self-improvement to set the bar higher than I ever imagined. So just 2 months in, all of this has happened, and I know in a year from now, I will be blown away knowing that I am on my way to truly building a legacy and empire!

— Sean Van Horn | Freight House Fitness | Kansas City, Missouri

Thanks to Gym Launch, I was able to move my gym from my garage to a huge waterfront location downtown! This has changed the game for me. I am living my dream.

> — Aaron Dawson | Hustle Athletic Training | Summerside, Prince Edward Island, Canada

Best thing about Gym Launch for me—not just having 200+ more clients my first year, but also the campaigns designed to deliver superior customer service to keep them. I am proud of my gym and what we have created. None of it would have been possible without Alex and Leila and the amazing team they have at Gym Launch.

> — **John Rudolf** | Iron Empire 24 Hour Elite Fitness | Dover, New Hampshire

Gym Launch Secrets has not only given us the tools to launch proper marketing advertisements but also gave us specific steps to follow to ensure the leads would get in front of us so we could sell them on memberships and challenges. The tech group at GL is top-notch and always available to help when we are in need of support. Though the systems are great, I have personally grown as an owner by engaging and befriending other gym owners around the country. From Texas to Canada to Europe to California, the bonds I've made are true and there is no competition. If a GL rep isn't available, I know I can count on the gym owner community to assist where help is needed. Thanks, Alex Hormozi, for always putting out a great product and constantly producing new material.

> — Steve Morici | Be1ST Fitness | Westbury, New York

Alex's program has changed my life from a 100-hour+ work week, scraping in £2–£3K a month, struggling to make bills, undeserving clients, and a lack of time, energy, and resources. I almost quit, got a "normal" job, but I wanted to change lives through fitness. With no idea how to run a fitness business, Alex showed me how. Now I can serve my clients at the highest level and give them the results they deserve. I can now spend time with my two-year-old son. I've made over £140K, opened a bigger location, and I still have only scratched the surface of his trainings. I can't thank him enough.

— **Chris Charlton | Boss Fitness | Durham, UK**

Using the tools and tactics taught by Alex not only saved my gym but in the first year, more than doubled my gross monthly revenue. The tools that are shared with you are not a one-and-done system. These tools help you become a better gym owner. This book will be invaluable to any business owner.

— **William Davis | Steel Mill Fleming Island | Fleming Island, Florida**

We had our gym for just over 3 years prior to joining Gym Launch and Legacy. We had about $22K in EFT and 8 people working for us. I rarely took time off, let alone days off, and felt very lost. With Alex and Leila's knowledge and support, we were not only able to hire but also to develop a full staff of nearly 20 so that we now have profit and also time off. I no longer coach, I have 2 part-time admins, and we love what we do again! Now we are at $28K EFT with front-end sales growing more than ever! We have been able to take a dream honeymoon, save cash toward a home, and feel positive for our future! They have taught me how to sell, how to lead, and how to own and operate a business that will make a massive impact on the community. What else could someone ask for?

— Brandy Martin | Feed Your Soul Fitness | Denver, Colorado

Too many great people and great professionals struggle to achieve a great business. The gym owner is no exception to this phenomenon! More likely than not, it is merely because what it takes to attain a business that works for you lives beyond sets, reps, nutrition, etc. Alex and his TEAM provide those necessary constituents so that you can acquire an optimal business model to both maximize profits and your purpose of helping others.

— Michael Ranfone | Ranfone Training Systems | Hamden, Connecticut

Before I met Alex, we were almost at rock bottom with expenses from a big move,. Since Alex, we have been able to bring in over $2 million in revenue. Being a very well-known strength coach, I figured people should come to me for my services, and Alex taught me how to actually get them to come through my door. We went from $20K/month in revenue to over $140K/mo. Forever grateful.

— Ryan Karas | Vigor Performance | Loveland, Colorado

Alex straight-up saved me from burnout. After 7 years in business, I was working a split shift 5x/week plus Saturday mornings, coaching every session, cleaning the gym on off-hours, barely paying bills. (In fact, the month I joined Gym Launch was the first time that I'd emailed my landlord saying, "I can't pay rent.") A year later, I doubled my number of clients and 3xed my gross revenue (thanks to raising rates), and I now have a staff of 5 who handle the day-to-day. To say this is a game-changer is an understatement—this is a LIFE-changer!

— **Paul Lyngso | Experity Functional Strength | Burr Ridge, Illinois**

Life-changing! I had been working a full-time job along with my gym full-time. We were making little to no income and had little time for family. Enter Gym Launch Secrets… We have grown 6x in the last year, I left my full-time job, my passion for helping my customers has grown, and most importantly, I have freedom and time to be with my loved ones. Forever thankful.

— **Josh Lynch | Ignite Training Facility | Salem, Virginia**

I had been training people for over 10 years and essentially was a one-man show. EVERY aspect of my business (from writing programs and training clients to cleaning bathrooms and taking out the trash) was dependent on my presence. Within a year of joining Gym Launch, we were able to grow to a team of 6 trainers and coaches AND 5x our gym's book of business. IN JUST ONE YEAR. These systems not only drastically transformed our business, but our quality of life as well. We will be forever grateful. Thank you, Alex!

— **Shawn Carlson | BodyFit Personal Training & Nutrition | Boise, Idaho**

For 8 years, we struggled to "outwork" our problems and hoped that our community and high-quality coaching would save us. Since meeting Alex and implementing his step-by-step methods, we are finally armed with the weapons and tools necessary not only to generate tons of cash and new clients, but also to fulfill our service to a level previously not possible. Thanks to Alex, I now have a solid understanding of the steps that I can take to achieve long-term, stable prosperity for myself, my community, and my family. Thank you, Alex Hormozi!!

— **Jason Skeesick | Bucktown CrossFit | Chicago, Illinois**

Alex and Gym Launch Secrets have helped me systemize my lead gen and sales systems across my 3 locations and have given me the freedom to manage them from anywhere. Currently finishing a 3-week tropical holiday while my studios generate revenue and deliver great service. Alex and Leila are genuine and care about their clients' success. I'm super happy to be a Gym Lord. :)

— **James Tosoff | Kickboxing Victoria | Victoria, British Columbia, Canada**

We'd done pretty well before Gym Launch, had built up to 5 centers and had hit a million-dollar facility, but all the growth had left us cash poor, we weren't opening effectively, and quality was starting to suffer. We were at our wits' end when it came to continually providing lead flow to keep all our centers humming. Enter Gym Launch. Now, we'd worked with a bunch of business mentors before and had some pretty good success, but nothing compared to the plug-and-play tactical action that Alex and Leila provided. This was a new beast and better than any "mastermind." Gym Launch has given us our guiding principles of always putting the customer first and creating an abundance of clients who genuinely want to work with us. We now have 6 centers, all continuing to grow at paces I would never have believed were possible. We are just kicking ourselves we didn't sign up with them 9 months earlier when we had our first call.

> — James Buchanan | The Body Consultants | East Perth, Australia

In over 30 years in the fitness industry, I can honestly say that Gym Launch has been the single best investment I have ever made in myself, and that in turn has had a direct impact not only on my financial well-being but more importantly in my life. In one year's time since joining GL, not only have I increased my annual gross revenues by over $200,000 a year, I have increased my net profit by $100,000 and grown my monthly EFT by over $25,000 a month. I went from being a solo studio owner teaching every class, doing everything, and working entirely *in* my business to now having a staff of 7 coaches and being able to work *on* my business. But even more importantly, Gym Launch helped me find the people whose lives I could touch and change! So thank you to Alex Hormozi and the whole team behind Gym Launch, who have helped me do my purpose work by reaching, touching, and changing so many lives!

> — Barbara Vinciguerra | Fit House New York | Ardsley, New York

After nearly 30 years in the fitness industry, I was about to throw the towel in, as just couldn't make it work—and I had hired all the best gurus. But 12 months down the line with Alex, GL, and Legacy, it's been a game-changer! Now I have a business that works from lead gen to nurture to sales to fulfillment, retention, and beyond! #highlyrecommend

— **Spencer Cuckney | Fit Body Bournemouth | Bournemouth, England**

I remember standing in my gym a few years ago. Frustrated, thinking, "Man, I wish someone could just come in here and show me what to do!" We were working our asses of, but not seeing the results for the effort. Getting conflicting advice from different coaches and mentors. That's when we first heard about Gym Launch. I said "Fuck it. Let's do it! What we've been doing isn't working." That's when the whole game changed. Everything plug-and-play, tactical information. Don't get me wrong, it's work. But it's like, how long would you stand at a cash machine where it continuously popped out $5 or $10 bills? You would literally stand there until you couldn't anymore. That's the description that comes to mind. We more than doubled our income within a few months. Alex and Leila are thought leaders who truly care. They are changing the industry and serve from the heart. I'm just thankful to be a part of the winning team.

— **Rob Grupe | Twice Bitten CrossFit | Oklahoma City, Oklahoma**

Passion doesn't pay bills, up-to-date systems and strategies do. Gym Launch took me from being ready to close the doors to opening a second location within 6 months. Thank you, Alex and Leila, for all you do.

— **Matthew Boccaccio | Republic of Fitness | Westport, Ireland**

I was working a "real job" 50+ hours a week, coaching 11 classes and handling all the leads each month. Alex and Leila have helped us grow from 20 members to 250+ in 8 months. And I can pay myself.

— **Daniel Romigh | Redemption Fitness Mason | Mason, Michigan**

I already had a successful studio…or so I thought. My members were never able to get over 150. I have been there for years. Alex helped me understand why this is and that the structure of my business model was broken. I am still not there yet, but I have been working on the stability and the machine so that going into the new year, I have the system in place. I was also in a previous business group that took me for a financial ride. Is Alex expensive? Yes. But when you're picking your dentist or doctor, you want the best, and you pay—no questions asked. There are many turds out there copying Alex and claiming they are original. Don't fall for it. And to be honest, I wasn't 100% sold because of how many times I had been burned. Facebook shut me down months ago. I had spent thousands with them, and they didn't care. I lost a massive amount of money. Most coaches would ignore this. [But] Alex personally contacted me to help me resolve [the issue]. Not an assistant, Alex himself. I plan on staying with GL as long as I can.

— **Bill Bennett | Bill Bennett Boot Camps | Orlando, Florida**

Gym Launch has helped me grow my business from $15K recurring to $25K–$30K recurring in 4 months! I have gained more freedom to do more of what I love to do and less of what I hate! The cool thing is, I am only just getting my feet wet with all the value provided. Thanks, Alex Hormozi!

— Riley Trombley | CrossFit Landmine | Las Vegas, Nevada

When Josh and I learned about Gym Launch, we'd had our gym for 4 years and we were doing okay, but could not figure out how to take our gym to the next level and push over 120 members. We would run marketing for challenges and would have 5 people show up to the orientation and 1 or 2 complete the challenge. After implementing the 6-week challenge that Alex created, we started consistently running 30-people challenges with a 90% success rate on those people finishing and getting results. This doubled our member EFT base in 6 months and renewed our passion for helping people live their healthiest lives!

— Stephanie Sweeney Commons | West Carmel Fit Body Boot Camp | Indianapolis, Indiana

We had been in business for 8 years before realizing that while we were surviving, we weren't on the path to freedom. What I mean is that I was striving to acquire clients, fighting to keep them, all the while missing the whole point of building a business. If nothing changed, I would be doing the same stuff in another 8 years, waking up at 3:30, training clients until noon, doing marketing and sales until our evening sessions. Either that or I would have quit. I was working a job. Working with Gym Launch isn't JUST about making a wild amount of money (although that happens), it's about building a legacy. A business that will support you when you can't physically be there or don't want to be there. Recently, we had our second daughter, and not only was I able to stay home with my family after she was born, but the business still grew. That's not something I could have said before working with Gym Launch. This group of people and the systems they provide will move you forward and provide a better life than you can imagine. I'm talking to the guy who has been doing this training thing, who knows that the next big swing in their business is right around the corner, but that corner keeps getting a little further away. That was me. And I'm telling you, it won't come on its own. I'm proud of my business and what we are able to accomplish, the lives we are able to change.

— Kian Ameli | Training For Warriors Concord | Concord, California

Although I have paid over $50K to Alex and Gym Launch, it has truly been FREE, as all the systems that Alex graciously shares in this book have generated a 10x ROI for my gym and gave me the freedom to do what I choose to do.

— Manzanares Logan Lee | Big Sky Barbell | Big Sky, Montana

Gym Launch Secrets gave me the freedom and courage to walk away from a 15-year+ career! For the first time in my life, I actually feel like I'm living my purpose. My business went from $25K to $45K a month in less than a year. I'm actually glad that I hired a coach before I met Alex Hormozi. I appreciate Alex 100x more because I know firsthand that this program delivers more value than anybody else in the industry!

— Joe Green | Sweat Heroes Boot Camp | Vacaville, California

If you want to 3x your company, 5x your skill set, and want to change your business, your relationships, and your mindset forever, what's in this book is comparable to bricks of gold. Don't just buy it—live by it.

— **Ally Johnson | Ninja Fitness Academy | Albuquerque, New Mexico**

I had no gym and zero clients when I came across Alex and Leila Hormozi. In fact, I was working at a big-box gym selling personal training because the last "fitness guru" had put me out of business (I was doing online training). I ran out of ALL of my family's money (investments, savings, EVERYTHING). My wife and I took the plunge, and within our first 13 days of working with Alex, we landed 70 grand-opening clients and over $34,000 in revenue. We were in over our heads for sure, and spent the first 6 months at an abysmal 25% close rate. But after grinding through 800 in-person sales appointments with Alex's proven processes and systems, we finally improved our skills to close more than 50%, which is where we've been at ever since. In the first 9 months of being open for business, we grossed over $200,000, but more importantly, we just had our most profitable month ($13,000 IN ONE MONTH, even after paying ourselves $4K salary). As a side note, before Alex & Leila, I always wrote off being a gym owner, because I looked around my community and saw that most (okay, all) were broke and exhausted and running themselves into the ground. Alex has reignited my wife's and my passions to help people and create a culture of weapons-grade compassion. Please don't just read this book. Quit perpetuating the stereotype of the overworked, underpaid gym owner, and join us in our movement in bringing this industry from its knees to its feet.

— **Cody Weber | Elevation Performance | Wichita, Kansas**

This is literally a blueprint for where to get the winning lotto ticket and how to cash it. Then he teaches you to get someone else to find the next winning lotto ticket and have them cash it for you! Because that is what we gym owners are doing each week. I've gone from 67 EFTs and charging $125 to $147/month to 165 EFTs and charging $200/month in one year's time. That doesn't even include the up-front cash or internal plays or supplements that he also sprinkles into the mix!

— **Kyle Barker | Training For Warriors East Bay | Pleasanton, California**

Gym Launch took us from bringing in $27,000 in 2016 to bringing in $250,000 in 2017. In 2018, thus far, we have hit over half a million, and 2019 will be our first million-dollar year!

— **Dean Trinklein | Muscle Monkey Functional Fitness | Pueblo, Colorado**

My first experience with Alex Hormozi was when one of my clients told me, "Hey, there's some young kid opening a gym down the street." I was in Huntington Beach, CA, the toughest market in the US. I wasn't too concerned. Gyms opened all the time there. Within a year or two, he had 5 gyms (and probably a few of my old clients.) Fast forward 4 or 5 years. I had hired and worked with every guru and coach in the industry, all telling me they would pack my gym, while spending tens of thousands of dollars for advice that sounded great but rarely worked. When a friend suggested Gym Launch, I won't lie—my ego popped up, "Oh that young kid that stole my clients, not gonna pay him nothing." But then too many people I knew began to explode their gyms, and so I finally took a leap. In September of 2017, we were at about 60 members on EFT, making $16K a month, barely paying ourselves, doing all the work from janitor to coach, and just stuck. From Jan-September that year, we grossed $148,000 with nothing to show for it besides credit card bills. Fast forward to the same period the next year, and we had $368,000, a full team, and my wife and I actually got to be home with our 3 kids (ages 5, 3, and 2). It is still hard work, but just this October, we took the entire month off and drove cross country with our family, all while our team ran (and grew) the gym for us. We set a record sales number that month, with $55,000 in gross sales. Oh yeah, we are in 1,600 square feet too. When I first saw Gym Launch, I knew about Alex, I knew all about the 6-week thing, but when you get inside and realize it's about the business, the systems, the training, all from someone who has done it, the game changes. I told Alex I was mad at him for publishing this book, because what cost me tens of thousands of dollars to glean from him in coaching over 18 months, people can now get for next to nothing. Look at my numbers—in my mind, there is over $300,000 worth of information in these pages, if you implement it.

—**Justin Lesh | Training For Warriors Estrella | Goodyear, Arizona**

Gym Launch was our last-ditch attempt! Had spent thousands over the years on so-called mentors, and never really made any progress, because they wouldn't show me how! What Alex has created is a "business in a box" on steroids. No stone is left unturned. My business has tripled in 6 short months. The future is bright…the future is Gym Launch.

— Russ Lubin | 30+ Men's Fitness Essex | London, England

Gym Launch Secrets took us from a small local boxing gym with 150 members at reduced rates to a well-known brand in our area. With proper social media marketing tools and sound business advice on pricing and how to create value and fulfillment with our clients, we were able to grow our membership base to over 450 members and increase our rates by 400%. After a year of following the Gym Launch Secrets program, we have 5x our year-end and continue to grow our business. We have also successfully added 3 new income streams to our business and have become the go-to facility for rapid, sustainable body transformations! Thank you, Alex, Leila, the Gym Launch family, and all the Gym Lords.

— Cody Thompson | White Collar Boxing Company | Airdrie, Alberta, Canada

Gym Launch and, most importantly, Alex were the catalysts of transformation in all areas of our business. In a year's time, not only have we more than doubled our monthly revenue and the number of recurring clients, but we also tripled the size of our staff and now have the freedom to enjoy our lives as business owners. Alex has shown us what true leadership means, and we are now more equipped than ever to create a massive impact on countless lives. Alex is truly changing the fitness industry for the better. If you're not on board, you will get left behind.

— **Nicole Race | Elevate St. Pete | Saint Petersburg, Florida**

When I was introduced to Gym Launch Secrets, I was about to lose everything—my business was losing $15K a month, I was unable to pay my 3 part-time employees or my rent. I was about to lose my house and my car. (Sounds like a sad country song.) I needed something…anything…to turn it all around. Enter Gym Launch Secrets. Within 14 days, we brought in 68 new clients and over $30K in front-end cash. Fast forward to a year later, and I am still following the Gym Launch Secrets model and crushing it. I have retired my husband and perhaps even saved our marriage, grown my team to 9 employees, bought a new car, aggressively paid off debt, and had the best year ever after struggling to win in business for 7 years. It finally feels like I have some momentum.

— **Sara Goossen | Fit Body Boot Camp Cheyenne | Cheyenne, Wyoming**

"Oh! So THIS is what it's like to ACTUALLY make money doing what you love!" Me every day since joining Gym Launch!

— **Nathalie Huerta | The Queer Gym | Oakland, California**

Best thing for me as a non-salesperson was being given the tools to feel confident in selling. And now I hear fitness is the hardest thing to sell? Feel like I could sell ice to Eskimos now! And actually, as a teacher, I'm using some of the things I've learnt in the classroom. Who would've ever figured on that happening!!

— **Gill Mills | Trimnasium Performance Gym | UK**

In January 2018, I didn't know how I was going to make rent for February. I joined Gym Launch on the 12th. By the end of the month, I was able to pay the next 2 months' rent and write myself a paycheck for the first time in 4 years. The best decision I ever made was to join Gym Launch!

— **Andrew Resendez | Beast Mode CrossFit | Friendswood, Texas**

The month before I had my first phone call with Alex, our gym was a month or two away from just closing it all down and giving up. I think we had fewer than 20 students at the time. But then I found Alex and learned about Gym Launch. I believed in what he said he could help us do. It was the absolute best decision of my life! 72 NEW Students came through the doors and signed up in the first 3 weeks we were with Gym Launch. What Gym Launch has done for our business allowed me to retire from the fire department. It was when I started and has continued to grow beyond my wildest expectations. It is amazing! I'm in for life.

— **Matt Carter | Training For Warriors Firehouse Fit OKC | Del City, Oklahoma**

Alex gave me a clear step-by-step program to follow that was more detailed and specific than anything I had ever seen. There was never any question of what to do, how much to do, or when to do it. I had all the answers right in front of me. If I was ever in a position where I wasn't getting the results I wanted, I knew it was directly related to my ability to implement what I had right in front of me. The level of clarity in both the tactical and the strategic sense gave me the feeling of control again. We literally doubled our revenue and tripled our profits using the techniques in this book.

— Austin Michael Hair | 9 Round Williamsburg | Orlando, Florida

In 2011, I started working at my gym, putting in the long hours and doing all the day-to-day tasks. I worked at my gym for another 6 years until 2017. While attending another "guru conference," I saw a friend of mine sit back and enjoy himself the whole weekend while I tried to fill up 3 notebooks that I would prolly never look at. I asked him why he was so relaxed and he simply said, "Gym Launch Secrets." Obviously, I did some research and ended up signing up 5 days later. From that point on, I no longer worked at my gym—I now owned my gym. Gym Launch Secrets will give you a blueprint for success and all you have to do is put in the WORK.

— Joshua D Rupprecht | Training For Warriors DuPage | Villa Park, Illinois

We were on our last dime, or should I say credit card. We had used other fitness gurus who overpromised and underdelivered, just to clean us out. Then Alex and Leila exploded on the fitness world to help gym owners who were broke and on their knees just trying to keep food on the table and the lights on.

Their company Gym Launch and their world-class team help gym owners by teaching them the 5 core functions that all businesses need in order to be successful. And they do this with a step-by-step method that anyone can do. We increased our revenue $20,000 in 3 months! This company is going to revolutionize the fitness industry!

— **Willis Renee Hicks | Gracie Jiu-Jitsu | Fort Wayne, Indiana**

We were with a coaching business before Gym Launch, but never learned how to run the business like we do today. We knew very little about how to really get leads in the door. Gym Launch Secrets has taught us to hire more people to relieve us of coaching duties so that we can focus on the big picture and actually grow the gym. We went from 2 very part-time coaches to a team of 5! We learned how to increase our revenue to get to this point. The things I learned about marketing and sales are invaluable!! I even majored in marketing in college ha ha. Thanks, GL Secrets!!

— **Shawna Frank | CrossFit Slake | Aubrey, Texas**

We tried other coaches, programs, books, everything…and we struggled! With four young kids, we needed to make ends meet and things weren't adding up. It was a risk to hire a coach, to spend money we didn't have and possibly still be in the spot, but that's not at all what happened. We gained the most knowledge, and my husband turned our studio around instantly. Alex Hormozi has built and packed in so much knowledge to make you successful, to give you financial freedom and peace of mind! You're not paying for them to do it for you, you actually learn how to do it, while always getting the best and most recent and applicable information to crush your gym and life! This book will change your life forever, and you will never look back! We are forever thankful for Gym Launch Secrets!

— **Heather Dunham | Redzone Performance Fitness Center | Bradenton, Florida**

Congratulations, Alex! Your tools transformed a stressed-out and overwhelmed gym owner to one who has the exact blueprint for a 7-figure, life-changing business. People, process, profits, baby!!

— **Heather DeWitt | EvoFit | Dover, New Hampshire**

Gym Launch, in a nutshell, saved our business and our lives. We were just tipping away, not doing too much, but now we are absolutely flying, with loads of members and a fantastic business. Gym Launch saved us. Simple.

— **Gary Dempsey | Match Fit Fitness | Wicklow, Ireland**

Alex Hormozi and Gym Launch Secrets changed my mindset on being a rural gym owner. He taught me that it doesn't matter what your market is, his system works. Thanks to Gym Launch Secrets, our gym went from $2K a month to $30K a month in only 60 days, living in a town with a median income of only $21K per year. You opened a gym to help people, so let Alex help you make that happen.

— **Jonathan Serrano | CrossFit Dark Zone | Hudson, Florida**

Thanks to Gym Launch, I went from a very tired, beat down, frustrated gym owner ready to throw in the towel to increasing our revenue (more than 10x!!) in just a few short months. Not only that, but I have found that burning desire deep down in my soul again, which is why I originally got into the business in the first place. This has been a game-changer for sure!

— Kattie Fleece | Fleece Fitness | Pittsboro, Indiana

Before Gym Launch Secrets, I was a semi-successful biz owner with a $30K run rate, 4 employees, a modest paycheck, and 12-hour+ workdays. This was after 2 years of running my own business and over 20 years total in the fitness business. In the year since getting my hands on Gym Launch Secrets, I am rocking an $85K run rate, I have 12 employees, and I get to eat dinner with my family every night—GOOD dinners! In one year, my life changed. And with the easy-to-execute tactics Alex shares, I anticipate life improving even more this year and in the years to come. Because of Gym Launch Secrets, I will finally "help millions of people while making millions of dollars."

— Tom Miller | Lifelight Fitness | Pleasanton, California

In 2017, all of my old ways of getting leads were NOT working anymore. I was lucky to get 30 leads per month!! Now, I easily get 300 leads per month and sometimes over 600 using Gym Launch! I also needed help with my organizational structure and all of the details on how to properly lead my team and keep clients!! So I joined Gym Legacy and got all of that plus more. I am better at sales than I have ever been because of Alex Hormozi and Gym Launch. I used to hate sales, but now they are okay (LOL), and I do really well with them using

Gym Launch. I have increased EFT at one gym by $10,000/month this year using his system! And revenue has gone up by over $400,000 in a year!

— Stephanie Flynn | Bixby & Owasso Fit Body Boot Camp | Oklahoma City, Oklahoma

Gym Launch Secrets was directly responsible for 5x-ing my gym's revenue in 10 months. Looking forward to implementing all they teach for another 5x!

— Patrick Reid | Grounded CrossFit | Hanover, Maryland

When I started Gym Launch, my gym was bringing in a third of the revenue compared to my bills. I was losing money quickly but, within the first month, I brought in $15,000 in new business. Following Alex's system saved our ship, and we have been growing ever since. Thank you, Alex!

— Mollie Estes | Training For Warriors Lee's Summit & Overland Park | Lee's Summit, Missouri

We invested more in Alex's programme in a few short months than we had ever spent on anything in 12 years of being open. Yet within 3 of those months, we had doubled our turnover from more leads than we had ever seen, who were paying 4x the price to start with us than anyone we had ever taken on. The shift in mindset this programme gives you will transform your business.

— Craig Kinsey | Kinetics Gym & Personal Training | Lytham St. Annes, Lancashire, UK

I believe I'm one of Gym Launch's OG clients. I've always been a skeptic, because I've wasted a lot of money paying "gurus" for outdated information...well, until I paid Alex. I've watched Gym Launch grow and help thousands of people. I've been with them for years, and they've helped me in so many more ways than just making more money. If you want to be an entrepreneur, they're a great team to have in your corner.

— **George Perelshteyn | Gravity Training Zone | Multiple Locations in New Jersey**

I took a leap of faith with Gym Launch, and it has literally transformed my studio. We went from a place that held classes to an actual total wellness facility. After being underwhelmed so many times, I am wonderfully overwhelmed by the support, systems, and tools we have now. It's well worth the investment. I finally feel like a solid business owner.

— **Tiffany "InMotion" Lymon | Emerge Wellness | Joppa, Maryland**

GLS completely changed the trajectory of my life. As I write this, I look back over the last 18 months and can't believe what's transpired. Going from about to close my doors to having a full gym and staff running everything like clockwork. Went from never seeing my family to working from home. From scared to swipe my card at the grocery store to buying a house. It's hard to put into words how life-changing Alex and GLS have been!

— **Cale Owen | The Exchange Fitness | Saint Augustine, Florida**

This is by far the best investment in not only my business but in myself. It has made running our gyms amazing. Just learning how to properly run Facebook Ads has been a huge game-changer. It will 10x your life.

— **Joshuah Ackiss | Washington, DC**

Using Alex's systems and advice, in a year and a half, our churn rate of members has gone from between 12% and 20% to between 4.5% and 9%. Our actual price each customer pays per month has gone from $80/pc to $150/pc. And our weekly payroll has gone from between $4,500 and $5,500/week to between $1,900 and $2,200/week. Alex and Gym Launch/Legacy have helped save my gym and remotivated me to have the best facility possible. HIGHLY RECOMMEND

— **Kirk Huggins Rogers | Heroic Fitness | Charlotte, North Carolina**

Gym Launch helped me to more than double my gym business in less than 4 months. But Alex & Leila teach far more than just how to run an extremely profitable gym. They teach the essential skills of entrepreneurship. Tools they don't teach you in school that can and will level up any venture. Pay attention, friends, you are in for a ride.

— **Ben Chew | CrossFit Ashland | Charlotte, North Carolina**

I jumped on Gym Launch before I even opened my gym. I went from zero clients to a break-even point in a single month. It was the easiest launch of a business I have ever had. The experience Gym Launch gave me showed me that it is possible to have massive, fast growth. Not only was it fast, but the type of clients we got were amazing to work with.

— Luke Elrod | Champion Karate Winter Park | Winter Park, Florida

In 8 months, Alex's program took our gym from $10,000/month in revenue to $65,000/month, and we are still climbing!

— Sam Grantham | Whole Health Club | Littleton, Colorado

Every chapter in this book is must-read. With Alex's systems and support, our revenue is up over 300% in 18 months with a retention rate over 96%. The plan is, this book can take your business and life as far as you want in exactly the direction you want to go. Oh, and the icing on the cake—Alex genuinely CARES.

— Dave Regula | TrAk Athletics | Akron, Ohio

Between August 20 and 31, my universe changed for the better. We made enough to cover rent on the premises, my mortgage payments, bills, cards, etc. In fact, on September 1 (long weekend), we made enough sales to cover that month's rent, which usually takes us a week to make. For 2019, with EFTs factored in, we are on track to more than triple our pre-GL run rate, become markedly more profitable, and have the proper systems in place so I can spend far less time operating this studio while focusing on enjoying my life and work. Thank you, Alex and Leila!

— Cyrus Osena | Spartan Krav Maga | Burlington, Ontario, Canada

Alex Hormozi has helped me take my business to the next level. Just one of the dozens of tips and tricks he has given me has made me tens of thousands of dollars. All together, he has made me hundreds of thousands of dollars and FAST. No joke. And he has put all of those lessons into this book, which gives you access to what all the category killers are doing right now in their businesses. Even just one tip from this book will make you thousands of dollars. It would be the best thing you have ever purchased for your fitness business. I only wish I had this book sooner.

— Ben Krymis | Strong Together Byram | Stanhope, New Jersey

Because of Gym Launch and Alex's team and their support, we've gone from "How do I pay all the bills?" to "How do I hire people fast enough to keep up with growth and good processes to implement?" In the first 3 months, we netted 40 members at a much higher price and better experience for them. If I could do it all again, I would start the gym from the ground up with what's in this book! Would have saved me 4 years.

— Jeff Stoffel | Centripetal CrossFit | Erie, Colorado

In just over a year with Gym Launch Secrets, we have grown from 4 to 14 full-time employees in our 4 locations and have increased our revenues up to 50% per location, all while keeping our monthly attrition below 5%. This step-by-step system is the thing that every microgym owner needs to be successful for the long term.

— David Rubin | CrossFit Durham | Durham, North Carolina

When I signed up with Alex, I was broke…and broken. Since that time, I have doubled my monthly income, created a business I can be proud of, and built the gym of my dreams.

— Daythan Nottke | Body Burn Women's Fitness Center | Kankakee, Illinois

Gym Launch Secrets not only doubled our revenue ($250K to over $500K) in a short 12 months, it also took me from physically training 8 hours per day to ZERO. It taught me how to run a profitable business instead of being RUN OVER by my business. Forever grateful to the GLS team.

— John Madsen | Athletic And Fit | Salt Lake City, Utah

I thought I had a handle on client-financed acquisition and retention until I met Alex. He showed me a new level. Culprit Athletics, my staff, my clients, and I have him to thank for $20K added to our monthly EFT. We have more time, more freedom, and more stability in all of our lives. 12-month EFT prior to Alex: $186K. 12-month EFT after Alex: $450K. Thanks again, Alex Hormozi!

— Austin Culp | Culprit Athletics | Dalton, Georgia

Gym Launch has been the equalizer for our bootstrapped gym to keep up with the corporate giants. They basically equal our Research & Development department. We used to throw away thousands testing ads on a small scale, but now we have all our ad copy written and tested on an enormous scale to ensure we always get the most bang for our ad-spend buck!

— Evan Daiber | 2 Tone Boxing Club | Beachwood, Ohio

We jumped into Gym Launch as a last-ditch effort to make our passion profitable. We were frustrated, defeated and desperate for a guiding light to profitability. In 6 months, we have been guided to more than doubling our EFTs, hiring 5 coaches and a general manager. More than anything, we were given a path to follow to continue the growth and success. We can't thank Gym Launch enough for all they do on a daily basis to strengthen beliefs and guide us to a fruitful future.

— Larry Ramey | Power Performance Strength & Conditioning | Loveland, Ohio

When I started with Alex, I was making a whopping $25K a year and was drowning in debt after 6 years of being in business. In the year since hiring Alex, we are over $120K for the year and counting, and most importantly we have a TEAM of people from GL that support our "particular brand" of fitness and help keep us growing while we look like the geniuses!

— Drew Reddish | Zoo Fit | Fayetteville, Georgia

We always struggled with lead generation, and for 6 years couldn't break past 40 clients. There were times we slept in the gym. We lost our apartment. It got rough. We moved the gym to a better location 7 miles away and lost half of our clients in the process. So when we started with Gym Launch Secrets, we had a new lease, were underpriced, and had only 20 clients with no lead generation system. We were running on borrowed money and losing each month. Within 3 months of starting the lead generation systems we learned, we had grown from 20 to

150 members, and had our strongest year in business. All thanks to Gym Launch Secrets.

— **Ashe Starbuck | The Nerd Gym | Tucson, Arizona**

Ever since I met Alex over a year ago, my gym business has gone crazy. Can't wait for the next year—it's going to be a fun ride. The training and support are unreal. I always thought my gym would just be a hobby, but now I see a huge future for my family. Thanks, team.

— **Scott Labeda | CrossFit Uncensored | Lake Elsinore, California**

My wife and I started our fitness business over 8 years ago. To us, it was never just a job, or even a career. Helping others achieve their health goals gives us greater purpose in life. We're both highly passionate and we work hard. Before we joined Gym Launch, we were struggling to keep our gym alive. To give you an idea of how bad it was before we joined: we owed more than $70K in debt, and we knew that we would have no choice but to close our doors in just a matter of weeks. We would have also lost our house (and home for over 10 years) to loan providers. Thankfully, Gym Launch found us, and when we took the leap of faith, they helped us turn our business around fast!! In only 5 short months, we 3xed our revenue (from $20K to $66K+ monthly) and we cut our debt in half!! We're currently on track to be 100% debt-free next year, and we both cannot say THANK YOU enough to GYM LAUNCH SECRETS and their amazing team for helping us to turn our business (and lives) around.

— **Silas & Amy Robinson | Lift Personal Fitness Inc. | Fredericton, New Brunswick**

Gym Launch helped me go from £2.5K revenue per month to £15K! Also, when I started, I was on my own wearing all the hats, but now I have a team of 7 including an operations manager! Thank you, Alex Hormozi, Leila Hormozi, and the GL Team.

— Jack Rigby | Strength Camp Chester | Chester, Cheshire

In 12 months of using Alex's Gym Launch system, we doubled our membership, cut our monthly cancellations in half, and built an unbelievably great culture in our facility. Alex is the best innovator in the fitness industry, and the best part is, he's just getting started. #gymlordforever

— Donnie Jaeger | Detroit Thrive | Detroit, Michigan

Gym Launch saved my business, saved my marriage, and saved my passion. I would never have lived my life the way I truly desired if it were not for Alex and Gym Launch. Saved and changed everything!

— James McQueen | Fuel Fitness Boot Camp | Tallahassee, Florida

Gym Launch has saved my business. Legacy is the blueprint to freedom for the gym owner. The support and consistent innovation are impeccable. Words are lost on me for how grateful I am to be a part of this team. Thank you, Leila and Alex. I appreciate you both!

— Yano Anaya | Crew Core Fitness | Woodstock, Georgia

If you're looking to take your business to elite-level status, Gym Legacy is for you. I've been in the fitness industry for over 38 years. I've seen A LOT. My mindset has always been "To be the best, you must surround yourself with the best." Alex has brought together THE best minds in fitness to deliver everything a gym owner needs to achieve elite-level status. I've been blown away by Alex's relentless drive to continually provide new strategies and innovations that ensure my gym is always #1. He leaves no stone unturned. From new customer acquisition to handling personnel issues, GL has your back. I wish I'd had access to a program like this when I first started!

— **Steve Baum, owner of athlete success | Iron Tribe Fitness | Brentwood, Missouri**

Before GL, I never would have considered myself a salesperson, which meant I was at the mercy of whoever was currently employed by me. I quickly went from no control to absolute control and freedom because of Alex's training and systems. Alex has given me more than just 4x our training revenue (that happened too). He has given me the confidence to sit in front of anyone and empower them to take action at our facility…and at a premium price. Because we're worth it. There's no better feeling than TRULY changing others' lives and also FINALLY making an income in doing so. Thank you, Alex and team!!

— **Beth Dazé | Workout Anytime Lenexa | Lenexa, Kansas**

I'll never forget the day I joined Gym Launch. I was sitting in Chipotle with my wife late at night waiting for my call from Alex. Our gym at the time had a small membership, but it was extremely disorganized and barely profitable. At the time, we were working every role in the business and living out of a tiny closet I had built in our studio. We were extremely skeptical as we'd had many terrible experiences in the past from other "fitness gurus." We felt hopeless and alone but knew we had to try something different. We decided to invest what was at that time our entire life savings into the program. Within 30 days, we had made enough money to move into our own apartment, pay off $15K in personal debt, and hire a small team.

Since then, we have doubled our business and [now] have a small team serving our members better than we ever could have. We now have the systems, resources, community, and clarity to build the gym I used to dream of and make the impact in our community that I always wanted. We still have a lot to learn and a lot of ways to grow, but with what Alex and Leila have created, we know it is only a matter of time before we get there. With what Gym Launch is doing and has done, we truly feel like we are a part of history in the making and are blessed to be involved with it. We are forever grateful. Fitness entrepreneurs, these are "your people" who always put your business and success first—get in now or get crushed.

— Ryan McCarthy | True Strength Fitness | Scottsdale, Arizona

We were six weeks away from closing our doors after almost ten years in business. Fifteen months later, we have signed a new five-year lease and are profitable and doing better all the time. It's a lot of hard work and Alex and Leila don't sugarcoat that, but it is worth every minute. We had our best month ever with GL—$52K—and are looking to do even better next year.

— **Maximus Lewin | Ascension Fitness East Bay | Oakland, California**

Gym Launch Secrets saved our business. We went from stashing things on credit cards and grossing $10K/month to closing in on a $500K business. We've built our team to eight amazing professionals to help Nashville become a healthier community. Thank you, Alex and Leila!

— **Mark Molinyawe | Nashletics | Nashville, Tennessee**

After 10 years in the business, Gym Launch made me realize that I barely knew anything. This is the blueprint to run your operation as efficiently and profitable as possible. After one year with Gym Launch, my wife and I have doubled our revenue, made a second location profitable in less than a year, and most importantly, we have learned how to build a team that cares about our mission and to deliver an incomparable experience to our members that makes them want to stay for life. I am in love with my business all over again. This program will ignite your passion and will harness the spirit of why you started in the first place. Sign up and make your dreams come to fruition. We are forever indebted to Gym Launch.

— **Vinay Chary | Triumph Krav Maga | New Orleans, Louisiana**

Alex Hormozi , Leila Hormozi, and Gym Launch Secrets have completely changed the course of my LIFE, not just my business. From attracting new clients and help to running a business for actual profit (so that I can keep doing what I love and helping others) to becoming an even stronger leader and having better life/business balance. YES, ALL OF THAT! And I can NOT believe you are getting ALL THESE secrets for the cost of a book! CRAZY awesome, no-brainer purchase!

— **Rebecca Tabbert | RT Fitness Calimesa | Calimesa, California**

So Alex is pretty special to me. I've never been someone to have heroes in my life or felt a strong connection to any one individual. I've never had someone make such a drastic impact on my life in such a short period of time. Alex is the person who changed that. I had an ego and a closed mindset where I thought I really knew how to grow. He also changed that. Thanks to Alex, he changed my life and has given me and so many others I care for a sense of new momentum that I can now use forever.

— **Thor Christerson | Pro-TF Fitness | La Mesa, California**

Gym Launch gave my business more predictability than anything else out there. It gave me the confidence to know that I was covered and because of that, my entire outlook toward my business has forever changed for the better. I went from a hit-and-miss lead gen system bringing in maybe a few hundred a month to a machine that produced upwards of additional $8K+ month over month in revenue on demand. Thank you, Gym Launch.

— **Adrian Shier | Kalamazoo Fit Body Boot Camp | Kalamazoo, Michigan**

Thanks to Gym Launch Secrets: Alex Hormozi, Leila Hormozi, their amazing team, and every amazing gym owner who has shared their ups and downs and everything that has worked and failed and what to try and not to try ! I have become a better person overall, which is the biggest profit for myself on this journey! It has opened endless possibilities and doors! I will forever be part of this team and do whatever I can to stay part of it! They are family, and everyone has your back! I went from very few to no clients my first three years on my own, zero community, couldn't pay bills, extreme debt, borrowing money to get by, literally my back against the wall and nowhere to move! I was done, and this was my last chance! DO OR DIE!! After my first five months in joining the Gym Launch Secret Team, I had broken my first six-figure numbers EVER in a small 800-square-foot studio! Now I own a real business and am learning to become a business owner and a leader, changing people's lives daily and building an amazing community that I couldn't be more proud of! Thank you, I am forever grateful!

— **Michael Bilow | Shore Movements | Bradley Beach, New Jersey**

GYM LAUNCH
SECRETS

The Step-By-Step Guide To Building
A Massively Profitable Gym

Alex Hormozi

Copyright © 2019 by Alex Hormozi

All rights reserved. No part of this publication may be reproduced, distributed, or transmitted in any form or by any means, including photocopying, recording, or other electronic or mechanical methods, without the prior written permission of the publisher, except in the case of brief questions embodied in critical reviews and certain other noncommercial uses permitted by copyright law. For permission requests, write to the publisher at the address below.

Print ISBN: 978-1-7329330-0-2
Gym Lords Media
Gymlaunch.com

Cover Design by Eled Cernik
Interior Layout by Soumi Goswami

DISCLAIMER

The content provided in this book is designed to provide helpful information on the subjects discussed. This book is not meant to be used, nor should it be used, to diagnose or treat any medical condition. For diagnosis or treatment of any medical problem, consult your own physician. The publisher and the author are not responsible for any specific health or allergy needs that may require medical supervision, and are not liable for any damages or negative consequences for any treatment, action, application, or preparation to any person reading or following the information in this book. References are provided for informational purposes only and do not constitute endorsement of any websites or other sources. Readers should also be aware that the websites listed in this book may change or become obsolete.

Two Guiding Principles

A business wins by making the same prospect more valuable to his business than to that of his competition.

We question all of our beliefs, except those we TRULY believe. And those, we never question at all.

Dedication

I want to thank my unbelievable soul partner, my ride-or-die, Leila.

You found me at my absolute worst, and you have fought beside me shoulder to shoulder ever since.

You said you would sleep with me under a bridge if it came to that, and I have never forgotten it. You stood tall when everything was crumbling around me.

I would go to war with you. I would die for you.

If the world were a hurricane, standing with you is like being in the eye, calmly observing the beauty with the storm raging around.

There's no one else I'd want by my side to watch my back and fight the battles that come.

Being with you makes the stars look within reach.

Here's to a life filled with the impossible.

Contents

Introduction lv

Section I: Acquisition: Get More Clients 1

   1. The Broken "Sell Your Soul" Acquisition Problem. . . . 5

   2. A Client-Acquisition Model That Works 9

   3. Get Paid To Acquire Customers. 23

   4. Get Them To Show Up. 33

   5. Get Them To Buy 41

   6. The C-L-O-S-E-R Formula. 49

Section II: Ascension: Make More Profit 65

   7. The Broken Profit Model 69

   8. Price-Profit Levers. 79

   9. Capacity-Profit Levers. 103

   10. The Overhead Lever 121

   11. Your New Gym On Paper. 131

   12. Making The Shift 145

Section III: Retention: Get Them To Buy More. 159

   13. Attrition: The Hole-In-The-Bucket Problem. 167

   14. How Retention Multiplies Revenue 177

15. PROCESS: How To Give Consistently Amazing
    Customer Experiences.........................185
16. PROCESS: The Five Horsemen Of Retention.....191
17. PEOPLE: How To Build Your Dream Team......205
18. PEOPLE: Communication Cycles And Cadences...211
19. PEOPLE: Five Things Every Role In Your
    Gym Needs..................................217
20. PRODUCT: How To Motivate Unmotivated
    Trainers...................................225
21. PRODUCT: How To Run An Amazing Session
    Every Time.................................233

Section IV: Baking The Cake 241
22. The Wedding Cake Gym Profit Model...........247
23. Tier 1: Large-Group Training................257
24. Tier 2: Semi-Privates (1-On-4)..............273
25. Tier 3: Supplement Sales....................287
26. Sprinkles: Internal Plays...................297

Conclusion......................................309
BONUS: Obstacle Overcomes.......................313
Appendix..349
Acknowledgments.................................365
About The Author................................367

Introduction

I heard the repeated dull thud of knuckles hitting against the glass front door of my gym.

"Hello? Alex?"

I opened my eyes. It was pitch dark.

I instantly felt my stomach sink. *Sh*t. Did I miss my alarm?* I peeled my face up off the floor mat in a panic. I checked my phone: 4:27am. I frantically flipped on the lights as I passed them, pacing toward the door. I rubbed my eyes so I would look less exhausted.

As I approached the front door, all I could see was female silhouette outlined by the harsh white fluorescent floodlight in the parking lot. I recognized her—Hilary. She had just signed up last week.

As she saw me approach the door, she took a step back. My "Beast Mode Engaged" shirt clung to my torso, soaked in sweat from yet another night of stress-sleep.

"I couldn't remember if the first session was 4:45 am or 5 am, so I figured I'd come early," she said.

I mustered the world's weakest attempt at an understanding smile.

"No problem. I was already up." I'm pretty sure we both knew I was lying.

We made small talk. I didn't know her that well. She was a coworker of one of my members and was coming to "see what she was talking about all the time." I don't think I did a very good job of impressing her. The rest of the morning was a blur of people filing in and out, Lululemon yoga pants, neon tank tops, colored water bottles, repeated playlists, and the humid smell of sweat mixed with rubber.

After the last morning session finished, Jill, one of my first members, came up to me and said, "Are you ok? You seemed a little short today."

Jill was small but fierce. She had just had her second child and had signed up to lose the baby weight. She was an entrepreneur and respected the fact that I was "fighting the good fight" starting out my little business. But she looked genuinely concerned.

And I heard what she was really saying: "This business isn't going to grow if you act like this to paying customers." And she was right. Something needed to change…but what?

I was four months into opening up Transformation Center Huntington Beach, my first gym. I had one part-time employee who would take two of the morning sessions. But I still slept at the gym, so it didn't give me that much time back, since I had to be up either way.

The only way to describe how I felt at that time to people who weren't there is: "I was the kind of tired that a good night's sleep couldn't fix." I knew that the path I was on was unsustainable. But the only way I could make ends meet and cover rent was by literally doing everything myself. It was the classic rock-and-hard-place scenario. I needed to get out of the business to work on it, but I couldn't get out of it, because if I did, I wouldn't be able to make rent.

Six months earlier, I had sold my condo and quit my swanky consulting job in DC that I had landed after graduating college. I was applying for business school (I had scored above Harvard's average GMAT score and was really proud of that) and realized I really hated my job and didn't want to keep going down that path. So, to the shock and horror of my family, I decided I was going to do something I loved instead and open a gym. I packed everything I could into my car and drove to California—the land of fitness opportunity. If I could make it there, I could make it anywhere, I told myself.

The truth is, I didn't know anything. I was incredibly ill-prepared to run a business, let alone a gym. My only saving grace was a crippling fear of failure and insecurity that drove me. I didn't want to hear "Told you so" from anyone in my family or my friends or anyone who knew me. I didn't want to give anyone the satisfaction of being right when they asked, "Why is he throwing away everything he worked so hard for?"

I wish I could tell you it was my love of transforming bodies and lives that drove the early success of my gyms, but it wasn't. The thought of facing my dad's judgement as a failure was more unbearable than anything I would go through. At least, that's what I told myself. I didn't want the people who had bet against me to be right. It was my ego, my pride, that drove me.

It's embarrassing to me now. I'm genuinely ashamed that this was the mental space I was operating in. But entrepreneurship is about growth and shedding old identities and beliefs for new ones. I've grown a lot since then (I think), and I don't want to sugarcoat anything in this book or come off as "holier than thou." I've got a lot of flaws. I've made bad decisions with good intentions. But that was the energy source that kept me going early on when I didn't want to anymore. Maybe it is for you too.

If I knew then what I know now, I would have told myself NOT to open a gym. But I didn't know what I didn't know. And sometimes blissful ignorance is the only way we take the risks that grow us the most.

Besides ignorance and crippling insecurity, my last advantage was that I knew no one in Huntington Beach. And this meant that when everyone left the gym each day, it was just me. My phone didn't ring. Just empty silence. I was on my own. No kids. No wife. No girlfriend. Just me. This freed up time for me to research everything and anything I could about "how to run a gym"..."how to get gym clients"..."how to sell memberships"..."how to make rent without killing yourself"..."how to work without sleep"..."how to not smell bad if you haven't showered in five days." (Kidding on the last one—I already knew the answer. Febreze, deodorant, rinse face, brush teeth.

As you probably gathered, I did end up figuring out, piece by piece, how to fix my gym. And a lot of what I discovered flew in the face of conventional practices and the "business truths" I had been taught.

The truth is...we were all sold a lie.
We were told that we could make six figures as fitness professionals by trading our hours for dollars. If we just worked long enough and hard enough, eventually it would all pay off and we'd have the business of our dreams.

I'm here to tell you that your work ethic will not save you. Most people in this industry have more work ethic than any other. It's why I love gym owners. We are the best clients. We are growth-oriented, we understand the value of coaching, and we will work our asses off.

Twelve-hour days are routine. Sixteen-hour days six days a week are not at all uncommon. Years without a vacation or time off. All totally normal.

The fact is, we make up for lack of business acumen with sheer effort. But we are holding on for dear life, waiting for our hard work to pay off and our business to turn the proverbial corner that never comes.

The good news is, there is a repeatable process to go from that rock-and-hard-place scenario to true business ownership. It's how I grew from one location to six before my fourth year in business, all opened off cash flow. It's the framework we teach that grew our current business from $0 to a $50 million+ run rate in less than 24 months.

And it doesn't take long. It's just *different* than you'd expect.

What is Gym Launch Secrets?
At some point, every gym owner had a moment when they said, "I'm going into the fitness business so I can do what I love as a career."

Some got into it through personal training.

Others got into it through a franchise opportunity.

Others were clients of a gym, got certified, then decided to open their own facility.

And some just jumped in with two feet, signed the lease and said, "F*ck it—let's do this. I'll make it work." And work we did.

Most of us opened a facility with the intention of helping people go through the same personal transformation we went through ourselves. Our lives were changed, and we wanted to help others change their lives too.

Many of us thought owning a gym would be one of our crowning accomplishments—a final destination—when in reality, it was just the beginning.

Somehow, in the process of going from "passionate to help others" to "owning my first gym," you slowly come to the realization that you don't even have the most basic skills for running a business, let alone a gym. We may know a lot about fitness, but that doesn't mean we know anything about running a fitness business.

What you have in your hands is the culmination of my work to date with 1,200+ gym owners and 50+ franchises in a bazillion different markets—small, big, saturated, empty, rich, poor, all ethnicities, north, south, east, west, UK, Canada, Australia, Ireland, New Zealand, Germany, Belgium. I made every mistake in the book running my gym. And now you can read and practice what I learned, so you don't have to make the same mistakes I did.

Gym Launch Secrets is the handbook we should have all received when we got into the fitness industry. My intention was to distill as many lessons as I could fit into a logical and digestible format for gym owners who want to experience a sustainable workload and soaring profits.

The Three Main Problems With The Fitness Business

There are lots of problems in the gym business as most people traditionally practice it. This book will focus on the three biggest ones: the broken client-acquisition system, the broken revenue model, and the hole-in the bucket attrition problem.

You already know the problems, right? It costs too much money and time to bring in new clients, because the usual acquisition system is broken. Even when your gym is full at the popular times, you're barely making it, because the typical gym revenue model is also broken. And it seems like you can't hang on to clients more than a few months at a time, because attrition happens.

If you're struggling with one or all of these issues, I want you to know you're not alone. I've been there. Heck, I think *every* private gym owner has these same challenges.

I also want you to know that it's not your fault. The models we're following weren't designed for microgyms. They were designed for giant big-box fitness centers that can afford to wait months to be profitable. They have huge marketing budgets and a big corporate safety net.

We've got none of that.

But what we do have is smarts. And the ability to pivot and turn things around really quickly.

It took me years of studying things like revenue models, client generation, and marketing to understand why my business wasn't working. And then it took years of me testing theories on my own gym to find out what really DOES work.

This book is the culmination of all that work. I've distilled everything I know about successful gym ownership and written it down in this book. It kills me to see gym owners struggling, because I know there's a better way. I know how it felt when I was literally sleeping at my facility. It was a dark time in my life. And I don't want anyone else to feel like I did if I can help them avoid it.

As of 2018, my company Gym Launch has helped over 1,500 gyms turn themselves around and become massively profitable. Our community is responsible for over 4,000 new jobs and over $1 billion in revenue (according to an extrapolated average from our internal surveys in 2018). We've helped gym owners regain control over their time, make more money, and—best of all—find the fun in fitness again. Because that's why you got into this business in the first place, right? You genuinely love working out and helping people feel better.

You've already got the heart.

Now all you need to be wildly successful is a little of the right math.

Don't let the "m" word scare you. If you're not into numbers or business models, that's okay. I'm going to walk you through each concept step-by-step. I'm going to explain each of the big three problems in detail, including why they don't work. Then I'm going to show you the solutions. And to wrap this adventure up, I'll explain the $100K/month Wedding Cake Gym Profit Model. We use this model for every gym we work with, and it's amazing how fast things can improve with this system.

What's In It For You?
If you are willing to exchange the time it takes to coach two sessions and really study this book—and if you IMPLEMENT even a portion of the techniques I describe—I can guarantee you will add more revenue to your gym. Nothing else you could do in that amount of time will help you more than picking up what I'm laying down here. That is a promise.

I can make such a bold promise because most of the gyms I work with have only implemented about 30% of the techniques I present. And every single one of them has seen a subsequent explosion in top-line revenue (sales) growth and bottom-line (profit).

What's In It For Me?
My end goal is simple: trust. I'd like to earn yours. No small feat in this industry, but what can I say? I've got big dreams.

So I'd like to earn your trust by making you money first, if that's okay. I want to give you *results in advance*. Try just a couple of tactics from this book, watch them work, then try a few more, watch them work…and so on. The more you see results in your own business, the better.

I remember how it felt to wake up in the middle of the night in cold sweats, wondering how I'd make payroll.

And I know how security and peace of mind feel.

I want the ladder for you and for every gym owner on the planet.

Sound good?

Cool. So let's get to it.

SECTION I

Acquisition:
Get More Clients

This is going to seem pretty obvious, but here it is…

You can't have a successful gym business without gym customers.

So the first thing you need to understand is how to successfully get qualified customers in the door and buying your services. This first section is going to cover what we've discovered about the best ways to attract people to the services you offer, get them into your facility so they can talk to you or a member of your team, and convince them to spend the money to reach their fitness goals.

Most gyms struggle because the normal cycle of a gym includes attrition, or "churn," aka the percentage of people who leave your gym each month. If you're spending money continuously getting people in the door, but then the same number of people leave, you're just spinning your wheels for nothing. With this client-financed acquisition model, though, you get more people in than your churn rate, so you grow. And the best part? After your initial ad campaign, you don't have to spend any money out of pocket to get your customers coming in.

Let's dive in.

CHAPTER 1

The Broken "Sell Your Soul" Acquisition Problem

Gym owners often start out making false assumptions about what will work to bring in new clients and what will keep them coming in. After making all those same mistakes myself, I realized that the model of client acquisitions I had used was fundamentally flawed, and eventually I figured out a new way.

But first, let me describe the problem.

The "Sell Your Soul" Problem

Maybe you're starting from scratch with no marketing strategies at all. But here's where most gym owners start out…

They spend their "marketing budget" (I'll explain why that's in quotation marks later) on ads for a low barrier-to-entry offer (LBO) like a $21 for 21 Days promotion. Fairly typical.

Then they get some leads—let's say 100 for this example—and call them up. (Or maybe they pay someone to do it, but that means more payroll expenses.)

Then they make some $21 sales—great. For this example, let's say they sell 30 of their 100 leads the $21 offer.

Then they start the clients up…wait 21 days…and see who sticks.

Then they count their shiny new recurring memberships (also known as EFTs, or electronic funds transfers). The industry average conversion from a trial to a membership is 35%, but let's say they're above average, so they keep 50%.

This means they actually acquire 15 new EFTs—in other words, members who sign up for automatic payment—from their 30 trials. (Of course, three of their trials probably dropped off and never even showed up to start—but we'll ignore that for now.)

So now they added a total of 15 EFTs to their recurring revenue. So the gym grew. Success!

But hold on a minute...when they look at their bank statement, the total EFTs are the same as last month. There's been no increase in money coming in.

Why? What gives?

They haven't actually increased EFTs, because during the 14 days it took for them to sell and run the campaign, the 21 days it took to fulfill, and the 7 days it took them to track everyone down and get them signed up and resold on staying, their gym membership attrition rate kicked in. Typical churn in this industry averages 10% per month. And they've been working for six weeks, so that churn happened one and a half times.

This means their original 100 clients (industry average) became 85 during those 6 weeks of running the campaign, and their brand-new 15 clients merely offset their attrition.

So they are back to where they started...except they've spent $1,500 and hours of their time.

Here's an image that summarizes this information.

PROBLEM #2: THE "SELL YOUR SOUL" PROBLEM

LOW BARRIER OFFER
(21 DAYS FOR $21)

SOFTWARE	-$199	
FACEBOOK ADS	-$1000	MONEY IN VS MONEY OUT
LEADS	$100	(+) (−)
COST PER LEAD	$10 / LEAD	
% OF LEADS CLOSED	30%	
NUMBER OF 21 LBO SALES	30	
PRICE	$21	
REVENUE	+$630	
COMMISSION ???	$21 x 30 = -$630	
NET	-$1199	

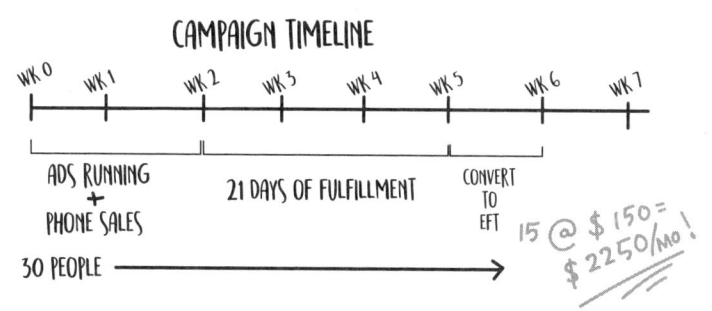

CAMPAIGN TIMELINE

WK 0 — WK 1 — WK 2 — WK 3 — WK 4 — WK 5 — WK 6 — WK 7

- ADS RUNNING + PHONE SALES (WK 0–2)
- 21 DAYS OF FULFILLMENT (WK 2–5)
- CONVERT TO EFT (WK 5–6)
- 30 PEOPLE ⟶

15 @ $150 = $2250/MO!

BUT WAIT... DURING THOSE 6 WEEKS YOU ALSO LOST THE INDUSTRY AVERAGE OF 10% PER MO WHICH MEANS IF YOU HAD 100 EFTS TO START... YOU LOST 15 DURING 1.5 MONTHS BRINGING YOUR NET GROWTH TO <u>ZERO</u> AND COSTING YOU $1199 TO STAY THERE.

Depressing, isn't it?

A Different Set Of Rules

If the scenario above seems at all familiar to you, you're not alone. This is how we were taught to market from our forefathers, the big-box mega gyms like 24 Hour Fitness and LA Fitness. It's all we've ever known.

The idea is to give a bunch of services, time, and money away on the front end, and make it up on the back end. The problem is that this model doesn't work unless you have deep pockets (in other words, lots of capital, aka cash on hand).

And what you may not know is that each of those companies I just listed is actually owned by private-equity groups—big-money guys who can afford to spend, even if it takes them a year to see a return. They play by a different set of rules.

This means that if we are trying to play their game by their rules, we are going to lose. Every. Single. Time.

So then how do you get people in the door, without LOSING money getting them in, while actually growing your EFTs?

Believe it or not, it's actually really simple. I can't believe how long it took me to figure it out. But once you understand this concept, you will never—and I mean NEVER—have to worry about a marketing budget ever again.

Does that sound good?

Then let's get to the solution right now.

CHAPTER 2

A Client-Acquisition Model That Works

Now I want to show you a concept that can literally change your life.

Are you ready?

There are only three ways to grow your business. ONLY THREE. No joke, I didn't sleep for a day once I understood this, because my mind was racing so fast with the possibilities.

THE ONLY 3 WAYS TO GROW YOUR BUSINESS

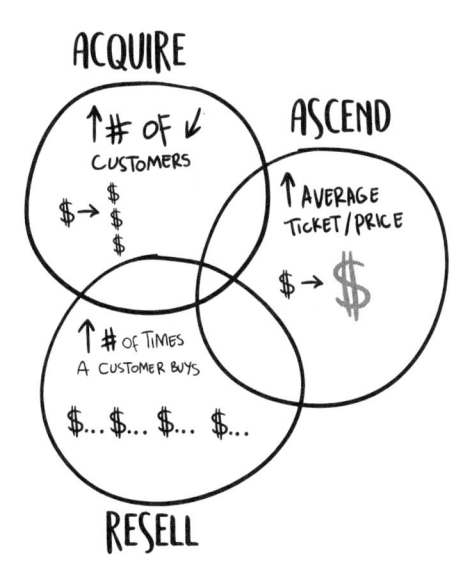

ACQUIRE — ↑ # OF CUSTOMERS — $→$$$

ASCEND — ↑ AVERAGE TICKET/PRICE — $→$

RESELL — ↑ # OF TIMES A CUSTOMER BUYS — $...$...$...$...

Business Growth Path #1: Get more clients.

Business Growth Path #2: Increase the average purchase, by increasing prices or a combination of cross-sells and upsells.

Business Growth Path #3: Get people to buy more frequently. In the gym world, this is called retention—the client buys month after month.

That's it. All you need to do is find ways to leverage one or all of these growth paths, and you're golden. I've found several that work so well in our industry that I trademarked the name Gym Profit Levers™. You will learn about them in Section II. There are three lever types: price levers, capacity levers, and overhead levers. When you implement one lever, things will start to improve for you. Implement them all in combination, and your life will completely change.

But enough dillydallying—let's dive in.

Here's how we fix the broken acquisition model:

1. Create a high-ticket/premium front-end offer.
2. Get paid to acquire customers (no joke).
3. Get them to show up.
4. Get them to buy.

There's a lot I want to show you here, so stick with me.

Let's go through these steps one at a time over the next few chapters.

Create A High-Ticket/Premium Front-End Offer

The reason you can't acquire customers profitably is because you are competing at a price that is too cheap. You're selling a commodity, something a consumer can use to hold your gym up to another one and say, "Yes, these two are similar enough that I will simply compare on price and choose the lower one."

This is what happens when industries, and the players within them, begin a race to the bottom. There are no winners in this race, only frustrated and broke people living on ramen noodles and sleeping on the floor. I was one—maybe you are too.

So the way you get out of that is through decommoditization. In other words, making your offer unique enough that there is no way to compare it to anyone else. By combining your services and products in such a way that they become unique, you become immune to price comparison.

The easiest way to do this is by making an irresistible offer. (Mind you, I didn't invent this concept—I just studied a lot and put the pieces together for myself and the other gym owners we serve.)

Here's my checklist for how to create and sell an irresistible offer. My favorite is a free six-week challenge. It's the exact same offer that most of our Gym Launch clients use successfully, so feel free to just copy and paste it into your own business.

Now, it's not enough to simply have an irresistible offer—you also have to sell it. There are eight steps to setting up your offer so it converts prospects into buyers.

1. Pre-Frame
2. Price Anchor
3. Splinter Stack
4. Scarcity
5. Urgency
6. Crazy Guarantee
7. Bribe
8. Downsell Your Upsell for Continuity

Cool. So let's dig into each step and see how they help make your offer even more amazing.

First, I want to say that we charge between $500 and $600 for this FREE six-week program.

Huh?

Let me explain.

The way it works is that we offer them the opportunity to try and lose X pounds or Y% body fat within six weeks. If they succeed, we give them their dollars back as cash or credit toward staying at our facility. It's a cool offer, people dig it and get great results, and it's *different*. But check out how you make it even more irresistible.

① PRE - FRAME
Ⓐ AUTHORITY
Ⓑ SOCIAL PROOF

The **pre-frame** happens on the phone. You ask them questions and give information that positions your gym as busy and highly desirable. You do this when setting the appointment and before they come into the gym. To pre-frame your gym in the best light, say things like:

- Did you hear about us from the local news story on best bootcamps?
- Have you heard about our owner from all the articles he's been featured in?

- He doesn't have a lot of openings for the next three weeks, but I may be able to get you in tomorrow night, because there was a last-minute cancellation.

Pro Tip: The sale has already started. It started before they even picked up the phone to contact you. This is always good to remember.

You also want to pre-frame their reasons for calling you in the first place. People reach out to a fitness professional because they have some kind of pain having to do with their body. Not necessarily physical pain, it could be mental. They've gained a lot of weight, they don't like how their body looks, they feel sluggish and flabby, and they want to feel good about their body again. Maybe they used to be an athlete and hate how they feel now after years of being sedentary. They want to live a longer, healthier life so they can be there for their family, and they worry about dying and leaving their kids alone. Whatever it is, those pain points are going to help you get them into your program.

Always have your potential clients fill out an intake questionnaire before you ever start pitching your program to them. This helps you understand the client and their goals, but just as importantly, it helps you understand their pain points—the reasons they've contacted you and want to make a change. And it keeps that pain in the front of their minds. It will also help you pre-sell your program by making them want to work with you…and only you.

You can have them fill out the form as soon as they sign up online by using an automated responder, email it to them once they've contacted you, or hand it to them as they walk into your facility. If you hand it to them personally, let them finish it first, and take a few minutes to review it before you start talking to them about your services. This pre-frames you as a person who genuinely cares about their challenges (which of course you do).

Here are some suggestions for questions to ask and the typical client answers. I got this from Dustin Napier and Dallas Wicker primarily, but a bunch of other great gym owners had questions and thoughts that likely influenced this list as well. These are people who close 85% of COLD TRAFFIC, as in people coming in the door wanting something for free and walking out $600 lighter and with the conviction that their life is about to change for the better.

It's important to state the qualifications of your program right up front. Make sure they meet those minimums before moving any further. Some of those might be…

- Are you able to commit to working out twice a week?
- Are you in good general condition?
- What injuries do you have that might hinder your progress?

Then you can continue with the questionnaire. Some of these may seem repetitive, but that's because you want the customer to touch their pain points multiple times as they answer the questions.

Intake Questionnaire With Sample Responses

- What are you here for?
    - I want to lose weight/get fit/be more athletic.

- What's your current fitness situation?
  - I'm a mess. I'm 40 pounds overweight, and my body hurts all the time.
- What's your dream goal?
  - I'd like to lose 40 pounds and fit into my old clothes again.
- How long would it take to accomplish this on your own?
  - Forever.
- Do you want to sustain your goal after you achieve it?
  - Of course.
- How long have you wanted to [*goal*]?
  - Since I had my last child. It's been 10 years, and I just can't get rid of the weight.
- Why do you want this so badly?
  - I have a 10-year reunion coming up, and I want to look good.
- You already know it's not easy to drop the weight. Will you take our recommendations and do what we ask in order to help you reach your goal?
  - Yes.
- Why are you applying now?
  - I want to lose weight, and I'm tired of struggling.
- Why do you think you'll succeed this time?
  - Because I'm committed, and my friend lost weight after joining your gym.
- Our average client loses 10 or more pounds with us in the first 3 months. Are you okay with this?
  - That would be great.

- What's your current state? What is your desired state?
  - I'm currently 40 pounds overweight. I want to be down to my college weight.
- Have you struggled to lose weight in the past?
  - Yes.
- Have you struggled with maintaining a self-directed fitness program in the past?
  - Yes.
- Do you think you'd lose the weight faster with an expert helping you along the way?
  - Yes.
- Do you think you'd lose the weight faster with daily accountability?
  - Yes.
- Is it more important that you lose the weight quickly or that it's permanent?
  - Permanent.

Answering these pre-framing questions forces them to slow down, gets them in the right frame of mind to make a purchase decision, and reminds them of their real pains and priorities.

② PRICE ANCHOR ~~$10,000~~ → $99

A **price anchor** is a higher price that you want the client thinking about before you present the current price. So as you go through your sales script, somewhere along the line, you want to drop that higher price point. It might be your regular price or it might be how much other gyms charge for a similar service, or even how much they might pay to do it all themselves. It just needs to be a much higher price than they will pay if they sign up today. You can even give them some bonuses when they sign up right away, to make the price seem even more irresistible.

I'm not going to go in-depth on the hand-to-hand combat of sales here. You can get more of that throughout the rest of this book. Just use the price anchor and see how much the sales resistance drops when you talk to prospective clients.

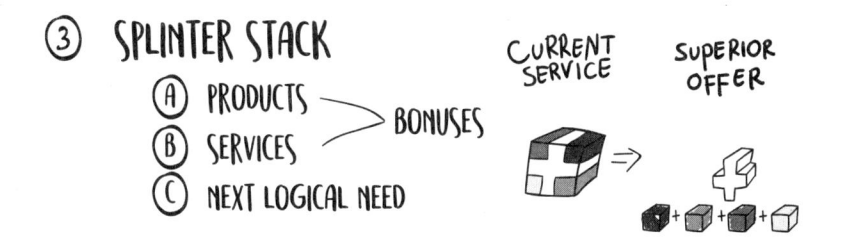

③ SPLINTER STACK
- (A) PRODUCTS
- (B) SERVICES → BONUSES
- (C) NEXT LOGICAL NEED

CURRENT SERVICE → SUPERIOR OFFER

The **splinter stack** strategy allows you to charge a premium for services that you're probably already doing as part of a bundle. You can think of it as "unbundling" if you like. This is where you take all the things you already do, but separate them out to offer as bonuses or special items.

Which is more appealing: a bootcamp membership or a six-week challenge with the following perks?

- Personalized meal plan
- Personal grocery list
- Local restaurant guide for eating out and special occasions
- Recipes specifically matched to your meal plan
- Accountability coach
- Three workouts per week with a trainer
- Online accountability group

- Online platform for permanent weight-loss education
- Super shake guide
- Bomb-ass breakfasts
- Lick-your-fingers lunches
- Delectable dinners

Now, you might include the exact same things in both programs. But when you splinter out and list each individual service in the challenge, people feel like they're getting so much more. Just because the list is longer, it's psychologically more appealing.

If you don't have all those things, like the grocery list and meal plans, go make them. It's not hard to do. I think I made all of ours over about a week (while taking a lot of stimulants). But once it was done, my offer was unique and special, incomparable with what other gyms were offering, which allowed me to charge premium prices. And you can also use half of those as same-day bonuses for signing up immediately, which pushes the potential new client to act fast.

④ SCARCITY (X LEFT / Y SPOTS)
↳ # OF UNITS/AVAILABILITY

Sold Out!

Scarcity means there's a limited supply. As in, "We only have X products left/Y spots available." A lot of people will want your most popular session times. So if you know what time the client wants to come, you can use it as a scarcity tactic to get them to act that day. They'll be afraid of missing out on that time slot. You really do have scarcity, so you might as well use it to your advantage in the sale. Just say something like, "You should grab your spot today, so we can make sure we add your name before it fills up."

⑤ URGENCY (BY X DATE) 5...4...3...2...1...DONE!
↳ RELATES TO TIME

Urgency means time is almost up. They need to act right now and not put the decision off, even for an hour. Lots of marketers lump scarcity and urgency together, but they are two different beasts. They're both necessary, but they're different. Urgency is a component of TIME. For example, you might say, "This program starts tomorrow, so you're gonna have to decide now if you wanna get in, and I don't know when we're going to run this promotion again."

We started a new challenge every week, so we could always say, "This program starts tomorrow, so you should sign up now to get in with this group." It's a small push, but it works.

⑥ CRAZY GUARANTEE 2x DOUBLE YOUR MONEY BACK GUARANTEE!

Crazy Guarantee: Many people feel like guarantees are risky, but they're not if you're good at what you do. Most clients are pretty good-natured at heart (in my opinion). So they're not gonna screw you, unless you really screwed them. This was my guarantee—swipe it if you'd like.

> We are so confident in our ability to blow you away with our world-class service that I offer a personal

satisfaction guarantee. If you get to the end of this program and you feel as though you did not get the level of service that was equal or superior to the investment you put in financially, I'll write you a refund check myself. Best-case scenario, I change your life; worst case, you worked out for free. You have no risk.

I used this guarantee to make hundreds of thousands of dollars. But the number of times someone took me up on the refund? Twice.

Was it worth it? I think so.

You don't have to use mine. I could write an entire book on guarantees, but in general the more creative, the better. Mine wasn't all that creative, but it was definitely effective.

⑦ FOR CONTINUITY GIVE HIGH VALUE PRODUCT/SERVICE AS FREE BRIBE TO ENTER CONTINUITY.

Get Our $2000 Program FREE Today When You Become A Member!

Bribe: People like to get things for free. Who doesn't like a good bonus incentive? So you can entice the customer even more during the sale by offering things you normally charge for as a bribe if they sign up as a member right then and there.

This is called an either/or, or an "assumed close." You give someone the final option of two choices, both of which involve buying from you. One high-ticket choice and one low-ticket with continuity or monthly commitment. Do NOT underestimate the power of this concept.

This strategy is popular and successful in many industries, and it works beautifully for gyms. You can offer a

6-Week Challenge that normally costs $600 as a free gift if they just sign up for a membership today. Beautiful. Elegant. Mind-blowing.

The famous marketer Frank Kern used this to build his eight-figure newsletter by giving away all of the digital products he had ever made (worth more than $16,000) as a bribe for people to subscribe to his $400/month newsletter.

⑧ FOR CONTINUITY DOWNSELL YOUR UPSELL ...

$\$ \rightarrow \$...\$...\$...$ ↘
SAME SERVICE FOR LESS BUT LONGER

Downsell Your Upsell: A lot of people give me credit for this concept and cite me as the creator. I definitely didn't invent it. But I've made a tremendous amount of money with it though, and I would highly recommend using it in your sales and pricing process. However, it can really only be used with a high-ticket front-end offer. If you aren't sold by now, this should be the clincher.

Downselling your upsell relates to the back end of the offer, converting people to the monthly membership (or continuity), which I will get into more when I explore the attrition problem. But the main nugget I will give you here is this: no one wants a membership. They want a result and a deadline. So you should give it to them. You can do it with a bribe as mentioned above, but most times, you need to sell them a defined-end program (DEP), one that last for X days or Y weeks. Why? I have no idea. But I know it works.

People will pay two to four times the price for something if it is NOT on continuity. So why not charge them the most when they are the most excited and their pain is the highest? It makes more sense than giving them everything for free until their excitement wears off, and only then trying to upsell them. Right? But for some reason, we were all taught backward.

For example, someone starts a DEP that is $100/week for 12 weeks. Then when they reach the end of that period, they can continue on at only $50/week.

Read that sentence again.

You're charging double the price at the beginning, when they're most committed and excited, and will likely get amazing results. Then you're making the $200 monthly membership seem like a total bargain.

Gyms that use this technique keep double the industry average on the back end AND at a 58% higher price. (Yes, you read both those stats right.) Neato.

Summary

The irresistible offer is the first step to fixing your acquisition problem. You need to have something unique to sell in order to command unique prices. Sell normal stuff for normal prices and irresistible things for irresistible prices. And irresistible pricing is necessary in order for you to generate enough cash up front to buy ads.

The next step is to get paid to acquire customers.

And you'll never need a marketing budget again.

What?

Keep reading.

Chapter 3

Get Paid To Acquire Customers

Now that you have your offer, it's time to make it rain.

As I explained earlier, the reason those big-box gyms can spend a ton of money on advertising and marketing without seeing an immediate return on their investment is because they're owned by private-equity groups that have a lot of capital. Most individual gym owners don't have that, so they're stuck trying to throw their own personal money into marketing, and then they don't have the funds to actually operate the gym. But there's a way out of that vicious cycle, and I'm going to explain it right now. This is Step 2 in the client-financed acquisition process.

Time to fire away. Here is your pretty picture for an illustration of the concept.

CLIENT-FINANCED ACQUISITION®

① CREATE HIGH-TICKET FRONT-END PRODUCT

② MAKE MORE MONEY ON FRONT-END SALES THAN YOU DO ON LEAD COST/ADS

③ NEVER NEED A MKTG BUDGET EVER AGAIN

EX:

<u>100% PROFIT</u> →

	DAY 1	DAY 2	DAY 3	DAY 4	DAY 5
SPEND	$100	$100	$100	$100	$100
LEADS	10	10	10	10	10
SALES %	20%	20%	20%	20%	20%
SALES	2	2	2	2	2
PRICE	$600	$600	$600	$600	$600
REV	$1200	$1200	$1200	$1200	$1200
DEPOSIT	$0	$0	$0	$2400	$3600
BANK ACCT	-$100	-$200	-$300	$2000	$3100

NOTE*: I SHOW A DELAY BECAUSE MOST PROCESSORS TAKE 72 HRS TO RELEASE FUNDS. SO THIS GIVES YOU REAL CASH FLOW #s.

This is it. This is what has made me an obscene amount of money, more than I will ever need to live off of. This is what allowed us to go from being a complete unknown in the gym-education space to the biggest player in it. (And hopefully it will keep us there for some time to come, as long as we don't rest on our laurels and we stay humble and eager to serve.)

This is also what allowed me to bankroll the opening of each of my new facilities beyond the first one…**and to open them all at full capacity on the first day.**

I'm only telling you this because if you made it this far, you have struck gold.

The concept is simple and ruthlessly effective.

It works like this—follow along.

> On Day 1, you put $100 into paid ads for your irresistible offer.
>
> You get 10 leads at $10 per lead.
>
> From those leads, you schedule appointments with 7 of them.
>
> From those 7, 3 or 4 will show for their appointment.
>
> From the 3 or 4 who show, you sell 2 @ $600 for a 6-Week Challenge.
>
> So from 10 leads, you make 2 sales, which means 20% of leads closed.
>
> What this means is that it cost you $100 to make $1,200 (2 x $600).
>
> That is a 12 to 1 return.

This is not weird. This is common. And $10 leads are actually higher than most get, but I wanted to keep the numbers the same as the typical 21-day offer I used in the beginning for illustration.

In this example, by the fourth day, you will have made $3,600 (6 sales x $600).

But because I've done this so many times, I know that payment processors tend to keep money for two to three business days. So at the very least, on the fourth day of your campaign, the first one or two days of sales will get deposited into your account.

So that's $2,400 minus $400 in ad spend, for a net of $2,000.

Now with this $2,000, you covered your initial cost of acquisition (cost of getting a new customer), and everything else you spend on this campaign is **pure profit**.

And this cycle continues until you have made money getting customers.

Read that again, please. I want it to sink in.

Got it?

Good.

And you keep spending and making money until you have filled your gym.

Not until you run out of cash.

Not until your agency tells you to stop.

Not until a revenue share company says enough.

But until you darn well please.

And that is how we get the gyms full…and how we keep them full.

The gym—and your business, if you do this right—should never require money from your pocket to get new customers.

It's like going to the casino and only playing with winnings.

This is the secret to unending growth. It's called a **negative client-acquisition cost**.

You MAKE MONEY getting more people. So why would you ever stop?

Good question. Most of our gym owners only stop when one of their other systems breaks down (they hit capacity, they have to open more times, change up their service delivery, etc.). But I'll show you how to handle those problems later.

The Secret To Fantastic Lead Generation Is Great Advertising

So let's tackle the next challenge—creating the actual ad campaigns.

The big secret to making great ads is simply testing a lot of different ideas. You don't have to be super creative. You don't have to hire a crazy expensive agency. It's just trial and error and keeping track of the data so that your next ad works better.

I hope that saves you some headache. There are no magic ad-making genies. There's no silver bullet. It's just testing ads, picking the ones that work best, then testing some more. When we run tests for our gyms, we'll usually test over 150 ads to find 5 home runs (winners in every market) and about 15 triples (winners in two-thirds of markets). I spend about $100K out of my own pocket on ads in 100+ markets to test what's working. Only then will I hand those winning ads over to our highest-level gym owners (who we call Gym Lords).

So they hit home runs every time. They print money. They pay us so they don't have to test. Win-win.

If you ever run out of ideas for what to create for your ads to "make it rain," you're not alone. It took me a while to get the hang of it too. So let me help you out.

This is what I call my **Lead-Gen Scrambler**. Basically, you want to spend a little time coming up with as many headlines and images, and as much body copy, as you can. Then scramble them up to create fresh new ads.

LEAD GEN SCRAMBLER
NEVER STRUGGLE TO MAKE "FRESH" ADS AGAIN

① **HEADLINE**: -DURATION -GENDER -BENEFIT/STATUS ↑
-CURIOSITY -AGAINST FEAR -NEGATIVE -CHALLENGE

② **COPY**: -SHORT -LONG -FREE -NEW
-REASON WHY -BENEFITS -STATUS
-SO THAT YOU CAN -DESCRIBE, DONT TELL
-SCARCITY -URGENCY -IMPLIED AUTHORITY

③ **PAGE NAME/BUSINESS NAME**:
-HAVE MULTIPLE VERSIONS
-DESCRIPTIVE -3rd PARTY

④ **IMAGE**: -↑CONTRAST -BLACK/WHITE -BANNERS -DIAGONAL
-GROUP PICS -SELFIE -WORKOUT PICS -PEOPLE IN CLASS
-PEOPLE SWEATING POST CLASS -MEME -DOO-DADS

⑤ **VIDEO**: -FLASH CARDS -BACKGROUND -SCENERY
-PRO V. IPHONE -SUBTITLES -PITCHING -FACILITY TOUR -WHITEBOARD
-GROUP TESTIMONIAL -AVG JOE TESTIMONIAL -SELFIE TESTIMONIAL
-GROUP EXERCISE IN UNISON -GET CLIENTS TO SAY HOW GREAT YOU ARE

(Sidebar illustration: JOE'S FITNESS ad mockup — ① FREE 6 WK CHALL, with video play button and FREE 6 WK CH / APPLY button)

Use Headline 1 with Image 8 with Video 16 and test. Mix it up again with Heading 3, Body Copy 2, and Image 12. The more pieces you have, the more fun you can have scrambling them up.

(Please don't get overwhelmed here. You can start with a low amount and just a few different pieces of copy. Over time, you'll collect more and more pieces that work.)

So then I hand them all over to my marketing team to make our new ads. This technique gives you virtually endless variations. So even in your tiny seven-mile geographical radius, you can always create fresh new ads that convert. (That's the radius we have found to be the sweet spot for a local gym. You're welcome.)

There are entire books written on each component of the advertisement. What you see there are the variables. Each of the bullets are some of the best converting "nuggets" I have on each one. This is my surefire cheat sheet. Whenever I get stuck or I need a new idea for an image, a video, or copy, I look here to remind myself of the fundamentals.

Since copy can be one of the hardest parts to get right, let me expand on that topic. Here are the twelve copy commandments that I check off for every single ad we write. This is also the checklist I give my internal team. I'm holding nothing back here.

1. **Headline comes first.** It is the most read portion of an advertisement and must sell the prospect on giving yet another millisecond of attention. Curiosity is king. Different is ideal. And sexy works. Never run an ad without a headline.
2. **Say what only you can say.** If you have done anything remarkable or different, say it.
3. **Always call out who you are looking for** (and who you are NOT—this is even more powerful than the call-out).
4. **Reason why.** Always tell the prospect WHY you are running a promotion. The word "because" is one of the

most influential words in the English language. Use it. *Because it works.*

5. **Damaging admission**. Always own your flaws. Eminem figured out that if he said all the things that were wrong about him, no one could call him out. The other power punch of this tactic is that it makes the statements that follow more believable, since you are starting with truth. It also makes you *authentic*. If you can do this with humor, you get bonus points.

6. **Show, don't tell**. I wouldn't say "make more sales." Instead I would say, "You'll be amazed when you hear customers read their credit card numbers to you over the phone after reading two magic sentences. It'll feel like taking orders." Note the description and the emotions.

7. **Tie benefits to status whenever possible.** A lot of people talk about "benefits not features," which is true. But I like to take it a step further. "A cookbook so fast and easy, all of your friends will wonder how you find time to be fit AND cook for your family every night."

8. **Use urgency and scarcity whenever possible.** And make it legitimate. It will actually make you more money.

9. **Implied authority**. This goes back to #1. If you are the only double-secret black belt in the area, say it. If you have transformed over 1,000 people in 10 years, say it. If you have a pro athlete client, say it. It will imply authority. And people listen to and trust authority figures more.

10. **P.S. = power sentence**. The headline and the PS statement are the most read words in any advertisement. Always have them. And always make sure they are strong.

11. **Clear next steps**. Make. It. Stupid. Simple. "If you want X, click the button. On the next page, fill out your info. Then select a convenient time for you to come in that you won't miss." Step 1. Step 2. Step 3. They won't guess. It WILL sound stupid when you write it. But it WILL make you more money.
12. **Third-grade level**. Most copy doesn't convert because people have to pause to understand it. The sentences are too complex or they use big words. You're not writing a college paper. You're writing an ad that has milliseconds to catch someone's attention. Make the process as frictionless as possible. Fancy = friction. Simple = sales. I put every ad I have through a free reading-level tool and continue to edit the copy until it is at a third-grade reading level or below.

Hopefully I just saved you thousands of dollars on copywriting courses. Those are twelve best nuggets on writing great copy.

Swipe. Deploy. Enjoy.

Chapter 4

Get Them To Show Up

Still with me? We're solving the client-acquisition problem, remember? It's not enough to have an irresistible offer and a great ad strategy. Those got you leads. Great. But now what?

There are two challenges to this step: getting your leads to schedule and getting them to show up to their appointments. Obviously, you need both of these to happen in order to convert leads into actual paying clients. Here's how.

Get Them Scheduled

The easiest way to get people scheduled is to simply have an automated calendar app on your thank-you page. (Brilliant, I know, but I didn't do this for the first five years of business. Shame on me.)

About 70% of the people who hit your thank-you page will schedule if given this option, which is pretty good. But there's more you need to do to get them to show up. Remember that these clients probably clicked on that scheduler or the "Yes, I want to join" button on a whim. In that moment, they felt like they were ready to make a major change to their life. But a minute later, they probably forgot about the whole thing. The key is to get them into your facility quickly so they don't have time to get cold feet or lose interest.

Scheduling Best Practices

Allow same-day or next-day appointments only. I could go on and on about this, but not scheduling for the same day or the next day is risky. People should only be allowed to schedule three or more days out under extreme circumstances. Why? Because show rates drop dramatically after that. And when someone no-shows, three things have to happen in order to get them to become a customer:

1. They have to reschedule.
2. They have to show up after no-showing the first time.
3. They have to buy.

That's a lot of hoops to lead them through. So we really try to maximize our first scheduling so that we can get as many people in and buying as possible. Make a straight line to the sale.

If someone fights you on this, remind them that they have to work out daily or every other day. So if their schedule is so full that they can only make it in the following week, then when were they expecting to work out? Ask this, and it'll give you a back door to get them to come in.

Here's an example:

> You: "When were you planning on working out?"
>
> Tracy: "After work."
>
> You: "When do you get off work tomorrow?"
>
> Tracy: "Five o'clock."
>
> You: "Great. I'm booked out the next two weeks, as is Mark, but he actually had a last-minute opening tomorrow (and he never has openings). Do you want that 5:30 spot after you get off work tomorrow?"

Tracy: "Yeah, that works."

You: "Okay, is this your cell phone?"

Tracy: "Yes."

You: "Cool. I'll shoot you a text right now with the address and all the details. See you soon, Tracy." *Click*.

Then send the text. That script is also how you get off the phone fast so you can move on to the next lead.

Use scarcity and urgency. I tell the following story probably every other day to a new gym owner who joins our ranks.

Many moons ago, we used to have an eight-person sales team that traveled from gym to gym making sales for gym owners. It ended up being difficult to scale the business (hotels x 8, rental cars x 8, marketing spend x 8, commissions x 8, managing 800+ new sales billing-wise, etc.), but we learned a lot. One of the hallmark lessons I learned from this experience was that in a 21-day campaign period, our sales team would always do twice the number of sales in the last 5 days than they did in the first 2 weeks combined. Why do you think that was?

Because our sales team realized later in their work cycle that they had to get the clients in the door or they wouldn't be able to get the sales commission. As they neared the end of the 21 days, they changed the way they spoke to the prospects, because they were doing the calculations in their heads and realized they had to get more people to sign up. And that was a change of conviction, not scripting.

The sales people had urgency—they wanted a bigger commission check that period. So their TONES changed. They spoke to the clients differently. They closed faster. The scarcity and urgency became REAL. And as a result…THEIR SHOW RATES DOUBLED.

Inevitably, a gym owner will tell me, "I'm using scarcity, I'm telling them there aren't many spots left, but it's not working." Here's the thing: the human mind is really good at picking out BS. So you yourself need to be *convinced* that the urgency and scarcity are true.

Here's why I believe it: if someone doesn't make it into the gym, it is very difficult for us to help them. So the reality is that if that person doesn't make it in for their appointment, it really can be their last chance of having a spot. Because the likelihood that they reschedule, show, and close is only like 10%. So we use everything we've got to get them to show up the first time they schedule.

The best thing to discourage people from breaking appointments is to simply have a hard-line policy of not rescheduling. Most gym owners aren't comfortable doing this, but it can be as simple as saying, "We don't do reschedules because we're simply too booked up. And we only work with people who are serious and keep their word."

Which leads me to another little technique: the **Integrity Tie-Down**.

Here's how this script goes:

"Do you consider yourself a person of integrity?"

"Of course."

"Great. Because we only do business with people who have the same values as us, and when we say we're going to be somewhere, we mean it. So are you the type of person who keeps their commitments?"

"Yes."

"Great. We're going to send you three reminders between now and then, to do our part to help you keep that commitment. We're excited to see you. Is this your cell phone number?"

And the rest you know.

People don't like doing things against positive character traits they identify with. This is a psychological technique known as labeling. Essentially, you label someone with a positive attribute, get them to agree to it, then provide them with the desired action that is in alignment with it. When you do this, most people will take that action to reinforce what they believe about themselves. So at the gym, they will demonstrate the positive attribute that they are "a person who keeps their word" rather than just because they made an appointment.

Number Of Outreach Attempts: The number of times you contact potential clients is directly correlated to how many people actually walk in your door.

It sounds straightforward, but it is what I would consider a sales law. The more attempts to reach out to someone, the more likely they are to schedule and to believe it is important and show up.

Many gym owners are shy and don't want to bother people or they say, "I only want people who don't need reminding because it's important to them." Well, that's silly. Because no one knows who is calling them until they pick up and speak with you, at which point you can say something like, "I know. If this is how much I bug you to get in the gym BEFORE you're a client, imagine how much I'm gonna do to make sure you show up." And that's pretty much all it takes.

Think about this: if people forget their kids at daycare occasionally, they can easily forget your appointment. Don't be too proud to send multiple reminders.

I recommend 15 outreach attempts over the first 3 days (combo of text, call, and email) to get ahold of people. And once you schedule them, give at least one daily reminder until the day of the appointment.

This will help impress them. "Joe's Gym must be good at training—look at all they do."

Day Of Appointment: You should send two texts. One as a personal video text in the morning, which I outline below. The second should be a picture of you making a goofy face pointing to the front of your facility with a relevant landmark like "Across from the 7-Eleven on 8th" to reinforce that you're likable, real people.

Video Texts: I got this strategy from Grant Cardone. One of his sales guys sent me a personal video text where he USED MY NAME. I thought it was so powerful, we implemented it right away and saw an immediate lift in show rates. A simple 15–20-second video texted to a prospect the morning of the appointment does wonders.

> Hey, Tracy. It's Alex, one of the coaches here at 123 Fitness. We're real people and this is our gym (*show front door & signage*) right across from [*landmark*]. You are on my team for the [*defined-end program name*]. I see you are on the schedule for tonight at [*time*], so I just wanted to send you this video to introduce myself and let you know we are excited to meet you and introduce you to everyone. Text me back what size shirt you want, and I'll put it aside for you. Can't wait to see you soon (*big smile & wave*).

If this sounds like a lot of work…you're right. But being broke sucks too, so you can choose: work or bankruptcy.

The good news is that you can automate all of this. Yep. It's obviously beyond the scope of this book, and tech software changes almost hourly nowadays, but this entire process I just outlined is 100% automatable. (In fact, we show our gyms how to do it for themselves.) This process alone typically saves our gym owners an average of $30,000/year in payroll, and adds stupid amounts to the top line in increased show-ups and sales.

There is so much more—and it kills me to cut this short—but we have to get moving. I hope that gives you at least a primer on some best practices to get people to show up to your gym.

But now that they're in your gym, how do you help them?

Chapter 5

Get Them To Buy

This is the part that a lot of gym owners (and businesspeople in general) often say they hate. They don't want to bug people, they're afraid the customer will run away when they're being sold to, or they worry that the customer will say no. But to give your clients the best service you can—and to make enough money to keep your gym not only open but thriving for you and your staff—you'll need to learn some selling techniques. In this chapter, I'll go over a few of my favorites.

Get Them To Give You Money

I had an incendiary title for this section, "How To Take Money From Strangers Who Have Never Met You…And Like It" but I decided to go with the nicer one.

But make no mistake, in the beginning, you have to take money from strangers who don't know you. Again, this makes selling seem heartless. But please shift your thinking around this because otherwise no one will give you their money. You have to convince them (hence the "take"), and I also think people pay more attention with strong headlines, so there's that too.

At the end of the day, selling is serving. And you need to believe that for real.

If you don't like selling, it means you don't like helping people make decisions to help themselves—which of course you do, because that's why you got into the gym business in the first place. So you need to get over this false belief.

At the heart, sales is made up of just three transfers:

1. A transference of belief in the product (you believe in your gym and services)
2. A transference of confidence that the person can reach their goals (you believe in people making a change since you have helped yourself and others do the same)
3. A transference of conviction that the person can overcome circumstances (all the things people tell themselves that stop them from deciding to change)

Without transferring these three things, you will not be able to help people. So here are some ways to overcome people's resistance to change. These are not theories. They were forged from over 4,000 one-on-one closes. Yes…4,000. I sold for all my locations for an extended period of time because I'm a stubborn bastard and I like sales. And I like sales because I got good at it. And I got good at it because I did it 4,000 times.

The "How Much Is A Membership?" Problem

A quick story…

My friend Josh Price was one of my first clients. (I pick on him because he is one of the nicest, most down-to-earth people you will ever meet, and he doesn't take it personally when I poke a little fun.) Several years ago, I was helping him out with sales for his gym. I was with a potential gym member who had responded to some ads we were running, and I was about halfway through the sale. I was really getting into it—not at a point I could leave or bring someone else in—and while this was going on, someone just walked in the door.

Crazy, I know. A walk-in. As rare a sighting as anyone has seen.

Josh stopped what he was doing and greeted this unicorn.

> Walk-In Human: I'm new to the area, and I'd like to know more about what memberships and pricing you guys have.
>
> Josh: Awesome. Welcome. (*Hands Walk-in Human a clipboard.*) Here's our pricing sheet. Take a look around, and let me know if you have any questions.

Then Josh went back into his office.

It was like watching a car accident in slow motion and having all the power in the world to stop it, but not being able to make it over in time.

The guy looked over the clipboard then looked around the gym. He set it down on one of the couches in the lobby, walked out the door, and was never seen again.

CRASH

This is an extreme example, but it happens every day. Many owners say, "I hate sales" or "I don't want to pressure people" or whatever. But the reality is, we all hate things we're not good at, because we don't like failing. But failing, especially in sales, is part of the game.

You need to learn to sell so you can help people. And you have to suck before you get good.

I can't name anyone off the top of my head who is great at sales but hates it.

All you need to do is improve your hand-to-hand sales combat skills and expect to get beat up a little your first few rounds. It's all right. You're tough. You can take it.

As with so many skills, it's only a lack of practice not a lack of inclination that makes it hard. Once you learn the skill, you'll most likely start to enjoy it and get better at it.

And a solid sales framework will help you get better fast.

> **Pro Tip:** The reason you feel like everyone is saying you are too expensive or everyone is telling you they're broke is because when they ask for the PRICE, you answer with a number.
>
> The real answer to the question "How much does it cost to join your gym?" is "It depends on your goal." This gives pricing context, so you can actually sell in a premium-priced environment. This is the goal of the irresistible offer, right?
>
> Consumers only ask how much something is because they don't know what else to ask. Most people think Planet Fitness and Weight Watchers are the same thing. It's the salesperson's job to educate, provide context, and break beliefs for the consumer so they can make an intelligent and informed decision. And the easiest way to do that is to make all conversations exactly the same so you have a consistent outcome.

At the end of the day, you need to make selling easy for your team, so that when you're not there, the chips are stacked in their favor.

This is called a sales system. And sales systems equate to leverage and scale. Use them.

What's that? You don't have a sales system?

Well, why didn't you say so?

Here's mine...

(This isn't supposed to be a sales book, but I couldn't help myself.)

The Sales Greeting, Waiting Area, And Office

The first part of a consistent conversation is a consistent environment. Because whether you are actively thinking about it or not, your lobby and selling space are shouting clues at the prospect. It's up to you if you want those things to hurt the sale or help it.

I'll try and make this short and sweet. It's simple but extremely effective. So take the afternoon, do this once, and never think about it again.

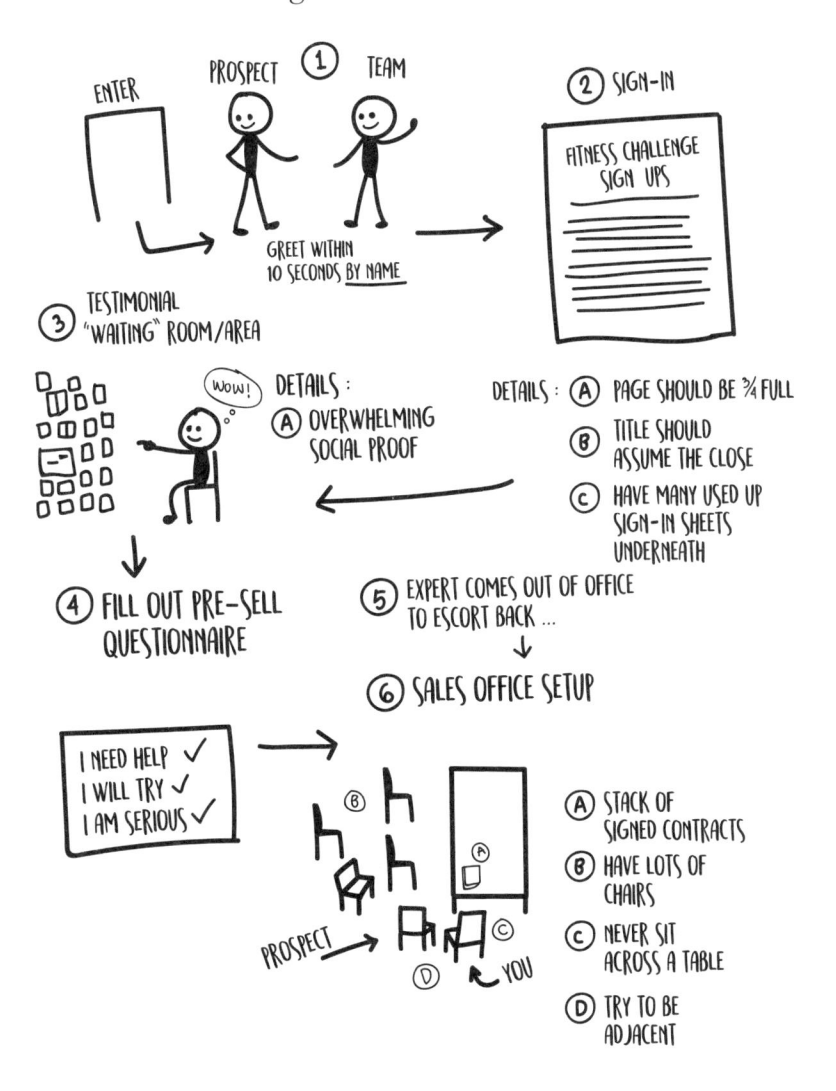

① PROSPECT / TEAM — ENTER — GREET WITHIN 10 SECONDS BY NAME

② SIGN-IN — FITNESS CHALLENGE SIGN UPS

③ TESTIMONIAL "WAITING" ROOM/AREA
DETAILS: (A) OVERWHELMING SOCIAL PROOF

DETAILS: (A) PAGE SHOULD BE ¾ FULL
(B) TITLE SHOULD ASSUME THE CLOSE
(C) HAVE MANY USED UP SIGN-IN SHEETS UNDERNEATH

④ FILL OUT PRE-SELL QUESTIONNAIRE
- I NEED HELP ✓
- I WILL TRY ✓
- I AM SERIOUS ✓

⑤ EXPERT COMES OUT OF OFFICE TO ESCORT BACK...

⑥ SALES OFFICE SETUP
(A) STACK OF SIGNED CONTRACTS
(B) HAVE LOTS OF CHAIRS
(C) NEVER SIT ACROSS A TABLE
(D) TRY TO BE ADJACENT

Let's start with the moment a potential customer walks in the door. Here's our preferred setup for your sales greeting and office to maximize your likelihood of making the sale.

Let's walk through this image one step at a time.

1. Greet the client emphatically by name within 10 seconds. Your team should run if they have to. This gives a solid first impression that tells them you care about high-quality service.
2. Make sure they sign in. You should have a stacked sign-in sheet. Make up names if you need to, or ask some of your current clients to write their names down.
3. Have a crazy testimonial wall or room as your waiting area. These are before and after photos of people you've worked with. Here are examples from two of our Gym Lords:

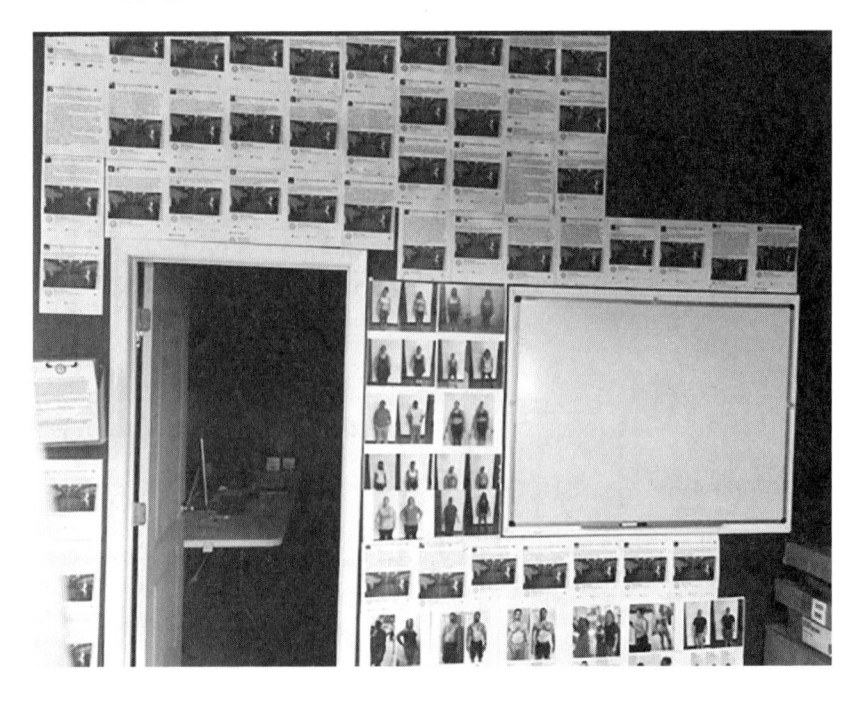

1. Have them fill out the pre-sell intake questionnaire. It will improve your close rate and that of your team.
2. After they've had a few minutes alone to browse the testimonials, escort them back into a sales area. Beforehand, you should set up your sales table so you NEVER sit across from a prospect. You should be shoulder to shoulder, on the same side. Have lots of other chairs in the room so it looks like you always have lots of people who want your attention, and a big ol' stack of signed contracts. (Go grab your EFT contracts if you need to.) These items should give off the impression that...

- You are in demand.
- You are an authority and an expert.
- Lots of people have come in recently.
- A lot of people have signed up for this offer. (People like knowing others have taken the same offer.)
- There's a lot of scarcity (because you are almost full) and urgency (because the program starts soon).

Some gym owners or sales teams have the customer fill out the pre-sell questionnaire (from Chapter 2) with them; others have their front desk people do it. Either way works—it's up to you. But if you're going to do it yourself, squat down so you are eye level and read the questions to them. It shows you care, and people appreciate when someone inconveniences themselves. It also makes you more comfortable, because you're on the same level and there's no perceived distance. Details matter.

Finally, you begin the sales conversation.

And, because I love you, I'm laying out our entire sales framework in the next chapter.

Keep reading.

CHAPTER 6

The C-L-O-S-E-R Formula

Want to see the framework I've taught to countless employees and over 1,500 gyms to get them selling cold traffic FAST? If you think you are good at sales but have never sold to anyone who wasn't a referral, you've never sold. In my book, sales is talking someone who is vaguely interested in what you do—who barely remembers opting in and who knows no one else who has worked with you—into giving you money. That is sales. And that is what I am going to show you.

It doesn't matter if you're the main salesperson or you have a team—you need to do at least some selling yourself so you understand the framework and how well it works.

Learn it. Use it. Profit from it. Then teach it to your team.

I use the acronym CLOSER to make it easy to remember. Here is the basic structure:

1. CLARIFY why they are there.
2. LABEL them with the problem you plan on solving.
3. OVERVIEW their past pains and experiences.
4. SELL them the "vacation."
5. EXPLAIN away their concerns.
6. REINFORCE their decision…WOW them.

Now that you have an easy acronym to remember, let's unpack it.

Clarify Why They Took Action / Showed Up

"What made you come in today?"

"What's your goal?"

"Why did you sign up for [*program name*] online?

I'll usually ask all three of these questions quickly and in succession, because some people need a few different prompts to understand what you mean. The point of this question is to establish a GAP. There's something they want that they haven't been able to achieve so far (or maintain after achieving), and the easiest way to find out is to just ask.

Sometimes they'll say something generic and not helpful like, "I just wanted to find out more info" or "I was just curious because it was a great deal."

To overcome that generic opening, say something like, "I'm sorry, I should have asked a better question so I know how to best help you get what you want. What are you hoping to accomplish or improve as a result of coming here?"

Then they will usually tell you their PROBLEM.

Label Them with the Problem You Plan to Solve

Here's where you highlight or recap their current state versus the state they desire. Get their stats.

- "Got it, so you want to lose weight. Well, how much do you weigh now?"
- "So you are currently 180 pounds with 28% body fat, and you need to lose 40 pounds to get your ideal body weight. Does that sound about right?"
- "So if we help you get there, you won't be upset with me? (ha ha ha)"

I know—lame. But I make the same joke, and everyone gives the same fake laugh every time.

Overview Their Past Pains/Experiences

In the next step, you review their past pains and failures. (Trust me, they have them—that's why they took time to drive their butts to meet with you, because they aren't already seeing amazing results elsewhere.)

- "Great, so I know where you are and where you're trying to go, but what have you tried so far?"
- "I can't help you get where you're trying to go until I know where you've been and what you've done."

Your client will most likely feel like they have failed in some way, and that's why they didn't succeed at past attempts to meet their fitness goals.

To convince them that you can help where others haven't, you'll want to categorize each of their problems with a little chart like the one below. (You can either do this mentally or write it down.) Using this visual will help you illustrate where the gap was so you can show them it wasn't THEIR fault, but the execution of a faulty plan.

You will then compare and contrast the things they did in the past, aligning yourself with the good and contrasting your services with the things they didn't like or with things that didn't work.

PROBLEM PAIN CYCLE : OVERVIEW OF PAST EXPERIENCES

① WHAT HAVE YOU DONE ? ←
② HOW LONG DID YOU DO IT FOR ? HOW LONG AGO ?
③ HOW DID THAT WORK FOR YOU ?

CATEGORIZE : ALIGN SELF WITH POSITIVES, REPEL SELF FROM NEGATIVES /GAPS

	FITNESS	NUTRITION	ACCOUNTABILITY
BIG BOX GYM	X		
PERSONAL TRAINER	X		X
WEIGHT WATCHERS JENNY CRAIG FOOD-BASED SYSTEMS		X	X
PILLS, SHAKES, SUPPLEMENT-ONLY		X	
WORKOUT FROM HOME	X		

④ WHAT ELSE HAVE YOU DONE ? ⎯

This little graphic will make you more money than I can tell you. It will shatter your client's beliefs around why they failed. I'll give you the script that explains this in the next section.

SELL THEM THE VACATION NOT THE FLIGHT

When going on vacation, no one wants to hear about TSA lines, baggage claim, delays, layovers, or time changes. They want to hear about Maui. So don't talk to your potential clients about your programming, exercise selection, the principles behind the nutrition plans, and things like that.

They. Don't. Care. They just want Maui.

So sell them the fun stuff, then teach them the rest later, once they'll actually listen to you (in other words, once they've given you their money).

When you transition to the sale, you'll want to tie in your core benefits against the pain points they experienced in the past and explain that the REASON they failed was due to a lack of combining the right components—fitness, nutrition, and accountability.

This is where we use all the data we've given clients and explain why each one failed within the larger context. They probably had a few things right in each circumstance, but not all. Here is a sample script.

> Well, I think I understand why some of the other programs didn't give you results, or the lasting results

you were looking for. And after hearing that, it makes sense that you're here today.

Good news—I think you're going to like our program. And, given your past, you're just like 95% of our customers who have seen crazy transformations using our programs. Can I tell you about those? (*Get customer buy-in with this question so they feel like they're on board with you selling to them.*)

There are three main pillars to our program: fitness, nutrition, and accountability. You need all three (*fingers and hand gestures work well here*) to have a sustainable transformation. Because if you have just one or two, then you get part of the way there, but it's a lot like an engine—if even one important part is missing, it won't work.

Use one of these scripts depending on which component they focused on primarily.

Big-Box Gyms (fitness only): "So when you went to the big-box gym, you got fitness from them. Sort of...except they didn't tell you how to work out while you were there, right? No, of course not. And they didn't help you with your food, right? And the only accountability call you got was if your card was declined (ha ha ha), am I right?" (Again, same joke every time...but it works.)

Weight Watchers/Jenny Craig (nutrition and accountability): "When you were with them, they gave you a diet and they checked in on you. So you lost some weight. That's great. The only problem was you didn't keep it off, right? Okay. Well, that came down to two things: 1) The diet wasn't sustainable (or you'd still be following it) and 2) when you lost weight, your metabolism actually went down because you weren't doing any resistance training.

Did you know you lose muscle when you diet? That's why so many people gain the weight back plus more. This is also why guys can eat more than girls do—they have more lean muscle, which burns fat for them. If you diet the right way, with a sustainable plan and resistance training, you can lose the weight and keep it off with all your newly built muscle. Make sense? That's what was missing before."

Shakes (nutrition): "Got it. So you tried a shake program, and you lost some weight in the beginning, then it didn't stay off. This is similar to Weight Watchers, except it had a little less on the nutrition side, a lot less on the accountability side, and virtually zero on the fitness side. You didn't get a meal plan made for you. You didn't have anyone check in on you. And you didn't have anyone waiting for you at the gym to show you how to work out for your specific goal. Correct? Do you think if you'd had all that you would have succeeded?"

The process you are going through with each of these is what we call the belief-breaking formula. I picked up this little five-step framework from my friend Linh Trinh. You can apply it to any business.

1. Say what they believe.
2. Say why it is wrong.

3. Say what is right.
4. Say WHY it is right.
5. Show proof (wall of testimonials behind you).

BELIEF-BREAKING FORMULA

EXAMPLE:

① "SO YOU BELIEVE CHEAP FRONT-END OFFERS WORK?"

② "THIS DOESN'T PROVIDE CASH FLOW TO MARKET OR ACQUIRE CUSTOMERS"

③ "USE A HIGH-TICKET FRONT END ACQUISITION"

④ "IT'LL ALLOW YOU TO SPEND WHATEVER YOU NEED TO GET PEOPLE IN PROFITABLY"

⑤ "DONT BELIEVE ME OR THE MATH?... BELIEVE 1000+ OTHER GYMS"

FORMULA

① SAY WHAT THEY BELIEVE

② SAY WHY IT IS WRONG

③ SAY WHAT IT IS RIGHT

④ SAY WHY IT IS RIGHT

⑤ SHOW PROOF (3rd PARTY STATS + TESTIMONIALS)

idonthatemoney.com

Hopefully, by now you're getting the drift. You need to highlight the good and the bad using the three key tenets of fitness, nutrition, and accountability.

Now, after you've broken all their beliefs around why they failed before, it's time to build them back up. They know why they failed in the past. Now we have to prepare them to succeed.

"I think you're gonna really like this program. In order to give you one of the spots, I need to know if you can do all three of the pillars I just talked about—fitness, nutrition, and accountability. Let's start with fitness."

FITNESS: "Can you work out here with a trainer three days a week for the next [*period of time*]? Great. That was easy."

Remember, they already circled times on the pre-sale questionnaire. Also, I don't say any more about the fitness, because it doesn't matter to them. They care about their end goal, not the programming.

NUTRITION: "Can you follow a meal plan if we make one for you? It's color-coded and so easy we've had children as young as 12 complete it." (Who's gonna say no after that? Ha ha.)

"We'll make you…

- A personalized meal plan
- A personal grocery list
- A personal dining-out guide
- Recipes specifically matched to your meal plan
- A super shake guide
- Bomb-ass breakfasts
- Lick-your-fingers lunches
- Delectable dinners"

Pro Tip: Don't take these items out if you have them. The prospect will want to look at them in detail (even though they don't know what they're looking for) It'll add time to the sale and often just lead to irrelevant questions that don't matter. It gives them more things to disagree with (despite the fact that most of them have zero information besides a Buzzfeed article they read once). Sell in the imaginary realm. It'll save you time and it works better, in my experience. If they ask to see these things, it's a red flag. I'll usually flash it and say this isn't the plan they would get, but just a sample. Do NOT hand it to them. Simply show it then put it away (give the vibe that it is a poor representation of what they'd get making it somewhat irrelevant).

ACCOUNTABILITY: "Okay, the last part is accountability. You can plan the best workouts and the best nutrition plan in the world, but if you don't follow them, ain't nothin' gonna happen, right? So we really pride ourselves on holding people accountable. We do that three ways.

- You'll be assigned a personal accountability coach.
- You'll be invited to join our online accountability group of fellow program starters and alumni. So you'll be shoulder to shoulder with other people going through this for the first time, but you can also learn from those who've already gone through it and will be shouting at you from the finish line.
- We also do weekly check-ins to make sure we're doing our job and you're doing yours. And if we need to adjust your food plan, we can. No more set-it-and-forget-it plans. The body adapts and we adjust accordingly. That's one of the main benefits of having a coach. Many people hit a plateau and get stuck. We've seen it a hundred times, and we know that making a small tweak can keep the weight loss coming so you don't lose momentum. Make sense?

Sounds amazing, right? Do you want one of the last spots?

Well, you're in luck, because I'm not sure how much longer we're going to be running this—we've had so many people sign up."

Here's how the rest of this transaction goes.

"Do you have your ID on you?" (I ask this because if someone takes out their wallet to get their ID, then they can't say they forgot their wallet [*wink*]. It's a micro-commitment. Then I start filling out the contract for them with the info from the ID they just gave me.)

Then I say, "Awesome—let me trade you your ID for the payment card you wanna use." And I hand them back their ID and gesture to their wallet. This is typically very laid back, and I chitchat as I sign them up. (Also to make sure I get the correct credit card number on the contract.)

??? Explain Away Their Concerns

There are only three obstacles (and one sort-of obstacle) you must ever overcome in a sales situation. Ever. For real.

They are…

- Stalls
    - "I need to think about it."
    - "I'll call you tomorrow with my card."
- Decision-Making
    - "I need to talk to my husband."
    - "I never make decisions alone."

- Price
  - "I can't afford it."
  - "I don't have the money for that."
  - "It's not in my budget."

In terms of **fitness-specific obstacles**, here are some typical questions you should be prepared for:

- "I have a bad back."
- "I don't like waking up early."
- "I hate broccoli. I won't eat anything with broccoli."

These aren't really obstacles, so don't be weirded out when prospects say crazy things. They still want to buy.

Know how to get over those, and you'll make a lot more sales and help a lot more people get healthy. (For more info, see my Obstacle Overcome BONUS section at the end of the book. But don't go there now, you'll get distracted. It contains only overcomes we actually use to close a sale, none of the useless ones that no one would actually say yes to.)

Note: If you sell well, you won't need these. If you feel like you have to constantly battle people for the sale, there is likely something going wrong earlier in this process. (Usually you aren't spending enough time building up the gap and building the need and pain cycle.) But IF you accomplish all the processes before, and you are energetic (for real) and smiling (for real), then these things will help you help others make the decision you both know they should make.

And the more you practice these, the more fluid they'll become, and the more you can summon them upon command. The artist Eminem used to read the dictionary so he had every "weapon" in his arsenal—he knew all the words. For a salesperson, this list of closes is your weapon. Make sure you bring your A game.

Reinforce Their Decision

The last step of the C-L-O-S-E-R formula prevents backouts and is the beginning of the relationship. This gives people an amazing first impression. You only get one, so it might as well be spectacular.

The Trifecta: Our Weapons Of Choice
The three steps we take to reinforce a client's decision to join our gym are...

- A **handwritten invitation** to our next event
- A **call from the owner** welcoming them that night or first thing the next day
- A **t-shirt or swag**

Most of these can be done with systems and technology these days. But you should develop a choreographed experience for new customers, to help them feel special and confident that they made the right decision.

You know they've made a great decision to sign up with you. To make it stick, you just need to show how much you care with a personal touch. Use one or all of these items to really seal the deal and welcome your new client to the family. This goes such a long way toward keeping that client over the long term. Plus, it's just a damn classy thing to do.

Let's Review

You're only a third of the way through this book, and we've already solved one of the biggest problems with your gym. Are you excited yet? At this point, you have two choices. You can close the book now, go implement this new way of acquiring clients, make a bunch of money, and then come back and read the rest. Or you can keep reading and solve all three problems simultaneously. Either way, you're in for some fun.

Before you do either one, let's review what you've learned so far.

Client-Acquisition Process That Works

- Cheap front-end offers don't work for you or the client.
- Client-financed acquisition® is the new way to acquire customers…at a profit.
  - The High-Ticket Irresistible Offer
  - Evergreen Lead Generation Using the Lead Gen Scrambler
  - Getting Them In
    - Scheduling
    - Showing Up
  - Getting Them to Buy
    - Pre-Frame Questions and Intake Questionnaire
    - Sales Office
    - The Sale
      - C-L-O-S-E-R Formula

Okay, ready to tackle the second major problem in the gym industry?

Read on to learn why your revenue model is broken and how to fix it.

Section II

Ascension:
Make More Profit

I'm sure you know what a lever is: a simple tool designed to help you move or shift a load that's too heavy to move with normal human strength. It's probably one of the first and most powerful tools that humans invented. For businesses, levers are ways to create massive shifts by making small simple changes to how the business operates.

In this section, we'll first establish the problem with the current gym model that most people use. Once that's clear, I'm going to talk about the three macro levers you can use for your gym to increase your profits while offering more and better services to your customers. **Macro levers** are the major initiatives that will move your gym forward. Within each macro lever, we'll dive into the smaller **micro levers** that will help you pull the larger macro lever and reap the rewards. Micro levers are the smaller (yet just as important) elements within the macro levers.

Think of these levers like the handles on the side of a slot machine (your gym). Pull them all and pull them right, and cash will start flowing out.

The three macro levers are as follows:

- Macro Lever #1: Price Levers
    - This lever relates to pricing, packages, and memberships.
- Macro Lever #2: Capacity Levers
    - This lever is the beefiest one. This will break down all the different ways to increase your facility's capacity. This is critical, as it will allow you to make a lot more money with your existing gym.

- Macro Lever #3: Overhead Levers
    - This is the unsexiest of the three levers, but it's still important. It's not what you make, it's what you take home that matters. So we'll explore compensation, fulfillment strategies, and other pieces to streamline your gym.

To wrap this whole section up, I'll show you how to communicate these changes to your staff and clients to encounter the least resistance and highest adoption rates.

Sound good?

Cool. Let me show you how we make unprofitable gyms profitable…fast.

Chapter 7

The Broken Profit Model

So by now you've got the client acquisition thing down, right? (If not, go back and read the previous six chapters.) But just getting boatloads of new clients isn't going to help if you run out of space or if your model isn't set up to maximize profit.

Capacity is a real problem that limits your ability to make money. Again, it's a problem of scale. But you can totally fix it by using a different revenue model and making a few tweaks to how you run your business.

Ready to learn this part of the equation? Let's start by reviewing the problem with your current revenue model.

My Story, Maybe Yours Too

If you were like me, when you first started out, you did the math and thought, "If I only have 200 people at $200/month, I'll make $40,000/month and be rich." So you signed your lease with an "if you build it, they will come and tell all their friends" mentality, like so many of us do.

Then reality hit: rent, payroll, admin work, software costs, cleaning costs, admin work, broken equipment, production costs for marketing materials and merchandise (shirts, events, signage, posters), advertising costs, and did I mention admin work? I never really thought beyond the rent. I had no idea how expensive it would be to run a business.

And there were other problems.

- I had to fight clients to get them to pay $120/month.
- My main class times (5:30 am, 5:00 pm, 6:00 pm) were getting packed.
- There were A LOT more fixed costs than I anticipated (email auto responders, landing pages, texting, CRMs, and more).
- Some costs increased as my members increased (more admin payroll, more cleaning, more equipment breakage/purchases, higher levels of software, more coaching hours).
- When I ran marketing campaigns, most people didn't stick past a few months. And the main members of my gym were the same 70–80 OGs (original gangsters) who had started with me.
- And even with a gym whose main times were packed, **I was still barely getting by.**

I was trying to run my business with a broken profit model. My mighty dream of owning a profitable gym, of helping people reach their goals, was fading fast as I became more and more burned out. When my client said I looked grumpy, I decided to take a long, hard look at what I had gotten myself into. And figure out how to get out of it.

If you can identify with these problems, you're probably running on that same broken model. The good news is we're about to fix that. But before we go there, take a look at your numbers. There's nothing like seeing the problem in black and white to motivate you to fix it.

Here's a picture of a younger, less wrinkled version of me. I can almost taste the hopefulness I had back then. It was only matched by my ignorance about how to run a business.

And yes, that picture on the next page is where I slept for the first six months. I didn't have enough money for an apartment AND a gym. I lived out of my car and showered at LA Fitness down the street.

I show you this to say that I've been in the trenches. This is no ivory-tower sermon. This is real. And this stuff works.

I've been there closing a credit card and signature while I had the prospect's six-year-old drawing on my wall in permanent marker—and trying not to freak out about it because I needed the $300 they were putting down that day to make payroll.

I get it. I've been there. But like I said before, there's a better way.

Onward.

The illustration on the next page shows the main problem with the microgym industry. Simply stated, the number of members at the industry average prices required to make a gym profitable is usually beyond its reasonable capacity.

Classes get crowded and full, but at the industry average price, the gym isn't profitable.

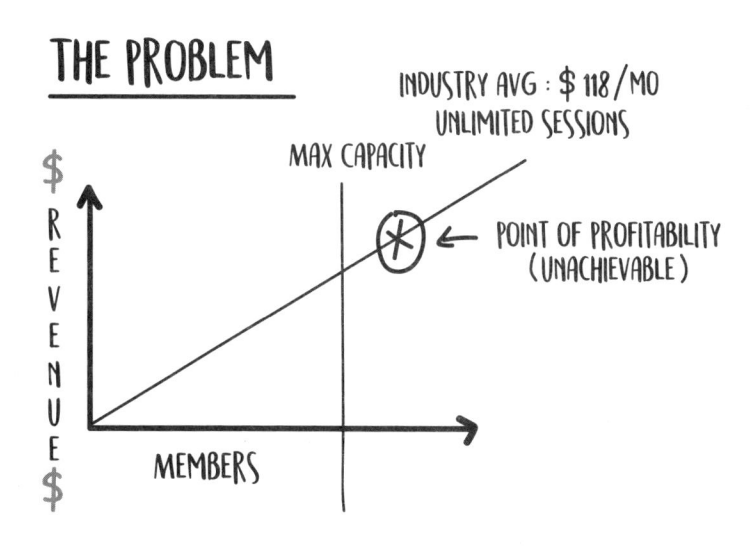

THE PROBLEM

INDUSTRY AVG : $118/MO
UNLIMITED SESSIONS

MAX CAPACITY

$ REVENUE $

POINT OF PROFITABILITY
(UNACHIEVABLE)

MEMBERS

EX : A LARGE GROUP TRAINING FACILITY HAS A CAP OF
16 PEOPLE / SESSION
AVG EFT = $120/MO
CURRENT = 100 MEMBERS
DAILY SESSIONS = 7
MAX CAP_1 = 114 (ASSUMING 100% COME DAILY)
MAX CAP_2 = 134 (ASSUMING 85%* INDUSTRY AVG ATTENDANCE)
MAX REV = $16.000/MO (134 x $120)

$14.500
{
 RENT = $4250
 PAYROLL = $4000 (163 SESSIONS x $25) + $2750 ADMIN
 MKTG = $1000
 UTILITIES/SOFTWARE/CLEANING = $1750
 MISC = $750
}
OWNER PAY = $1500
PROFIT = $0

Let's look at the example in the illustration.

I'm going to break this little analysis into three parts, in accordance with the three macro profit levers I mentioned earlier.

- Price Levers
- Capacity Levers
- Overhead Levers

They are all interrelated, but I will do my best to keep them separated so I can explain them more easily. Within each lever, I'll describe what most gyms do, and then I'll explain the micro levers you can pull on to influence the macro profit levers, and by extension, the profit of the gym business as a whole.

Macro Lever #1 Price Levers

The gyms we typically encounter have these average numbers: 100 recurring members paying $120 per month. This means they are grossing $12,000 per month.

Some do private training on the side, which is really where they make their money to feed themselves, and the gym acts as a nonprofit to cover itself, but that's about it. For the sake of the illustration, I'm only going to talk about the large-group training component.

The micro levers that affect your macro price lever are…

- Number of members
- Billing cycle (for example, weekly vs. monthly)
- Price

Macro Lever #2 Capacity Levers

The average gym we encounter has the following picture for capacity:

They're actively teaching seven sessions a day Monday through Friday and usually three over the weekend, split between Saturday and Sunday. The membership most gyms sell is unlimited, meaning clients can come as often as they like. On average, they can service 16 people per session, depending on their exercise selection. They run hour-long sessions and typically have 85% daily attendance.

The micro levers that affect the macro capacity lever are...

- Number of sessions per week
- Duration of sessions (length of the session itself and the break in between sessions)
- Membership levels (how many sessions someone can attend)
- Attendance (percentage of scheduled sessions that are actually attended)
- Physical space (amount of useable space available for fitness activities)
- Exercise selection (because walking barbell lunges take up more room than sit-ups)

Overhead Levers

The average gym pays $25 per session in payroll costs and fulfills 38 sessions per week.

Gym costs include rent, utilities, marketing, and software. But we can only affect the following three micro levers:

- Number of sessions fulfilled
- Total work hours
- Cost of those work hours

Note: The number of sessions will also be affected by the changes we make in the capacity macro lever.

Now back to the illustration.

The point I want to emphasize here is that the average gym, even if taken to full capacity, does not produce the profit the owner desires. It reaches capacity BEFORE the point of adequate profitability, which means that something needs to change or the business will not survive.

Here's how the math breaks out.

If you can train 16 people per session and you have 7 sessions a day, you can train 112 people total per day. That is assuming PERFECT fit for all the sessions, meaning that every class is at full capacity, which rarely happens in the real world.

So assuming the industry average of 85% daily attendance, you could stretch the total number of members in this perfectly distributed client base from 112 to 131. (I got this by dividing 112 by 85% attendance.) This means you could have more people on membership than you can fulfill. And this is common in the gym space, since we know not everyone works out every day.

But even with 131 members—at a completely maxed-out facility, with PERFECT distribution of people between session times—you would still only be making $15,720 per month in gross revenue once you take out the following costs:

- $4,000 for rent
- $4,000 for payroll, since we have 163 sessions per month at $25 per session, once you include payroll fees
- $800 in utilities (phone, Wi-Fi) and cleaning supplies
- $2,000 for your customer relationship management (CRM) system, software, and processing fees

- $1,000 for marketing
- $1,000 for miscellaneous expenses

    (You'll know what I mean here if you have a gym—broken equipment, speakers, t-shirts, events, etc. If you don't, just look at your bank statements for the last three months…you'll find them.)

So you're looking at $2,920/month in profit ($15,720 - $12,800 for the expenses listed above). And that is for a fully maxed-out facility in a perfect world with $0 paid for an administrative assistant or front desk person, $0 paid for sales commissions, and $0 spent on continuing education for your staff. And the list of things you SHOULD be spending money on to actually make this into a business that runs itself goes on. This means that even if you paid someone $1,000 per month to help with admin tasks, you're now taking home $1,920/month, which is barely enough for most gyms to survive. This is where most gym owners live…and eventually burn out.

I don't know about you, but working the average 80+ hours/week that most gym owners do means that your effective hourly wage is $9.13 ($2,920 monthly income/320 hours per month).

I don't know whether I speak for you, but I'm pretty sure that kind of take-home income is not what any of us signed up for when we took out a five-year lease and put our life savings into starting a gym.

But don't worry—there's a way out, and it doesn't take long to get there. In the next few pages, I'll share my experience, then I'll get into how to fix all this stuff.

CHAPTER 8

Price-Profit Levers

Let me tell you about Kirk Huggins. Kirk is one of the kindest human beings on Earth. If you think you know someone kinder, then I would bet you haven't met Kirk. He's truly one of the "good ones." He wanted everyone to be able to work out and have a trainer for an affordable rate. And so at his gym in North Carolina, he actually had some memberships as low as $49 per month.

And what's crazy is that those people usually were his biggest PIAs (pains in the ass).

Anyways, one time I got a message from Kirk saying he wasn't going to be able to make payroll—which, by the way, is a MUCH bigger deal than not being able to pay rent, if you are ever in hard times. The trust of your employees is everything. Landlords can be forgiving and allow you to make it back up over time. (Just an FYI, having been both landlord and tenant now.) Always choose your employees first.

So despite it really not being a good business decision for me, I lent Kirk the money to make payroll. And within five days, he sent me the money back in full (using the client-financed acquisition tactics from Section I).

But after that, we agreed that he was cutting it too close. People were paying too little for his business model to be tenable, and he was only one unforeseen cost away from being in dire straits again.

So we sent out a letter, text blast, video, and email to his client base explaining why he was going to increase his prices. We settled at $150/month, which was a MASSIVE jump. But he TRIPLED his prices in a market with one of the most depressed economies in the country. Kirk took action because he had no choice. Hopefully you do too, before getting to that point.

We also pulled on every single macro and micro lever all at once. (I highly recommend that you do it this way. Cut once, cut deep.)

In one fell swoop, Kirk's business went from losing $2,000 per month to NETTING $4,000 profit. And we did it in one week.

This stuff can change your life. And you don't have to be in trouble. You might simply be getting by or not making as much as you'd like. If that's you, then you may be able to make a swing from $4,000 to $10,000/month profit from the same changes. Hopefully, that gets you as fired up as it does me.

So let's dig in.

The goal with these particular levers is to increase how much money people are spending with you. We're working with Growth Path #2—Increase Average Purchase. So we're going to tweak how you set your pricing and packages. I'm going to show you three different levers you can use.

Price Micro Lever #1: Increase Profit Per Member

A while back, I encountered a single father of two beautiful girls. He had done everything to make his dream come true… but it had become a nightmare. He had just put his rent on a credit card. Like *that* kind of nightmare.

Just like Kirk, Josh Ponton was charging too little. His customers didn't respect his time or his expertise. And worst of all, they weren't getting results.

So since Josh was on his last leg and truly had nothing to lose, he decided to throw a Hail Mary and sign up to work with us using the last $1,000 he had on his card.

We told him to change his front-end offer from $21 to $600.

And all of a sudden, Josh had all these people showing up on time, following their nutrition plans, and getting amazing results. At first, Josh was reluctant, because he felt bad about charging so much. Then he made the realization that so many of our gyms make: if you want to truly help people, you need to help them make it a priority. And nothing does that better than money.

So if you want to actually help people, not just say you are, charge more. But how much?

The Big Secret

When most gym owners set prices, they open their doors, look around, see what everyone else is charging, then average it out and charge that.

But what most people don't know…

the big secret…

is that everyone else is BROKE.

So why copy them?

On some level, you may realize this, or you wouldn't be reading this book. Want to know another secret? The easiest way to make more money is to simply charge more for the same level of service. No shit. It's so simple, but no one does it.

People have a lot of difficulty with this concept, because it's deeply rooted in their own self-value and their personal beliefs around money. This is why broke salespeople don't sell well—people can *feel* desperation. But when you have money, more of it flows to you because you don't need it. There's no desperation. It's sad but it's true.

This is why the rich get richer and the great economic divide continues to grow. And the only way for you to cross the great divide is to understand that premium pricing is your friend. It allows you to overdeliver, pamper, and serve your customers in a way they have never been served before.

Here's a chart we use to illustrate the concept of virtuous and vicious price cycles. You can choose which one to use for your business.

VIRTUOUS VS. VICIOUS CYCLE OF PRICE $

⬇ PRICE	YOUR CLIENTS	PRICE ⬆
DECREASE	EMOTIONAL INVESTMENT	INCREASE
DECREASE	PERCEIVED VALUE	INCREASE
DECREASE	RESULTS	INCREASE
INCREASE	DEMANDINGENESS	DECREASE
DECREASE	REVENUE FOR FULFILLMENT PER CUSTOMER	INCREASE

⬇ PRICE	YOUR BUSINESS	PRICE ⬆
DECREASE	PROFIT	INCREASE
DECREASE	PERCEIVED VALUE OF SELF	INCREASE
DECREASE	PERCEPTION OF IMPACT (RESULTS)	INCREASE
DECREASE	SERVICE LEVELS	INCREASE
DECREASE	SALES TEAM CONVICTION	INCREASE

Here's how the **vicious price cycle** works (which MOST gyms use).

As you DECREASE your prices…

- Your clients' emotional investment DECREASES.
- The perceived value of your service DECREASES.
- Results DECREASE as a result of decreased investment and perceived value.
- Clients INCREASE their demandingness. (Ever notice how the cheapest customers ask for the most?)
- Clients get LESS service because you have less money to spend on them (a race to the bottom).

And as you decrease your prices, your BUSINESS…

- DECREASES in profit per customer.
- DECREASES in perceived self-value.*
- DECREASES its ability to create results for customers.
- DECREASES your conviction in the sales process, because you and your team are no longer sure you can even deliver what you promise.

*You feel like you are worth less because you don't charge much for what you do and constantly feel underappreciated, like you're "giving away the farm."

And here's how the **virtuous price cycle** works (which is what OUR gyms do):

When you INCREASE your prices…

- Your clients' emotional investment INCREASES.
- The perceived value of your service INCREASES.

- Results INCREASE as a result of increased investment and perceived value.
- Your clients DECREASE their demandingness. (Ever notice how the people who pay you the most are the most easygoing?)
- Your clients get MORE service because you have MORE money to spend on them and therefore RAISE your level of service (race to the top).

And as you increase your prices, your BUSINESS…

- INCREASES in terms of profit per customer.
- INCREASES in perceived self-value. (You feel like you are worth more, because you charge what you're worth and are able to serve more.)
- INCREASES its ability to create results for customers, because you can get the word out and actually help more people by reinvesting money into the business and marketing.
- INCREASES the level of service you render for each customer.
- INCREASES your conviction in the sales process, because you and your team are confident that you can deliver what you promise and even guarantee it.

If you only do one thing after reading this book, RAISE YOUR PRICES.

The Virtuous Pricing Model

If you need some average examples to get you excited, here's what I'm talking about with the membership model we recommend.

Large Group: 16+: $167–$225/month*

Medium Group/No-Man's Land: 5–15:

(In my opinion, these are NOT good class delivery options, which I will explain in a bit.)

Small Group: 1-on-4: $500–$700/month

*Note: We don't actually bill monthly—but it's helpful for this illustration. That's another lever, which I'll get to in a minute.

These are the prices you should be jumping to. And before you say, "But my market is different" or "People won't pay that" or whatever other gobbledygook you have, remember that gyms I've worked with have successfully used this model in EVERY market we've tried—more than 1,500 to date.

The reason everyone else is broke is because they're afraid. That's all.

They're afraid that if they shoot for something higher, they'll lose what little comfort they have now.

Simple is not necessarily easy, or everyone would do it. You might know this from your work with fitness clients. Lift weights. Eat more protein. Eat more veggies. It's not complicated. But hundreds of millions of people struggle, because it's HARD...simple but hard.

Making money in business is the same. And this first concept is no different. Raise your prices, or suffer burnout and make no profit.

Charge more so you can help more.

If you want to actually help people and not just say you are, you need to charge more. I used to say, "I want fitness to be affordable to everyone." But the problem is, if they don't value it, they won't use it. And people vote with their dollars about things they value. People will not give you their time until they give you their money.

Low prices don't leave any room to give people AMAZING experiences. Higher prices allow me to actually give people the support they need to get in shape, and in my case, help more gym owners transform their gyms. If I charged $1,000 for our service, I wouldn't be able to have a SEAL Team 6 support crew that answers questions in less than three minutes, guaranteed. And I wouldn't be able to market to get the word out. So I'd be sitting here with a mediocre product (because I'd have little money for support) with a mediocre price (because to be honest, it wouldn't be worth as much without the in-depth coaching and support to ensure victory) with no way to reach people and market because there is nothing left over.

Let the virtuous cycle work for you, so you can ACTUALLY help people, not just say you are.

As I tell our gym owners, you're going to have hard conversations either way—either with your spouse and landlord about how you can't provide for the family and can't pay rent, or with your customers about the higher rates. But only one of those conversations will make you more money.

Your choice.

At the end of Section II, I'll give you an action plan for how to best choreograph pulling all the levers at once for massive turnarounds. In my experience, they work best when done in unison.

But for right now...

Raise all your new EFT prices to the ones I just listed. No exceptions. Grandfather in the OGs until you hit capacity, then raise the prices on them as well. It's just basic economics, supply and demand. People understand that prices go up as supply goes down.

Price Micro Lever #2: Membership Levels → Increase Profit Per Member

Let me tell you a story that illustrates the pricing model I'm going to show you in this section.

I had a reasonably well-off client who had been working with me for a few months. She seemed happy. She was on a subscription, and her payment came through every month. There didn't seem to be any problem. But then one day, out of the blue, she canceled.

I asked her, "How can we do better? How could we have better met your needs?"

And she said, "Oh, I signed up with a personal trainer. I just wanted more personalized attention."

I was stunned. But I realize now that the whole time I'd been working with her and other clients, I'd been afraid to charge more money. Because I wasn't charging enough, I had to have more and more clients and had to hustle more. I wasn't giving this client the attention she wanted, because I was so focused on keeping my doors open. So I lost a valuable client to someone who had the time and the energy to give her a higher level of service. If I'd been charging four times as much and had devoted more time to working with her, I could have retained that client.

She was willing to pay more.

I was not willing to charge more.

But I fixed that…quick.

The Buying Curve

Every gym has their own take on membership levels and service structures. And as I mentioned earlier, many of them are ridiculous and nonsensical and reveal a misunderstanding of basic pricing principles. They price based on an average of what everyone else is charging. Or they start the race to the bottom and undercut their local competitors.

But they should be charging based on what the client is willing to pay to solve a problem or pain point, NOT what the market is charging or what it costs them to fulfill. People sign up for a gym membership because of pain points. These are what drive them to want to make a change. Maybe they gained a lot of weight and feel bad about themselves. Maybe they've tried other methods of getting fit that have failed. Or maybe they're worried about an upcoming event such as a class reunion or a wedding.

But the main thing to understand is that you want to charge what a client is willing to pay, not less.

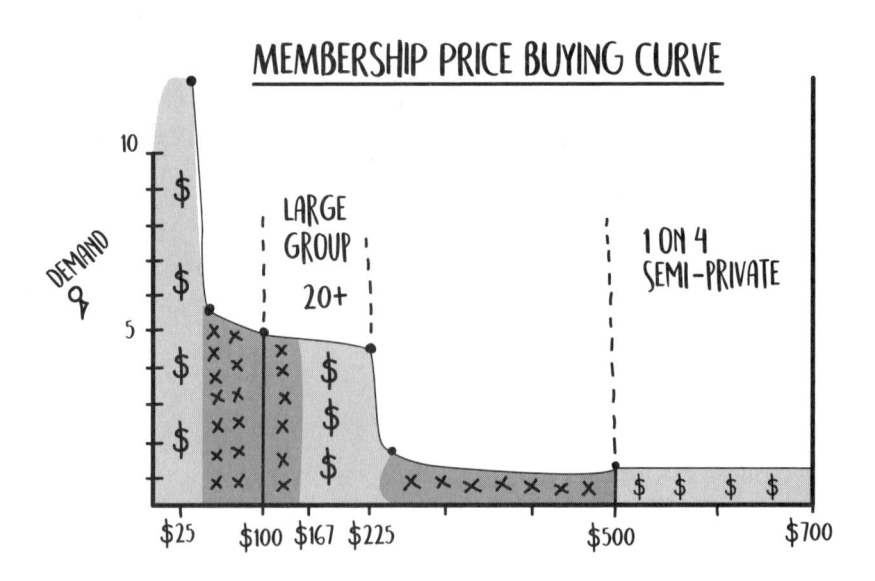

MEMBERSHIP PRICE BUYING CURVE

Okay, so I call this the watermelon curve. (The colors aren't visible in the book, but trust me—in color, the green and red look like watermelon slices with seeds in them.) This buying curve provides extremely powerful insights for your business.

Each of the dotted vertical lines separates fulfillment strategies.

- **Section A:** From the baseline at left to the first dotted line is where you essentially have **self-service**. This is Planet Fitness, LA Fitness…large-box globe gyms. They bet on the fact that 90% of clients will never use their gym regularly. This is how their model works. You cannot compete with them on price; they have a different model.
- **Section B:** From the first dotted line to the second one is where you have your space for **large-group training**. This is your typical 16+ per session model. Affiliate boxes, bootcamps, etc.
- **Section C:** From the second dotted line to the third is where you would have your **medium-sized class**. This would be like one trainer with between 5 and 15 clients.
- **Section D:** From the third line onward is your high-ticket group. This is your highest level of service, or **semi-privates**. You can typically do one-on-one to one-on-four in this range.

So now that we have the different levels of fulfillment mapped out, let me explain the colors and price points.

Anything with a $ sign is where you want to be price-wise for that fulfillment level. Anything with an X is where you don't want to be.

The reason for that is economics of capacity and profitability.

I also want you to notice Section C, which is full of Xs. That is the fulfillment zone for 5 to 15. This is what I call No Man's Land, because you COULD fulfill at that price point, but you would not be maximizing your business.

In this case, you would be splitting between two different tiers of buyers. You have people who can really only afford about $200/month feeling stretched to pay between $300 and $500. And you have people who are being undercharged, like in my story—someone who could and would otherwise like more service but isn't getting enough personal attention.

So what are the key takeaways from these four fulfillment zones?

Low Price, Low Service: $0 to $99 per month

You do NOT want to be in this space. It is heavily competitive, and you are competing against all the big-box gyms with multimillion-dollar build-outs. You would be competing on quality of facility at that point. And if you're the typical gym owner, you don't have the capital to fight that game. So I would suggest you steer clear.

Large Group

You want to be at $199/month here. In reality, $167 to $225 is the range we recommend, because we've seen it work. Anything less than that and you'll run into capacity and profitability issues. Avoid the $99 to $167 zone. This is where most gyms are, but it's not enough money to give the service needed. And **most people will pay more if they get more** up to this top tier...trust me. Between $167 and $225/month is where you need to live in the large-group world.

Medium Group

Although you can 100% fulfill at this level, the price points associated simply don't make sense. They'll be too high for some consumers and too low for the ones who can afford more. The solution? Don't live here. Instead, split your service into two tiers—large group and small group.

Small Group

This is 100% priced like personal training. But in my experience, clients like the small-group atmosphere just as much if not more—they still get the benefit of familiar faces and community, but also get personal attention. Anyone who has done one-on-one knows there's usually a lot of wasted time in a session. As a result, one-on-four is the perfect blend of great fulfillment and the same price points. So you essentially just 4x the amount of revenue per time slot. You need to live in the $500 to $700/month range here.

So at the end of the day, you can think of everyone in the X Zone as a buyer with a buying threshold that's either overextended or underutilized relative to the amount of fulfillment being provided. The $ Zones are the safe areas. This is where pricing, consumer buying patterns, and fulfillment exist in harmony.

So who fits where?

Pain points are helpful when deciding what membership levels to offer. The quadrant illustration below shows the relationship between pain points, demand, and pricing. A low pain point isn't causing a significant amount of distress, while a high pain point is really making the person suffer. People with high pain points are extremely motivated to make a change and will likely be willing to spend more to solve their problem.

There are two price points we'll use for this example: $199/month and $499+/month.

Now who makes up these price-point pockets?

- **$199/month pocket:** These are wealthy people with low pain points or average-income people with medium pain points.
- **$499+/month pocket:** These are wealthy people with normal or high pain points and average-income people with high pain points.

	PAIN/NEED HIGH	PAIN/NEED LOW
INCOME HIGH	$499+/mo	$199/mo
INCOME LOW	$499/mo	$199/mo

Of course, the definitions of "wealthy" and "low-income" clients will vary based on your location and particular market.

So with this information, you can create your membership tiers. (Again, we don't bill monthly—these are just examples.)

Lower Membership Level: $167–$225/month
1. A normal person with a normal pain point
2. A wealthy person with a low pain point

Service provided: 3x per week in large-group sessions (16+ people)

Higher Membership Level: $500–$700/month
1. A normal person with HIGH pain or HIGH need for your service
2. A wealthy person with normal OR high pain or need for your service

Service provided: 3x per week in semi-private sessions (one trainer with four clients)

You might be wondering, "Why is the second level three times the price of the first?" Great question.

First, because the buying pocket goes up that high, so you might as well charge it. Second, customers follow the famous 80/20 distribution: 20% of your customers are willing and able to pay more, so you should give them that opportunity. And in exchange, you should provide them with the service they really want and deserve.

If you can get 20% of your customers to pay you three times as much, then you can add 60% to your business while only serving one-fifth of them. That's the power of premium pricing.

As the story at the beginning of this section illustrates, if you charge a higher price, you can offer better service to your customers and retain them for longer.

No Man's Land

But why is there no middle price or middle level of people per session?

As I mentioned, I call this No Man's Land, and I recommend you avoid it at all costs.

It looks like this:

Price Point: $250–$399/month

Service Level: 5–15 people per session

Why do I advise against it? Because if you have a price point that is a stretch for someone in the lower buying pocket, you'll have more trouble collecting that money. That means constant billing issues and people dropping in and out. And at the same time, the price point isn't enough to provide a high level of service to that client. Either way, the client is dissatisfied, struggling to pay for mediocre service.

When gyms I work with implement this two-tier model, they increase their profit 3x–5x within a few months and see decreased attrition/churn rates. No joke—it works.

Takeaway On Pricing

Buying curves are a lot like accommodating strength curves. You want to optimize your resistance to the muscle's ability to generate force. You're strongest at the top of the squat, so you can add bands or chains to make it harder, and you're weaker at the bottom, where it gets lighter. Fitness theory is that you work the muscle at higher average intensities and thereby get stronger.

Think about your pricing the same way. Except the "strength" is your prospect's ability to spend money. You want your pricing and fulfillment to maximally match their ability to spend.

Keep It Simple

I've always believed in simple pricing models, for three reasons.

1. **They're easy for the customer to understand.** A confused mind doesn't make wise decisions. And if your prospect isn't sure which option is the right fit, they won't buy any of them. It's as simple as that. I recommend that gyms never offer more than three membership levels. Any more are simply too much for someone to comprehend.

    Ever noticed that Apple only offers a handful of colors with their products? That's because as the number of choices increases, customers' satisfaction with their choice goes down. There's more opportunity to second-guess themselves.

2. **They're easy for your employees to understand.** Have you ever gone to a gym and asked for pricing, and the front desk person stares at you like you asked them to name the planets in reverse order of distance from the sun? Right. Employees need to not only know what levels you have, but also to be able to explain them quickly and easily.

3. **Membership levels should be targeted according to types of buyers, not types of services.** Read that line again. Many times, I see gyms offering memberships like this:

    $119/month 3x/week and $139/month unlimited

    OR

    $129/month unlimited and $149/month unlimited, with nutrition

There are a million permutations of these depending on how many times a week the person wants to come. Then everyone winds up on a weird custom plan that only the person who signed them up remembers. And most people are paying LESS than they should be.

Actions To Take

1. Combine your membership options into two tiers to reflect the two types of buyers from the square visual.
2. Offer your large-group option for $199/month for 16+ people per session.
3. Offer your semi-private option for $599/month for one-on-four.
4. Get rid of any price points that are in No Man's Land.
5. If you can only fit 5–15 per session at your facility, don't worry. We'll talk about that in the next chapter.

Price Lever #3: Billing Cycle → Increase Revenue and Profit AND Increase Ease of Sale

Of all the levers in the book, this is the easiest to use. I would say almost 100% of our gyms adopt this within the first two months of working with us. It is that powerful. I usually like to start each section with an anecdote showing efficacy of the change. But in reality, this lever is so easy to pull, every gym we have in our network has switched over to it and seen the positive benefits.

This is also one of my favorite levers to pull, because most gym owners don't realize how much money they are leaving on the table.

First, let's look at the problems with the typical monthly billing cycle.

- **Problem #1 Inflow vs. Outflow Inequality:** Most gyms pay their employees every 14 days but get paid by clients monthly. This means that at the end of the year, they paid for 13 outflows of payroll (26 x 2-week cycles = 13 "months") but only got 12 inflows from EFTs (12 months). That means one entire month of payroll comes out of your pocket. Yep. Chew on that one for a minute.

- **Problem #2 Low Gross Margin:** The average gym only makes 12% profit per year, which basically means they are barely surviving and drawing only enough to make it to the next month. So if your gym grossed $250,000 but you made a 12% margin, you only made $30,000 take-home (.12 x $250,000). Pretty underwhelming for the amount of money, time, and risk you are exposed to.

- **Problem #3 Devil Is In The Decimals:** Most people assess pricing without realizing that there are four and one-third weeks per month. That one-third is important. It means that whatever people say yes to emotionally, that boundary can always be pushed another 8% or so by simply changing the cycle.

The biggest takeaway from this section is that **you MUST take your billing cycle OFF OF MONTHLY if you want to increase your profits** for no added cost.

If you're not going to bill monthly, what's left? You can charge every 7 days, every 14 days, or every 28 days. You can choose whichever you like. But make a conscious choice—there are advantages to each. I put them in a graph to show you how they stack up.

Considerations	7 Days	14 Days	28 Days	Monthly
Sellability	4	3	2	2
Admin Work	2	3	4	4
"Sick Days/Vacancy	1	3	4	4
Revenue/Aligned w Payroll	4	4	4	3
TOTALS	11	13	14	13
Billings Annually	52	26	13	12

Your New Billing Choices: Every 7 Days, Every 14 Days, Every 28 Days

Factor #1: Sellability

Winner: 7-day cycles

Loser: 28-day cycles

I know *sellability* isn't really a word, but it's the easiest way to explain the idea that a 7-day cycle is easier to sell than a 28-day option. The smaller the time duration, the cheaper a price sounds. I'm sure you've seen ads for insurance companies that say things like, "It costs less than $3.31 per day to take care of your family." They say it this way because $3.31 sounds cheap. A daily cycle would sound even cheaper, but that would be a pain to set up billing-wise and would require processing fees. But hopefully you get the point.

Time to get your hands dirty with a few examples.

Example #1: $200/month vs. $49/week

The weekly amount sounds like less, but $49/week is actually $211/month ($49 x 4.3 = $210.70) But because it seems like a lower amount, it's easier to sell.

Example #2: You want to raise your prices from $34/week to $39/week.

Doesn't sound like much, right? You might assume that none of your current clients would leave because of that, but it's actually a major increase.

$34 x 4.3 = $146.20/month

$39 x 4.3 = $167.70/month

That's a pretty impressive increase (15%), although as a weekly number it barely seems noticeable.

I don't know about you, but I'd much rather say, "We're going from $34/week to $39/week" than "We're increasing rates from $146/month to $167/month." That's the power of sellability.

A long time ago, I had a business mentor who told me, "You can shear a sheep for a lifetime, but you can only skin it once." He was a fan of lower, more frequent debits. It looks like less coming out from a member's account. They never take a big hit from their gym membership.

Factor #2: Admin Work and Freezes/Sick Days

Winner: 28-day cycles

Loser: 7-day cycles

The downside to more billing cycles is that the more transactions you have, the more billing work there is. So weekly billing creates four times the transactions. A lot of the downside, however, can be avoided by simply having a clear membership policy like ours.

> We don't have freezes for any time greater or less than one month. Specifically, being sick for a few days, going on vacation for a week or a long weekend, or being out of town for work do not merit a freeze or a reimbursement of any kind. If 123 Fitness chooses to, it may—provided the customer has a history of on-time payment and good standing—credit the equivalent number of sessions to be spread over the duration of 123 Fitness's choosing. This is to decrease unnecessary administrative work and keep people accountable to making sessions.

Why even bother jumping through all the hoops to change your billing cycle for "only" about 8% more revenue? Because business is a game of math, and the pennies add up…always. If the average gym works on a 12% margin per year, and they switch billing cycles from monthly to every 28 days, they boost profits by 7.7%. But in this context, **12% to 19.7% take-home would be a 64% increase in take-home profit.**

So let's talk real-world money.

The average gym does $12,000 per month in revenue, which means $144,000 per year. They are taking home the industry average of 12%, or approximately $17,280 per year. (Mind you, if some of these differ from previous examples by a thousand dollars or so, don't get bent. It's just an example.)

If you were to implement this change and go from monthly to 28-day billing cycles, you would go from $17,280 to $29,280 in take-home. And you will have changed NOTHING but the billing cycle. If you couple this with a rate increase, it gets really funky.

Now that is something to get excited about.

Have your cake and eat it too. When you sell, do so in the context of weekly amounts, but set up the actual billing as 28-day cycles to decrease your admin work. This gives you the best of both worlds. The only downside is you don't get the shearing effect of avoiding a big hit on their credit card. But besides that, this combo gives you all of the following:

- You are getting equal inflows and outflows.
- You have the benefit of weekly sellability.
- You have the same amount of admin work as you did monthly.
- You add 8% gross revenue per year to your income (assuming no added price).

So to put it all together…

Summary

Advertise your rates as $49/week for all your new people and set it up as a 28-day billing cycle. We use weekly in our business and we like it a lot. Either one will give you a MASSIVE increase in profitability. And if you couple the billing change with a price increase, then you'll see crazy 3x–5x increases in profit that a lot of our gym owners get.

You got this.

Price isn't the only lever you can use to fix a broken revenue model.

Next, we'll look at the magic you can create with capacity profit levers.

Actions to Take

1. Offer two levels of service: large group and small group (one-on-four).
2. Large group should be $39–$49/week or $167–$225 every 28 days.
3. Believe you can. Know that charging more enhances your clients' results and that you staying in business will help them more than anything.

Chapter 9

Capacity-Profit Levers

I had just landed at my first ever Gym Launch gym, which at the time was CrossFit WSA, owned by Josh Price in Towson, Maryland. We had been introduced by a mutual friend, and I was in the area because my mom had fallen very ill. If you've ever traveled to be with someone who was sick, and you only had a few visiting hours, then you know the last thing you want to do is to be idle. So I did what I do best—I found a gym to help keep my mind and my hands busy.

After a four-hour meeting, Josh and his partner were battling me and wanted to call the whole thing off. They had 70 EFTs at an average of $100 per person per month, so $7,000/month total, and they had 3,000 square feet of usable space. But they were insisting that they couldn't handle the influx of members I was promising.

And I was like, "Wait…what? You guys are losing money on your classes, yet you're at full capacity? Pick your problem."

After a lot of back and forth, they said they could only service 14 people per class maximum, despite their 3,000-square-foot floor space. It all came down to one thing that was limiting their class-size: double unders.

If you're not familiar with this term, a double under is an exercise popular with affiliate box gyms where you twirl a jump rope under your feet twice before you hit the ground. They're a brutal and effective tool for conditioning, but…

- They take up a ton of space.
- People always end up hitting each other or hitting each other's ropes.
- Most people can't do them well.
- There is a real risk of people tripping and eating floor mat.

I was so frustrated with their insistence about their limited capacity, I finally went and grabbed a jump rope, held it between my hands in front of their noses and said, "This is strangling your business. Are you going to let a jump rope kill your gym?"

They finally accepted that mathematical reality, and things began to improve with their business. Exactly one year later, WSA Fitness (they had disaffiliated) averaged $45,000/month in revenue with over $30,000 of that from recurring EFT.

Maybe your gym doesn't have a jump-rope problem, but chances are you've got some sort of blind spot about where you could be making changes to drastically improve your bottom line. Let me show you how we systematically increase floor capacity and streamline fulfillment.

Maximizing Your Capacity

The problem with Josh's gym was that they were allowing one exercise to limit their capacity and bottleneck their entire business. So they were making less money than they could have from their space per square foot. For your gym to be as profitable as it can be, you need to use your space efficiently and effectively.

Here are the five micro levers that maximize capacity:

1. Membership Levels: how many sessions someone can attend
2. Attendance: percentage of scheduled sessions that are actually attended
3. Duration of Sessions: length of sessions themselves and the breaks in between
4. Physical Space: amount of useable fitness space
5. Exercise Selection: exercises available for your clients to perform (because walking barbell lunges take up more room than sit-ups)

Let's look at each one more closely.

Capacity Micro Lever #1: Membership Levels

→ Increase Capacity Per Square Foot

→ Increase Profit Per Session

The "Unlimited" Problem

This is controversial, but I believe anything that's unlimited is perceived as less valuable. Gym owners make services unlimited with the intention of increasing value. But I would argue that they're telling their customers they value themselves and their product so little that they're willing to give away as much as people want.

Think about some examples of "unlimited usage" services.

- Netflix $9.99*/month
- Planet Fitness $10/month
- Globo Gyms $29/month

Rates as of 2018.

Have you ever heard of unlimited personal training? No, of course not, because personal training is valuable.

I believe the service we provide is valuable as well, and therefore should not be offered as unlimited, except under very specific circumstances (which I'll get to in a minute).

The Unlimited Problem → Solutions

6. **Call them sessions, not classes.** Because language matters. You need to begin to value your time and effort more, and that starts with you and your team using premium language. People can get "classes" anywhere for next to nothing. If you want to set yourself apart, use a term associated with personal training and defined-quantity services. This will become a part of your culture, and then people will value your time as much as you do.

7. **Go from unlimited to 3x/week.** This one tweak will double how much your facility can make overnight. Switch everyone to either Mon/Wed/Fri or Tues/Thurs/Sat sessions. When you sign people up, start by asking, "Does Tuesday, Thursday, and Saturday work?" Because if either option will work, they'll take the first one you offer. But if you start by asking about Mon/Wed/Fri, everyone will want to take that one and your Tues/Thurs/Sat will be less filled.

   If anyone asks why you don't have unlimited sessions, you can say something like...

   "We have people commit to certain days because if you can come whenever you want, it really becomes never. So we have people schedule their sessions just like appointments, so they're more likely to make them."

OR

"We added these times to keep track for accountability. We know when to expect you, so we can reach out if you don't make it for some reason. That way, we can hold you to your commitment and help you reach your goals."

8. **Charge more.** Yeah, I know. I've already said this. But remember, when you switch to limited sessions, you are providing more service and attention. People value limited resources more, I promise. Try it and see. I've had more gym owners than I can count switch from struggling to sell unlimited memberships (at $118/month) to making easy sales at 3x/week (at $49/week). That little adjustment simultaneously doubles their profit and their capacity, which means they have the potential to quadruple future profit without opening another gym. That's the kind of math I like to see from a single change.

And if you are nervous about raising prices, you can always just do it for new members. Then when you get capped out, introduce the new structure to your OGs.

Capacity Micro Lever #2: Attendance

This micro lever has two components to it:

A. Percentage of people who are supposed to show up every day and actually do

B. How well are they spread out between available times

So obviously with this lever, the intention is NOT to get people to come to the gym less often. That would mean your attrition would go through the roof, and you would be worse off than where you started. Besides being ethically uncool, it's just not good business.

So you have to focus on affecting #2, member attendance spread and the average "fullness" of every session. This allows you to maximize teaching hours per day relative to your membership level.

The problem is, if this percentage is off, you have too many sessions, and your overhead creeps up. This is the issue with most gyms. They simply have way too many sessions given their membership numbers. (We'll address that more in the overhead section.)

That being said, how do you smooth out attendance more evenly along the class times?

Restated, the key goals here are to **get them to show up and to spread out as much as possible.**

The idea is to increase the efficiency of each session.

Solution #1 → Get them to schedule ahead of time when it best suits YOU.

To piggyback off the previous lever, having three sessions per week forces people to schedule during those session times. This will help you put people where it makes the most sense for YOU.

Tell them the times they will get the most attention—in other words, the sessions with the least filled time slots—and you can help spread out those members throughout your mornings and afternoons.

When signing up a new customer, or meeting with current customers to introduce a new membership structure, offer session times in reverse order of popularity. People will make things work if they are asked to solve a problem. So start with your least crowded session, like Tues/Thurs/Sat 8:00 am. If they say yes, you just added a member but didn't add to your busier class times, which allows you to grow further before hitting capacity.

This little hack is really effective. Use it.

Solution #2 → No-Show Fee

This one I 100% stole from Orangetheory Fitness. I don't think they were the first to do this, but from my perspective, they were the first to do it well.

The idea is, people get charged a fee if they don't show up. From a selling perspective, you tell people, "This is your extra nudge to get to the gym when you don't feel like it." And from a business standpoint, you can also follow up with, "We are also very busy, and you would be taking a spot that otherwise could have been given to someone else."

Typical cancellation fees are $15 per no-show. Call it an accountability measure. But in one fell swoop, this practice does the following: 1) increases attendance at desired sessions; 2) decreases attrition because the more people come, the longer they stay; and 3) becomes a separate revenue stream for you.

From a technology perspective, having a CRM tool that offers online scheduling will make this much easier to manage.

Just from these two hacks, you should be able to spread the butter out more evenly and get more out of the rent you're already paying.

Capacity Micro Lever #3: Duration

I believe the general population can achieve amazing results by working out 3 days a week for 45 minutes nonstop, or even 30 minutes of high-intensity interval training.

They are not us.

We are obsessed. We program. We plan our cycles way in advance. We cycle our macros.

The average client is just trying to look good and make sure they actually show up to the gym. Our services should meet *their* needs, not our own. Especially if meeting our own needs sacrifices margin and profitability.

The solution is to increase the efficiency of your operation. The more people you can service in the same amount of square footage, the more dollars per session and per square foot you generate. This allows you to get MORE from LESS.

The 60-Minute Workout/15-Minute Break Problem → Solution

The solution to this problem is simple. I recommend that virtually every fitness facility run 45-minute back-to-back sessions rather than the standard 60-minute sessions with a 15-minute break.

This allows you to strategically split packed times into two so you can further increase your facility capacity. Here is an example to show you how this breaks down.

Problem

> 5:00 am
>
> 6:15 am **PACKED 23/20**
>
> 8:45 am
>
> 4:00 pm
>
> 5:15 pm **PACKED 22/20**
>
> 6:30 pm

Solution

5:00 am

5:45 am < This splits the busy hour, but payroll costs stay the same.

6:30 am

8:45 am

4:00 pm

4:45 pm

5:30 pm < This splits the busy hour, but payroll costs stay the same.

6:15 pm

Going from three sessions in the morning and three in the evening to four sessions in the morning and four in the evening, with no increase in payroll, increases your capacity by 33% when done on its own and 66% when done in unison with the 3x/week change (since you get the boost 2x). I know that's a lot of math in one sentence, but isn't it awesome?

But what about those extra 15 minutes of workouts?

Good question. Short and sweet answer: it doesn't matter. You may hear some whimpering from your OGs, but they'll get over it eventually. People hate change, even if it's better and more convenient for them. This is why I recommend that when you switch, you switch it all. Do it all at once so you can deal with the kickback and get over it. Cut once, cut deep. (I'll talk more about the switchover in Chapter 11.)

When clients ask, "Why are you doing this?" you say something like…

- "We wanted to add more times to make it convenient for everyone. We realized that some session times were more packed than others. By offering more time slots, we can help more people."
- "By providing a few more options, especially at the busiest times, we're able to have fewer issues with an overcrowded parking lot."
- "We realized there was a lot of dillydallying in between sessions. This way, you can warm up and hang out with people when you get here, but the moment the clock strikes, we'll get right into it."
- "Split session times allow us to give everyone more individual attention since we have fewer people per session."

Special note for small facilities: If you can only service 15 or fewer people at your facility, I would highly recommend switching to 30-minute sessions. Why? Because if you have 30-minute sessions and can only service 12 people, for example, then you could effectively get in 24 per hour. That is a BIG improvement in capacity.

And at the prices we're charging, we need to be able to get 20+ people per session however possible.

Otherwise, it may be wiser for you to keep two sessions of one-on-four running at the same time and specialize in high-ticket services ($500+/month) only. But I would recommend selling the shorter time slot. This is also easier to sell. Remember, effort is a COST, not a benefit. If people can achieve results in less time, they are happier, so don't let it trip you up mentally. You can also make those sessions balls-to-wall hard and have everyone leave in a daze of endorphins without being crushingly exhausted.

Capacity Micro Lever #4: Physical Space

At my facility, we ran into capacity issues early on, and I could not figure out a way around it. I was also running out of equipment. Most gym owners in this type of situation immediately assume their situation is unchangeable and start looking for another location to grow into. But this can be problematic for a variety of reasons.

- **Lease reasons:** Lots of landlords don't want to let you out of your lease.
- **Moving reasons:** You lose people when you move. Moving costs money. All in all, it's a lot of headache for not a lot of benefit. I advise against it unless it's absolutely necessary and you've pulled and maximized every single lever.

Our gym ran into capacity issues early. Here's what we did.

Solution #1 → Use partners.

Luckily, the solution hit me like a stack of bricks one day while I was working out with one of my trainers who was spotting me.

Partners.

One of the easiest things you can do to double your capacity is partner everyone up. One person rests, spots, or cheers while the other does the programmed exercise.

When I sold the partners idea to our customers, they loved it.

Partners increase safety, increase community, increase encouragement, and allow for adequate rest while strength training.

And, most importantly for the business, partners DOUBLE the number of people you can have in your space.

Solution #2 → Convert office to fitness space.

The next thing you can do takes a little bit of effort, but this is typically the next step we suggest for gyms who outgrow their current space.

We get rid of any offices.

The "sales room" becomes a portable cubby you can shove into the corner of your lobby.

It'll still get the job done. And you can display the social proof in the waiting room/lobby.

Getting rid of an office will usually allow you to accommodate another 4 people per session. Over the course of 7 daily sessions, this gives you 28 more slots per day, and with 3 weekly sessions per person instead of 6 (you 2x capacity again), increases your EFT max capacity by 56 people, or another $11,000/month. Not too shabby.

Now if you're thinking, "But where will I work?" the answer is…anywhere but at the gym. If you're doing everything outlined in this book, by the time you hit capacity, you should be out of your daily gym operations and fully into gym ownership. That means your gym should run without you needing to be there.

By all means, go in and check on things, but don't feel guilty about not being there. You will better serve your business by working ON it, not IN it.

Capacity Micro Lever #5: Exercise Selection

→ **Increase Capacity Per Session**

→ **Increase Profit Per Session**

→ **Enhance Experience**

Okay, so this last micro lever is a big one. It's one of the things so many gyms struggle with and one of the biggest obstacles my team encounters on sales calls.

"How will I make sure new people can get acclimated to how we do things?"

New people coming into the gym should be a great thing. But it's often a source of stress, for a number of reasons.

- You want to impress new clients the most because you NEED them to stay on, but you have a hard time getting them integrated into the moving machine.
- OGs (your original members) complain about how newbies slow them down.
- It's often necessary to offer inconvenient skill-practice times like 7:00 am or 8:00 pm to get them prepared for higher-level workouts.
- You need additional payroll for special times when a promotion comes out, which further decreases your profitability on the front end for any low-barrier offers.

This problem appears more often with facilities that have more of a barbell and strength emphasis than it does for bootcamp-style ones. But the problem can creep into any type of gym. The big issue is that new people have a hard time integrating into the community. They're literally segmented with their baby exercises at weird hours, if they show up to them at all, before falling off. And nowadays, there are "pre-beginners" who can barely do a bodyweight squat.

It's hard to keep people coming back when they don't feel welcomed into a facility and when there's a steep learning curve to get them up to speed. (This is central to the attrition problem that I'll get to in later chapters.)

Sometimes it feels like you just can't win.

> ROCK: You water down your classes and spark a revolt with your OGs, who pay next to nothing but are the heart and soul of your gym.
>
> HARD PLACE: You have a weird few sessions per week where only newbies can go for their first two weeks, or whatever arbitrary timeline you choose, which isn't convenient or fun and costs you even more money to get someone going.

So how do you actually win?

The first thing to do is recognize that you've got two problems here:

1. Onboard Problem: Getting "pre-beginners" and other new clients integrated into your gym so they are most likely to stay, while minimizing extra overhead. This problem affects client acquisition and attrition.
2. Jump Rope Problem: Exercises where your return on space is very low, which hurts gym session capacity.

The good news is, we figured out a way around these problems with my gyms, which you can model.

Solution → Set Up Regressive Two-Tier Programming

For every workout, create a second easier one that's done in parallel with the first. This allows you to have new people with no fitness experience get their time in, while also offering workouts that your more advanced OGs can do. The workouts should be

100% in parallel—same muscles and movement patterns, just regressive. This also gives new people another metric besides body composition they can use to measure their progress.

> Sara, when you started here just six weeks ago, you could barely finish the Tier 2 workouts. Now two-thirds of your exercises are from Tier 1. And that's just in six weeks. Imagine where you could be in six months.

Example Using Two-Tier Programming

Tier 1: BB Back Squat, BB Bench Press, BB Row

Tier 2: Goblet Squat with KB, Push-ups From Knees, Double KB Row

Here are a few hints to make this strategy work even better.

Take out complex lifts and space-consuming lifts like double unders and Olympic lifts. This way, you'll need fewer trainers per person to manage each session. There will be less of a learning curve for new people. You'll have more space to fit people, which increases capacity, especially during your busy times. And really, most people don't need complex lifts to meet their fitness goals. They will feel more accomplished with simpler lifts they can master quickly.

Don't announce that you're making changes, just make them. It's rare that someone "remembers" that you haven't done something in a while. Just stop doing those exercises, and if someone confronts you about it, tell them the truth: "We believe there is a higher risk of injury and that the risk–reward tradeoff for noncompetitors is simply not there."

Use partners. Yes, I am repeating this idea. But I believe in having peer partners for all workouts, especially for bigger movements. A buddy system is motivating, and it saves crazy amounts of space, because one person is resting while the other completes the movement. You can sell it as "spotting for safety." A partner system also allows for great supersets and strength sets.

Have the strong help the weak. Have your OGs act as spotters and partners for newer members. This is motivating for both people. To sell the idea to your OGs, you can say something like this:

> At a certain point, you'll never be more fulfilled by getting fitter, but you can improve by helping others. That's why I opened this gym and why all our coaches here do what they do every day. To get to that next level, you have to pay it forward. Remember when you started? You could barely do a bodyweight squat. But none of us judged you, and none of the other clients told you to speed up or said that you were holding them back. Why? Because the strong help the weak.

This system also helps with morale, because the OGs who might have complained before are now proud mentors. They become brand ambassadors for your gym. And the newbies make friends with their new mentors. There's no adversarial atmosphere where everyone is competing for the coach's limited attention.

> Hey, Sarah—meet Tiffany, one of our rock-star clients. Not only has she lost 20 pounds, she can also

do 30 push-ups in a row! Tiffany, it's Sarah's first day. Would you mind showing her the ropes?

A few benefits to two-tier programming include:

Bank Account Confidence: It's not just morale that goes up—your bank account balance does too. There's zero cost for added fulfillment. The new members get a full, rich experience and feel taken care of. It integrates the whole community with no added staffing complexity. There's less risk of trainers walking away with clients. And it's a fully scalable solution. You can't beat that. And from a real human sense, having an extra $15–$30K in the bank gives you the power to make some harder decisions (such as raising prices or changing class times) and allows you to absorb any temporary chaos like OGs getting mad and leaving.

Limitless Marketing: When you sign up 50, 70, or 150 people in 8 weeks, it's all hands on deck.

It would break most models. The reason this model can handle a surge of customers (from marketing that actually works), and why I teach client acquisition first, is that you have a lot more credibility with your OG clientele when you say things are changing. It's hard to have semi-privates of one-on-four when your average class size is seven, ya feel? Being able to handle a new surge of customers allows you to create an influx of cash in your business. Having a cushion helps everything.

Actions To Take

Create two levels of programming for every session. One for new people and one for your more experienced clients. This allows them to tailor their experience to their confidence level while also decreasing your cost of acquisition/fulfillment AND allowing them to seamlessly merge with your existing clientele. It also allows you to get as many new customers as needed. Period.

I know that was a lot to take in. But I wanted this to be as actionable as humanly possible for you.

Capacity Profit Levers Summary

1. Membership Levels: Switch from unlimited to 3x/week as your core offer. Call them sessions, not classes.
2. Attendance: Get everyone to schedule in advance and ask them which session they want in reverse order of fullness. Implement a no-show fee for bonus points.
3. Duration: Switch to 45-minute sessions back-to-back (30 minutes if you can only service 15 or fewer).
4. Physical Space: Partner up. Blow out office walls and sell from a cubicle.
5. Exercise Selection: Swap out any space-consuming exercises for less space-consuming ones and don't announce it. Offer two levels of programming (hard and easy) so people can start in the same session.

Yowza.

I know that is a lot of stuff. Then again, being broke sucks too. So pick whether you want things to stay the same or you're willing to suffer the pain of change.

Now, there's one more macro profit lever I want to show you—the overhead lever. It's going to decrease your outflow and increase your profit per session.

Let's dig in.

Chapter 10

The Overhead Lever

It's not what you make, it's what you keep. The overhead macro lever is the smallest of the levers. But understanding this will help you keep your eye on the ball and the game that really matters—PROFIT.

And do NOT underestimate the power of this.

Back in 2017, I encountered a gym that was running 189 sessions per month. That is a LOT of sessions. But they only had 120 EFTs. And of course, they all had unlimited access.

The issue was that their sessions were never that full. The gym owner believed that his clients appreciated the smaller class sizes (and they sure did), but it was not a good business decision.

Clients would love $10 one-on-one training sessions, but that doesn't mean it makes sense business-wise. And if your average client comes 20 times a month and pays $120, then they are paying you only $6 per session.

This gym had an average of six people in their sessions, so he was barely breaking even on what was supposed to be his primary source of profit—selling service.

Needless to say, he wasn't going to make it much longer using this model.

We ended up cutting his classes from 189 per month to 100, while also raising his prices.

And guess what? Profitability went through the roof, and his blood pressure came down.

As a sad but true side note, and the reason I'm removing his name, this gym owner had been hospitalized only 9 months prior due to a heart attack at age 46. This stuff really can be life or death. Don't take it lightly. He has since enjoyed over a year of unbroken profitable months with consistent growth, and actually spends time at home now.

Hopefully you don't let your stress levels get that bad.

Now let's dive into the three micro levers surrounding overhead.

Overhead Micro Lever #1: Number of Sessions → Decrease Overhead and Increase Profit Per Session

Thanks for hanging in there. I hope you're enjoying the ride so far.

There's no secret sauce to making money with gyms (or really for any business). It's just about making mathematical decisions within the context of human psychology. That's the heart of all good business decisions. So let's keep going with the money math, okay?

The Empty Session Problem: Approximately 90% of gyms we work with are overfulfilling—and I don't mean their sessions are "too good," I mean they simply have too many of them. A lot of times this happens because a client will say, "I can't make it at six—do you have a seven o'clock?" And gym owners think, "Great. Another $120/month. I sure do. You're it." I say this half-jokingly, but for many, it happens exactly like this, until eventually they have a packed schedule but empty sessions.

This is a problem not only because of the added payroll, but also because you're burning through what should be productive time. You should be doing a million other things besides selling your time to two people who are paying you $6 each—yippee (that's sarcasm).

How can you tell if you're doing this?

I use an 80% service margin ([revenue - cost of trainers] / revenue) to create the gold standard for the gyms we work with. As soon as we get a gym past that point, it is profitable and self-sustaining. The only exceptions are gyms with a massive rent overhead, in which case they need it to be higher. But 80% should be your standard as you're starting out.

Here's an example of a bootcamp that has 100 EFTs, at the industry average of $118/month (blended average), and a total of 38 sessions per week. Let's fix this gym's margin piece by piece.

Here are the numbers we need in order to figure out their gross margin on service:

#1 Number of Sessions

This bootcamp has seven sessions a day M–F (5:30 am, 7:00 am, 9:00 am, 12:00 pm, 5:00 pm, 6:00 pm, 7:00 pm) and three sessions on Saturdays (8:00 am, 9:00 am, 10:00 am).

35 + 3 = 38 sessions per week

38 x 4.3 weeks per month = **163 sessions per month**

#2 Revenue Per Session

of EFTs (recurring members) = 100 @ $118 (industry avg.)

Now we multiply the number of EFTs by how much they are paying on average to get the monthly revenue.

100 x $118 = $11,800/month (assuming no declined cards)

Then we divide total monthly revenue by total number of sessions. This gives us the revenue per session. That is, how much their business is actually getting paid per hour of training.

$11,800 total revenue / 163 sessions = **$72/session in revenue**

#3 Cost to Fulfill Each Session

Now we calculate the REAL COST of each training session, which includes payroll. (I'm using the real amount my payroll company charged me in my California gyms.)

Cost Per Session: $20 per hour (x 1.22 for payroll costs) = **$24.40/hour**

We then multiply the number of sessions by the cost per session and get the **total training payroll**. (This is not to be confused with total payroll if you have admins or salespeople, etc.)

163 sessions x $24.40 per session = $3,977/month in session payroll

#4 Margin Calculation

Now we finally do the big calculation. We subtract how much money they made on each session (#2) from how much it costs the business to fulfill each session (#3), and then divide that number by #2 again. This gives us the percentage of money coming in that's actually margin to be used to pay other expenses and will eventually be left over for a crazy thing we call PROFIT.

Revenue - Cost to Fulfill = Gross Margin

Ex: $72 revenue per session - $24.40 trainer pay = $47.60

Gross Margin / Revenue = Gross Margin %

Ex: $47.60/$72 = 66% Gross Margin

Now most people see that and say, "Sweet, I'm just 14% off."

But the issue is this: the industry-average gym runs on 12% margins. Being off by 14% may very well be the entirety of your take-home income. It is a naive entrepreneurial move to think 14% of gross profit is not a big deal. It is game-changing, especially in an industry that has historically low margins.

Here's the problem: you aren't making enough per session to justify the costs. For many, doing less will actually earn the gym more. Only open new sessions when you are certain you can fill them.

Remember, if you have a 66% margin to start, there is barely anything left over for you after you pay rent, administrative costs, marketing, utilities, software, facility fixes, and miscellaneous expenses.

How do I fix this gym?

Stay with me—this is about to get funky.

So we only have three micro levers here: 1) number of sessions, 2) number of hours worked, and 3) compensation for those hours.

Now mind you, I don't like to adjust compensation unless it is absolutely essential. And even then, I still don't like to.

So I'll show you how I do the math to determine how many sessions the gym SHOULD have.

Solution → Cut Sessions To Maximize Efficiency

If we use the same numbers as above, we know that we only need to fulfill 100 clients.

If we have already implemented the 3x/week fix, then it means only 50 people per day at 100% attendance.

But since attendance is 85% on average, then we only have to service 42.5 people per day.

That means we could hypothetically get away with only 3 sessions a day.

In the real world, I wouldn't cut the gym to 3 sessions a day, but I would likely cut them to 4. This would allow them to service 64 people per day, and would still provide ample room for growth without them needing to re-add another session within a week or something.

So let's see what changing to 3x/week and cutting from 7 sessions per day to 4 per day really does.

We would have 4 per day M–F and 3 on Saturdays. This gives us 23 sessions per week.

Now multiply that by 4.3 to get sessions per month.

> 23 sessions/week x 4.3 weeks/month = 99 sessions/month

This would take our sessions from 163/month to 99/month, or a reduction of 61%.

So if this gym's training payroll before was 163 x $24.40 = $3,977, it now becomes…

> 99 sessions/month x 24.40 cost/session = $2,415/month

We just increased owner pay by $1,561/month and $18,732/year.

You may think that is not a lot. But these things add up. And the secret is, you need to become BETTER before you become BIGGER.

The last two micro levers—human hours worked and compensation per hour—are interrelated, so I'll just discuss them together.

Solution → Calibrate Trainer Pay

Now I hate—I repeat, HATE—decreasing pay. But sometimes it is the ugly truth. And sometimes—scratch that, a LOT of times—the trainers are making more than the owner.

So I am going to call this "calibration." As in, standardizing your pay. A lot of times, we deal with gyms that have multiple trainers at different compensation levels.

Say the compensation for trainers for large-group sessions is $15/hour. With payroll tax, it goes up to $18.30/hour.

If we applied that to the math we were just doing, this would further decrease our monthly overhead from $2,415 to $1,812 for a net decrease of $603/month.

This would increase the net income of the business by another $7,200/year and, in combination with the $18,732/year we just added, bring us to $25,932 per year.

Considering most gym owners net around that much currently, this single fix could effectively double their take-home pay.

Like I said, I don't LIKE doing this, but if the option is keeping the doors open or closing them, you need to feed the business first. That is your obligation as the owner. Otherwise, you should be fired. And if you don't, you WILL be fired by going out of business.

New Gross Service Profit Calculation

Remember the calculation we did before to get that 66% margin? Well, let's take a look at it again.

We are still making $11,800 per month in gross revenue, assuming we have done nothing else.

Let's look at our gross margin again and follow the same steps.

STEP 1: Calculate total revenue.

>(Unchanged assuming we did no price increases or anything.)
>
>Total Revenue = 100 EFTs x $118/month = $11,800/month

STEP 2: Calculate revenue per session.

>Revenue per session divided by NEW total number of reduced sessions = $11,800/99 sessions.
>
>This means our new revenue per session is $119. Remember the $72 from before? Big improvement.

STEP 3: Calculate cost to fulfill each session.

>$15 x 1.22 payroll fees = $18.30 per session

STEP 4: Calculate new margin with overhead lever efficiencies.

>Revenue Per Session - Cost Per Session / Revenue Per Session
>
>$119 - $18.30 / $119 = 84.6% Margin Per Session
>
>Note: If you didn't want to decrease your trainer pay, the margin would be this:
>
>$119 - $24.40 / $119 = 79.5% Margin Per Session

Kaboom.

Use the math above to calculate your own margin. And if you are below 80%, make the changes. Even if it is "only" 7% under, that could be HALF your net revenue. Said differently, these changes could increase how much you take home by 50%. That is something worth looking into.

Summary

1. Know your margin math.
2. Cut unneeded sessions.
3. Drop to 3x/week.
4. "Calibrate" trainer pay if needed.

In the next chapter, we're going to put all of this together.

That's right, we are going to pull on all the levers at the same time and see what we can do for your gym's profitability.

Chapter 11

Your New Gym On Paper

This chapter is the most mathematical, but I broke it down step-by-step so it will be easy for you.

It's fine if you're not a math geek, but you need to understand these calculations, because this is the lifeblood of your gym business. This is how you figure out whether you're going to make money, how much, and when. Mind you, no math we're doing here is above multiplication and division.

I wasn't good at math in school, but I know this stuff like the back of my hand. You will too. We only fear what we don't understand. So this is me…begging you…please learn to dig this stuff. It's important. Not only for you, but for the many lives that you impact. Your family. Your trainers. Your clients.

After that, it will be the end of the heavy math section of the book (*sigh of relief*).

The entire framework you were just dragged through in the last chapter was the result of everything I've learned from managing my six gyms, the many mistakes and heartbreaks, and the 1,500+ gyms I consult with actively.

I have gone step-by-step through this on the phone with gym owners, sharing a screen with all the numbers, going line by line. There was no formal process. It was sort of like me asking about all the different places where they weren't operating efficiently that I would typically see, then going from there. And we would always end up massively improving the gym's bottom line.

Over time, I went through all the calls, put all those action items together, and itemized them. Then I categorized them the way you see them now, as macro levers.

I want this part of the book to give you hope. These consultation calls are incredibly draining on the gym owner because of the amount of focus and attention they take. But after an hour's honest work looking at the numbers, you can turn a business around in a matter of days. I desperately want you to believe me, because you may only be an hour's focused attention and a week of implementation away from the swing you will see unfold in the pages that follow.

Remember, you are only a few hard conversations away from what you want. You can have them with your spouse and landlord, or you can have them with your trainers and customers. But only one of those will make you more money.

Nitty Gritty

Okay, this is where you get your PhD in Gym Turnarounds.

Or, if your gym is doing well, your PhD in Gym Launching, taking your gym into the stratosphere.

We have more seven-figure gyms in our Gym Lords community than a lot of "gurus" have in total as clients. It's no longer a pipedream in our world; it's just an eventuality. Think when, not if.

That being said, in order to win Super Bowls, you need to play fundamentals football. You need to score more than the other team. In the context of the gym, winning means making more money than it costs you to make it. And pulling on all these levers is the best way I know to make gyms pump out money, virtually overnight.

Over the last three chapters, we've taken a deep dive into each of the macro profit levers: price, capacity, and overhead.

And I hope you feel I did a good job of separating them. Because to be honest, I think of them all as one massive profit system. They work together like a football team, with blockers and passers and runners.

This section is what it looks like when the entire play is run together in unison.

The major purpose for this section is to show you how much profit you are leaving on the table, and to transform your gym from a job into a cash machine. I almost didn't include this content in the book, mostly because my editor said it was too much math. But I really wanted to show you that this isn't smoke and mirrors. This is REAL stuff. And I don't pull numbers out of my backside like I see so many others do.

I want to show you where the numbers come from, why they are believable, and how you can achieve a similar profit within a week, by doing nothing but improving your current model. So follow along, use the math from your gym (or be lazy and just read…for now), then see what your gym could look like after implementing these steps.

You will probably think, "But I don't know how to even begin." Then you will turn the page and read the next chapter, which explains step-by-step how to communicate the change to your trainers and staff. If you don't do it, then you have no excuse but fear, because all the steps are outlined for you.

Also, if the steps look familiar, I literally took them from each chapter ending. That way, you know exactly what's going on.

I am going to use our hypothetical average struggling gym numbers. Here they are again.

Current Gym Stats

EFTs = 100

Price = $118/month

# of Sessions/week = 38

# of Sessions/month = 163

Duration of Sessions = 60 minutes (with no breaks)

Max Cap Per Session = 16

Cost of Trainer Per Hour = $25 (including payroll tax)

# of Sessions on Membership Level = Unlimited

Billing Cycle = Monthly

Revenue = $11,800/month

Expenses = $10,000/month (This is minuscule, but I'm just taking industry averages here.)

We're going to use all the levers available to fix this hypothetical gym and make it profitable.
Ready?
Off we go.

Step 1: Define What You Can Control

Note: All items with checkmarks (✓) are under our control.

EFTs = 100

- ✓ Price = $118/month
- ✓ # of Sessions/week = 38
- ✓ # of Sessions/month = 163
- ✓ Duration of Sessions = 60 minutes (with no breaks)
- ✓ Max Cap Per Session = 16

- ✓ Cost of Trainer Per Hour = $25 (including payroll tax)
- ✓ # of Sessions on Membership Level = Unlimited
- ✓ Billing Cycle = Monthly
- ✓ Revenue = $11,800/month
- ✓ Expenses = $10,000/month

Step 2: Macro Lever #1 Price Increase and Billing Cycle Switch

1. Large group should be $39–$49/week or $167–$225 every 28 days.
2. Advanced: Offer two levels of service: large group and small group (one-on-four).

The first step is to increase prices and change the billing cycle. I know this can feel scary, but don't worry—you'll start to see an increase in profits within weeks. You may lose some clients, but that's just temporary. Believe me. I've seen this work a bazillion times.

Okay, yes, after you make this announcement, you will have fewer members. But you are going to be cutting the fat. I have rarely had any client lose more than 10% when making a massive switch like the one we are about to do with your gym.

Here's a little note to boost your confidence: I switched one of my own personal gyms from a $99/month bootcamp to a $299/month semi-private, and I lost 30% of my customers. But remember: we TRIPLED THE PRICE. And despite that jump, I still made more money each month serving FEWER customers. And they were the people who like me the most. That's still a win in my book.

You are adding $10–$15/week, so relax.

So the first two changes we make are pricing and billing cycle.

✓ Price = $118/month → $39/week
✓ Billing Cycle = Monthly → Weekly

Next, we're going to switch the billing from $118 per month to $39 per WEEK. (I could make this $49/week, which would definitely make this average gym owner even more "Excel rich"—that is, wealthy on paper—but most of our gym clients switch to $39/week initially.)

Effective monthly increase $39 x 4.3 = $168 - $118
= **$50/month increase per customer**

Assuming that the maximum we have ever seen leave (10%) actually left, that would leave you with 90 clients paying $168, and 90 x $168 = $15,120. That is an increase of $3,320/month from the $11,800 we started at (even with the 10% customer loss).

If you wanted to be extra bold, you could offer one-on-four semi-privates and sell just 16.6% of your remaining customers into it at $129/week. This would increase your effective EFT by an additional $388 per month for every client who signed up. In this case, that would mean 15 new high-ticket customers. The "added revenue" or marginal return of the move would be…

$555 - $167 = $388/month

That's how much EXTRA you would make by having a higher-ticket offer.

This single move would increase your gross revenue by $5,432 per month ON TOP of what you would have received if those people only stayed in large group. Did you get lost?

> 90 clients (left over from price change) → 16.6% (15 people) take upsell of more service
>
> 15 x $388 (the difference of what they would be paying you if you didn't have a higher-priced service) = $5,820/month MORE

That's an additional $69,840 per year. This is the power of premium services.

But if you want to stay with the beginner moves for now, that's 100% cool too. Just make the switch from monthly to weekly or 28 days, and make your effective billing rate $39 per week.

Step 3: Increase Fulfillment Capacity And Cut Overhead Capacity Profit Levers

1. **Membership Levels**
   a. Switch from unlimited to 3x/week as core offer.
   b. Call them sessions, not classes.
2. **Attendance**
   a. Get everyone to schedule in advance, and ask them which session they want in reverse order of fullness.
   b. For bonus points, implement a no-show fee.
3. **Duration**
   a. Switch to 45-minute sessions back-to-back (30-minutes if you can only service 15 or fewer).
4. **Physical Space**
   a. Partner up.
   b. Blow out office walls and sell from a cubicle.

5. **Exercise Selection**
   a. Swap out any space-consuming exercises for less space-consuming ones, but don't announce it.
   b. Offer two levels of programming (hard and easy) so people can start in the same session.

These are pretty much the same numbers as the overhead capacity lever example. The only difference is that I am also going to increase the CAPACITY of the session. I combined our last two micro levers because they go hand in hand. For example, when you switch to three days per week of fulfillment as your main offering, you simultaneously increase capacity while also decreasing overhead. So for the purposes of continuity, I am making this a single "step" in our new profitable gym money math calculations.

- ✓ Switch from Unlimited to 3x/week
- ✓ # of Sessions/week = 38 → 23
- ✓ # of Sessions/month = 163 → 23 x 4.3 = 99
- ✓ Max Cap Per Session = 16 → 20
- ✓ # of Sessions on Membership Level = Unlimited → 3x/week
- ✓ Use Partners

Third, we are going to cut some wasteful overhead. One hundred people do NOT need 38 session times a week to work out. So let's do the math. You're going to switch to 3x per week to increase capacity anyways, so that means you only need to service 50 people a day.

And if our "average" gym can train 16 people per session, then we're going to assume they have stretched their square footage, stopped doing double unders, partnered up clients, and gotten rid of complex barbell movements except for semi-privates.

So even though I'll bet you could push 24, I'm going to say 20. That would mean with "perfect" attendance, you could likely get it done in 3 sessions a day. Why? Because 10% will never show up. So 3 sessions a day with 60 members attending (3 x 20) would cover you.

But we're going to do one extra for good measure during this transition. So we'll change the schedule to 5:00 am, 9:00 am, 5:00 pm, and 6:00 pm. You can use your own wisdom here, but those are the biggest pockets at most facilities. That also gives you a projected 80 members you could service per day, more than enough to satisfy your current gym-goers.

You would have those training session time slots Monday through Thursday, then take Friday evenings off. (Enjoy, it's my gift to you.) Or if you prefer, keep them. So Monday to Friday is 4 x 5 = 20 sessions. (But I still say you should keep those Friday night sessions off since no one wants to do them anyways.)

Then Saturday morning, you would have 3 sessions, since again, attendance isn't as high as on a weekday. So that takes you to 23 sessions a week, and you take off Sundays. You should rest. It'll make you money. Trust me.

Last but not least...

- ✓ Duration of Sessions = 60 minutes (with 15-minute breaks) → 45-minute sessions with no breaks
- ✓ Cost of Trainer Per Hour = $25 → $18.30 (both including payroll tax)

This means you have 60 minutes (15-minute setup + 45-minute workout) in the early morning and 60 minutes in the late morning for the 9:00 am session. Then 2 hours at night (90 minutes of coaching and 30 minutes of breakdown and cleanup). This gives you 20 hours of training during the week and 2 hours 45 minutes on the weekends (technically 2 hours 15 minutes of sessions + 30 minutes of breakdown/cleanup).

This amounts to a whopping 22 hours and 45 minutes of payroll. But let's round it to 23 hours.

Now, the last thing you could do, which I have done, is to decrease trainer pay. As I mentioned, I absolutely HATE doing this, but if the option is to close the business or find a way to keep it open, then this might be something you have to do. (If you really don't want to cut trainer pay, I discuss another option below.)

I have found phenomenal trainers for $15 per hour. Also, consider that your trainers will have access to your gym clients for semi-privates. That being said, the net cost will be closer to $18.30 per hour if you include payroll taxes, which you absolutely should.

Step 4: Do the Math To See the Final Results On Paper
Large-Group Revenue

100 x $118 = $11,800 → 90 x $168 = $15,120

That's an increase of $3,320 while assuming a MAX loss of customers, which I have rarely seen any gym actually experience. If you manage to keep everyone during the transition, it would be an increase of $5,000 (100 x $168).

Large-Group Training Overhead

$25/hour x 1.25 hours/session x 163 sessions/month = $5,100/month

→ $18.30/hour x .75 hours/session x 99 sessions/month = $1,358/month

This last change cut your overhead by $3,741.

If you wanted to just cut the class times but keep trainer pay the same, then your overhead would go down to…

$25 x .75 hours per session x 99 sessions = $1,856.

This would be a net decrease of $3,244. Still a BIG reduction.

Advanced Move
Small-Group Revenue

$0 TO 15% of EFTs taking $129/week offer for one-on-four training

→ 15 x $129/week x 4.3 weeks/month = $8,320/month

Now we remove what you would already have been making from them doing large group. That way you don't get an inflated number. This will show you what revenue you would truly ADD to what you'd have already been making.

15 x $168/month (from above) = $2,505

This means ADDED revenue would be $8,320 - $2,505 = $5,815/month.

But no added revenue is cost-free. So here's what you would need to add to your overhead to fulfill on that level of semis.

Semi-Private Overhead

You would add 12 more sessions per week M/W/F, 2 in the morning and 2 in the afternoon.

If you choose to add this and pay hourly, this would add 12 sessions per week x 4.3 weeks per month x $18.30 per hour = $944/month in semi-private overhead.

OR if you decide to revenue share (which is recommended to encourage the switchover for staff), adding the 25% revenue share for the trainers makes it $2,080.

Now, to put a bow on this, let's add up how much we swung the NET PROFIT of this facility.

Check out the three scenarios below. (I included different ones to account for whatever route you may choose to take with your facility, depending on your level of confidence in what I am suggesting.)

Scenario #1: Advanced Perfect Swing (Semis Added, No Attrition, Decreasing Trainer Pay)

+ $5,800 semi-private revenue > 15 x $388 (difference between $168 and $555)

+ $4,250 large-group increase (85 x $50 increase in revenue per customer)

+ $1,660 in payroll savings (from $3,741 reduction in large group fulfillment cost but an increase in semis of $2,080, assuming rev-share model).

= $11,710/month extra profit > **extra $140,520/year**

Scenario #2: Perfect Swing (No Semis Added, No Attrition, Decreasing Trainer Pay)

+ $5,000 in revenue (100 clients increase EFT by $50 a month)

+ $3,741 in cost savings (decrease sessions and change trainer pay)

= $8,741 total per month, netting you approximately an **extra $105,000/year**

Scenario #3: Imperfect Swing (No Semis, 10% Customer Attrition, Trainer Pay Stays Same)

Even with some attrition and an unchanged compensation structure, it looks like this…

+ $3,320 revenue (with 10% loss of customers)

+ $3,150 in savings (decrease sessions, no change in trainer pay)

= $6,470 extra profit, netting you an **extra $77,640 per year**

Hopefully I didn't lose you with all the math. But this stuff is REAL. I tried to make as many accommodations for self-doubt and disbelief as possible.

Get out your calculator. Do the math over and over again until you're convinced I'm right.

If you STILL need convincing, go to IDontHateMoney.com and read all the success stories from Gym Launch owners just like you who are now running incredibly successful gyms. But only go there if you don't hate money (ha ha).

Actions To Take

1. Charge more.
2. Change your billing cycle.
3. Optimize your exercise selection to use your space efficiently.
4. Make the most out of your session times.
5. Schedule shorter sessions.
6. Set trainer pay to increase profitability and encourage semi-privates.

You may be thinking, "Alex, this makes sense on paper, but how would I even begin to communicate this to my community or my staff? I told them they would get their rates for life and I'd never change anything."

Well, you're in luck. In the next chapter, I will give you the exact schedule we lay out with our gym owners to communicate the change to their team members.

Now you have no excuses not to do it.

Chapter 12

Making The Shift

Now the next natural question is, "Okay, Alex…I'm pretty sure if I did this, my members would kill me and everyone would leave. But let's just imagine I did believe you. How would I go about communicating this?"

Glad you asked.

There are two main parties that you need to communicate with: trainers and clients.

(As an aside, you can never OVER-communicate. Communication in relationships is good, and in business, it's everything.)

Telling The Trainers

1. Frame the problem (for them, the business, and the customers).
2. Explain your thought process (what you considered, pros and cons).
3. Explain the solution (and what's in it for them).

The first thing to do is talk to your trainers individually. This is 100% a sale. You're making your employees aware of a problem, exploring potential outcomes, then coming up with a solution together. That's selling. So make sure you understand that you want their buy-in. The worst thing you can do is frame it as "my way or the highway." Your trainers already understand that your decisions are final, but in order to keep your community happy, buy-in is essential.

Note: If you have a certain trainer who acts like they own the place and second-guesses your every decision, it may be time to let them go. Before making a firing decision, think about these words from one of my mentors: "I have never fired someone and not found someone better to replace them." If you're even thinking about it, you probably already know you should do it.

I can count on one hand how many times I've thought about firing someone and didn't end up doing it. As soon as you think it, it's going to happen, so it might as well happen sooner rather than waiting until it becomes unbearable. (Or worse, they could decide to leave on their own and take half your customer base with them.)

The conversation with your trainers should go something like this:

> Hey, Tom. I wanted to reach out to you because we have some exciting new things coming down the pipeline regarding member services, pricing, sessions, and everything in between.
>
> I'm not sure if you know this, but the business is pretty much just breaking even every month and has been for [*period of time*]. Every month, we barely get by.
>
> It's incredibly stressful for me, and I'm sure that it has affected you in one way or another.
>
> So I hired some industry coaches and experts to help me with the business.
>
> And after reading and going through everything, it looks like there is a way for us to save the business

and give the customers a better experience, AND for the trainers to make more money.

But I want to make sure I have everyone on board, because there is going to be about one month of rockiness ahead before we are in the clear.

Can I share with you what they recommended?

Okay, so the goal is to switch us to a "bifurcated" or two-tier model, which basically means large group and semi-privates. This will allow you to make more money and the clients to get better service. I'm sure there are a few people you and I can both name off the top of our heads who would like to get more personalized service and are willing to pay for it.

So with the changes, you'd be able to make an extra $2,000–$6,000 per month and probably go full-time, but we're going to have to change a lot of things about the business in order to get there.

The first thing we're going to do is stop giving our lives away in the large group. And we're going to try and make those a little more personalized. So instead of giving away unlimited access, everyone will get three sessions a week. That will allow us to give them better service while they're here, and also raise the price of membership since they'll be getting more attention.

Don't think about it as how much workout time they're losing, but how much attention they're gaining. One session of private training per week should cost more than five group workouts, right? This is no different. And large-group facilities at our price point are a dime a dozen, so we need to differentiate by providing more value.

As a result of these changes, we can cut down on the large-group sessions to make room for semi-private sessions. This will allow you to fill up your time and off days with semi-private one-on-four sessions. We'll be charging $125 per week for three semi-private session times. This way, if someone wants to get even more workouts in, they can opt for semi-privates and get those on top of their 3x/week large group.

And let's be honest, a lot of people here have been using the gym as social hour. I want to make sure they're actually getting what they pay us for—results.

So the cut in large-group sessions would obviously result in fewer total hours, but it would open up more time for you to do semis and make way more dollars per hour. Does that make sense?

So if you get 15 people to do semis with you, that equates to about $8,000/month. And you get 25% of that. It's an extra $2,000 per month, and you get to actually serve people at a higher level. If you get 30 people to do semis, it's $4,000/month on top of what you make from large group. Think of large group as your way of generating leads to sell into your semis. That make more sense?

My goal here is for everyone to make a very livable wage wearing sweats and hanging out with friends at the gym all day, while having enough left over that the business can make it through the rough seasons without any anxiety.

I'm honestly a little nervous, but I need you on board with this so I can explain it to the rest of the team and present a unified front. If any member of the team questions it—or worse, creates doubt in the members—it could make this really difficult on the business, so I want to avoid that at all costs.

Are you on board?

Obviously, the talk doesn't need to be verbatim. That's just a general outline of points. Explain how the changes are there to protect the business and also provide more value and a higher level of service to customers. And make sure you tie everything back to the semis that are coming soon as a natural solution to those people who want to train more or get more attention.

Make no mistake, people hate change. There will be loud squeaky wheels. But better to have hard conversations with them than with your landlord or having to tell your team you can't afford to pay them.

Telling Your Members

So this is the big thing everyone is afraid of: "What will my team members say or think? Will the Facebook group blow up? Will they throw Molotov cocktails at my gym at night and burn down what I've created?" Like I mentioned before, clear communication is the best strategy.

You'll want to make your announcements over multiple mediums such as…

- Direct mail (old-fashioned, with a stamp)
- Email
- Social media post w/video (and comments turned off)

- YouTube unlisted video
- Text blast pushing to social media posts and YouTube videos

The letter might look something like this. Feel free to just swipe this whole thing—my treat.

Dear [*Name*],

As you may or may not know, we are going on [*years/months*] of being open as of next month.

As you most likely have seen, we have grown a tremendous amount over this period of time. A letter with black-and-white words can never communicate how deeply grateful I am to you for being a part of this journey. You have honored us with your patronage, and I want to honor you with transparency and with a significant improvement to the level of service you have been receiving. We want to truly transform lives, not just say we are.

To live up to this, I wanted to make you aware of the effort we put into this on a continual basis, and what is coming down the pipeline, which the coaching staff and I are incredibly excited about. A few of the upcoming improvements are as follows.

WHAT WE CURRENTLY DO

Hire and Retain The Best Coaches: We strive to hire trainers who are sharp and have tremendous work ethic and warm hearts. We strive to replace the traditional model of fitness—watching the clock, counting reps, lack of enthusiasm, lack of knowledge or personalization—with a friendly face that knows your name, top-notch coaching, and motivation to not only get you in the door, but also to keep you coming back.

Offer Continued Education: The best coaches in the industry are the best because they invest in their education. As a result, we continuously invest in our coaches' education like [*certifications/workshops*]. We train our coaches to provide the absolute best service in the region so you get the results you are after as fast as possible.

Provide New Equipment: As we continue to learn about new training systems and methodologies, we continue to invest in up-to-date equipment. This applies to new equipment like [*equipment*] we recently purchased, but also replacing malfunctioning equipment like [*equipment*]. In the next few months, we also plan on bringing in [*new equipment*] to give you even more to look forward to and to help speed up your results.

WHAT IS COMING

Facility Improvements: We're a lot like the *Millennium Falcon*: we ain't pretty, but we'll get you there… fast. While we don't provide cucumber-scented towels and marble bathrooms, you deserve working AC and showers. So our goal is to dramatically improve this facility or move to a new one to improve your training experience and have a gym whose quality matches the caliber of its members.

Member Events: To further build this community and connect you all with one another, we are planning on hosting events so you have something social to look forward to. (Don't worry—you can cheat on your diet every once in a while.) This is so you all can get to know one another like we know you, which I feel is one of the greatest benefits of owning this gym.

Specialty Programs: We will also be rolling out specialty programs to those members who would like more attention and individualized coaching to address specific needs for an even faster rate of progress than is possible in a large-group setting.

A MASSIVE Improvement to the Level of Service: This is the one we are the most excited about; it's also the one I am most petrified about announcing. We are planning on changing the programming from a "come whenever you can" to "you now have an appointment with a trainer 3x per week." This is with the full intention of making the class sizes smaller so that we can provide you even better service. It will also help with some of the parking issues that the city has been continuously reaming us for, so you won't have to fight for a space anymore.

Candidly, we never want to be a "get your sweat on" facility. We want to be a gym that prides itself on transformations (both internal and external). And we have noticed that making sessions "whenever you want" has become "never" for many people. And this does not sit well with me.

We have also noticed that people seem to get results in the beginning, but then they tend to slow down as the novelty wears off. You keep working out, which is great, but I want you to transform with continuous progress.

As such, we will be implementing accountability on top of our normal service. You will be checked in ahead of time, and if for some reason you miss your session, we will hound you and make you feel terrible about it (joking). But we really do want you to be here and treat it like an appointment with yourself.

Now, all of these continued investments and upgrades in the level of service we provide you will require significant funds to become reality.

And to continue to stay aligned with our mission to provide a remarkable experience for our clients, we will be implementing a change in billing structure. Instead of "unlimited come whenever you want," we will be switching to weekly billing. This switch will be an increase of about $10–$15/week depending on your current membership. But the final result will be $39/week with an effective date of [MM/DD/YYYY]. (*Note: You can also simply attach a letter or chart on the back if you have multiple levels to show where they will be. Break it down to weekly.*)

Since we will have these as scheduled sessions, we have a revised calendar, which I have stapled onto the back of this letter. Please check it out and take a picture of it. We will be following these hours effective

[*MM/DD/YYYY*]. This is partially due to the change in season and typical member traffic trends from last year.

[*Feel free to exclude this part if you did not give lifetime rates or promises recently.*] As you know, just a month ago, I implemented a rate increase in the business. And at that time, I made a promise that your rates would not change. So I want to address that with you now.

I have spent my entire adult life investing in myself to become a great coach. However, something I have not been very good at is being a good business owner and understanding the financial realities of running a small business.

That being said, like you, I am working daily to grow and improve. And just like we recommend to everyone at our facility, I have recently invested in business coaches and top consultants to review our business, know our numbers, and improve the product we are putting out to you.

Now that they have forced us to look at the numbers, calculator in hand, it is simply impossible for us to grow and provide the level of service and facility you deserve without this change.

For those of you concerned about the $10–$15/week, I want you to know we are simultaneously launching a Refer-a-Friend program where you get a full month of service for every friend you refer who signs up as a client. So refer 12 friends over the next year and get an entire year absolutely free, as our way of saying thank you for helping us transform more lives. I'll be announcing this in video format in the Facebook group as well.

Now, let's be super real. Human beings HATE change. But we also understand on some level that change is a part of growth. What I do NOT want under any circumstances is for a gossip mill to be started. So my team and I will be happy to address any questions you have related to the change in person.

Not via text…or FB Messenger…or Instagram DM…or email…or on a Facebook thread (God help us all).

We want to talk IN PERSON. That way, there will be 0% chance of miscommunication. So we will not be allowing any social media group posts related the "business side" of the gym. The group will stay focused on what it is intended to be—a forum for the community to connect and encourage one another on this path to transformation.

I hope I have your support in allowing us to continue to serve you in the best way we know how.

Respectfully yours,

(Hand-signed)

YOUR NAME

Owner, GYM NAME

P.S. I love you all, seriously.

Dealing With The Loud Customers

Adjust the script and letter content as you need to for your business. Include a change in schedule and a price matrix if you offer multiple levels. This should cover you.

That being said, here are some quick tips to make the transition easier.

1. When you make the video in your Facebook group, make sure you turn off comments on the post. You can reuse the letter content as the text for the video.
2. Send a blast out to push people to the Facebook group, and be ready to deal with LOUD customers for the next few weeks. But recognize it for what it is—NOISE. It is in their best interest to convince you NOT to change.

    It will be scary.

    You will wonder if everyone is going to leave.

    But they won't.

    The costs of leaving a community to find a new home, new friends, and a new routine are very high, much higher than $10–$15/week. If you do have people threatening to leave, remind them that the risk of falling off their fitness regimen if they leave will put them at risk for losing the momentum they've created while using your facility.
3. Remind people who worry about the added cost that there are ways to change their budget and spending habits in order to be able to afford the new rate, and that it's an investment in their good health. Tell them stories about people in harder situations who have been able to scrape up the money because their health is a priority.

4. And remember, above all else, if you do not make this change, your business will never get to the profitability level you want it to be, which is bad for you, your employees, and your customers. You're going to have to do it sooner or later, so you might as well do it sooner and start enjoying the benefits now.

You have two choices: the guaranteed path to burnout or the potential to transform your entire business. Both have risk, but only one can get you what you want.

Section III

Retention: Get Them To Buy More

You made it through the math-y section (sigh of relief). So you know how to get them in the door with client-financed acquisition from Section I. You know what you need to do to profit from them being in your gym by using the profit levers from Section II. So what are we going to talk about now? The silent killer of all gyms—attrition. Or as I called it earlier, the hole in the bucket.

I want to reach my hands out from this book and shake you so you'll fundamentally understand the next few paragraphs.

If Equinox and Life Time and other high-end multimillion-dollar facilities can offer high-level trainers and superior equipment and amenities at more flexible times with better parking for a lower price, how can you compete?

And if this trend continues and drives prices even lower due to commoditization, how can we possibly win?

How are you better? How are you different?

By realizing one simple truth...**you are NOT in the fitness business.**

You will never beat those facilities in terms of equipment, amenities, or sound systems—heck, even the sessions they offer are pretty top tier.

So again, how do you win?

By realizing the game that you ARE playing.

You are NOT in the fitness business.

> You are in the **accountability** business.
>
> You are in the **relationship** business.
>
> You are in the **community** business.
>
> You are in the **coaching** business.

If you do not have this portion of your business dialed in, systematized, and laid out with intention, you will FAIL.

If you ask your team what business you are in and they say "fitness," you will FAIL.

If you yourself don't fundamentally understand your primary competitive advantage and value proposition, you will FAIL.

Or you will keep going until you burn out or struggle forever (which to me is the same).

This is the common feature I see in gyms that fail—they don't know the business they are in.

The owners will say…

"We get people great results!"

"We have the most badass workouts."

"Our XYZ programming is so magical."

"We need more people to come in and experience us."

No. One. Cares.

Let's cut the sh*t for a moment. First off, your sessions are likely mediocre. How can I say that? Because most gym owners have access to the same talent pools, do not have strong onboarding or quality control, and have inferior compensation compared to these bigger gyms. So your sessions probably aren't any better than theirs.

Also, just saying "our community is like a family" does NOT make you special. Every single gym owner in the world thinks they have an amazing community. But if it were truly amazing, you wouldn't consistently have 10% churn month over month. The community happened by accident, because when people are in the same room repeatedly, they form relationships without you doing anything at all.

So I REALLY need you to internalize the following concept: you are in the accountability, communication, coaching, community, and relationship business. THAT is what people STAY and PAY for. That is the value. You just so happen to own a gym. Not the other way around.

If you shift your belief about what business you are in, you will be able to win; if you continue to cling desperately to why your workouts are badass, you will not. Period. I have seen enough gyms go out of business to tell you the common themes. Lack of understanding what business they are in is the primary driver. They don't pay attention to their customers. They let it happen by chance instead of design.

But you are different.

You are smarter than that.

How do I know? Because you made it past the first two sections of the book, which makes you a statistical unicorn.

Good news…

Despite this being the last "fix it" section of the book, this may very well be the most important. This should inform the *strategy* of your business. The GOAL should be to hold people accountable and deliberately create a community to foster and create new relational ties. People are lonely. They CRAVE attention. They pay therapists hundreds of dollars an hour to LISTEN. If you do this, you will never struggle with losing clients again, or with maintaining members far above market price.

But why was it so easy to retain customers in the beginning?

Because you were actively fostering each of these as individual relationships. But you did not continue that cadence, because it was random. It was not systematized. Everyone can do it with their first 40 customers (which is why they all love you and are still at your gym). Doing it at scale, with intention, is another matter entirely. It is what separates the winners from everyone else.

Retention Money Math

Using all the systems in this section, if you cut your churn from 10% (industry average) to 3% (what gyms using these systems achieve), you will 3.3x the lifetime value (LTV) of every client at your gym.

It costs about $10 per month to retain a customer (between cards and payroll minutes for reach-outs). But doing so allows you to 3.3x the amount of money that person spends with you. So if your average EFT stays 10 months @ $167 before implementing these systems, and after these systems you now retained them for 33 months (10 x 3.3), you would make an EXTRA $3,841 ($167 x 23). And to get this extra $3,841, you would simply need to spend $10/month for 33 months (because you can't just start at month 10, silly).

Rhetorical Question: Would you like to pay just $330 to get $3,841 in return? (Not to mention all the other things they will buy, people they will refer, and other services they will ascend to.)

Yeah, me too.

Here's an example.

Old Way (Don't Know What Business You Are In, Leave Retention To Chance)

Avg EFT Duration: 10 months

Price: $167

Investment in Retention: $0

Total LTV: $1,670

New Way (Know What Business You Are In, Implement Deliberate Systems To Retain)

Avg EFT Duration: 33 months

Price: $167

Investment in Retention: $330 ($10/month for 33 months)

Total LTV: $5,511

Additional Revenue By Using Retention Systems

New LTV - Old LTV = Additional Revenue From Retention Investment

$5,511 - $1,670 = **$3,841 additional revenue generated from $330 of retention spend** (not including referrals, other products, other programs, upsells, and cross-sells)

Does an 11:1 minimum return on every customer you have seem like a good ROI? I think so too.

Ethical Note: If you keep people exercising and working out 3.3x longer, don't you think you will ACTUALLY be helping people get healthy? Isn't that the whole point? You make money when you provide *value*. These are not tricks or hacks. This is how you provide great service and get people to improve and transform their lifestyles for real. That is what you wanted, right? Don't see this as a chore, see it as fulfilling the promise you made to these people when they gave you money and trusted you with their health.

I've said it before, and I'll say it again. Your customers come to your gym for one reason: to meet their fitness goals. But they *stay* because they feel welcomed, supported, and a part of the community. They stay because of the things they get from your gym that they didn't know they needed. That friendly hello when they walk in. That bit of encouragement from the other members. That invitation to come to the next gym event. That friendly internal competition. Knowing the staff by name and vice versa. The impromptu reach-outs they get. The handwritten holiday card. The call they get when they miss a workout to tell them they were missed and ask when they are coming back in. The pull-aside chat after class when they are stressed at work. The flowers they get when their mom passes.

In this section, I'm going to show you how to deliberately build the kind of community at your gym that makes your customers and your staff want to stay. One where your team is tightly knit, everyone supports one another, and people feel inspired and encouraged to do their best. And the systems to support this community and grow it, at scale.

Curious to know more?

Read on.

CHAPTER 13

Attrition:
The Hole-In-The-Bucket Problem

So just to recap the problems and solutions we've gone over thus far…

Main Problem #1: The Broken Acquisition System

Solved By: Client-Financed Acquisition

Main Problem #2: The Broken Revenue Model

Solved By: Gym Profit Levers

Main Problem #3 (*drum roll, please*)…**The Hole-in-the-Bucket Problem**

Getting people to sign up for your program and show up to their appointments aren't the only challenges that gym owners have. Another big issue is retaining members after they transition to EFT from whatever their front-end offer was.

Gym owners often ask me these questions:

- How did my gym grow so quickly in the beginning?
- Why is it that whenever I run marketing campaigns, I feel like these people don't stick like my OGs?

- Why does getting even 5 new EFTs of net growth feel like an uphill battle now that I have 80–120 EFTs?
- Why won't my gym grow anymore?

Remember, OGs are your "original gangsters"—the founding members, the heart and soul of your gym, the ones who absolutely love you—who you grandfathered in at $99/month, and who also drag down your average EFT to $118/month when you do the math, even though you say your rate is $139–$159/month. You know who I'm talking about.

EFT GOAL

ATTRITION

EFT MOUNTAIN

Meet Sisyphus. In Greek mythology, this dude was punished by the gods and sentenced to roll a giant boulder up a hill, only to have it roll back down again, continuously…forever. I think he best depicts the feeling of growing your EFTs when you aren't using the right processes.

And that's not your fault. You just didn't know, and that's fine.

Read on—then you'll know.

Then you can roll that damn boulder over the hill and breathe easy.

Let's do a little Q&A, shall we?

Why did my gym grow so quickly in the beginning but growth has slowed since?

The main reason you could grow it in the beginning, even just from word of mouth, is that the 10% churn (the attrition, or members who leave) hadn't caught up yet. When you only had 40 members, if you lost 10%, you only lost 4 people. Replacing that isn't too hard if you need to.

Members also told their friends about your "new gym with a great new owner who really cares and has great early membership deals" and you could offset any losses in membership quickly.

In the beginning, you were also the underdog. Because you were small, you knew everyone's names, clients received tons of personal attention, and you sold yourself cheap at $5/session.

Why don't new people stick like my OGs?

The main reason is that your level of service dropped as more people came in. That service typically drops off for most gym owners at around 70–80 members. That's when you just don't have the time or energy to keep delivering the same levels you were when you only had 40 members.

The other maybe 20–30 active members in your gym (if you have them) are there only for a few months, soon to be replaced by new people who are trying the gym out.

These people are transient, because they never really "get it." They don't get involved in the community, they see a clique that hangs out by themselves and who mostly ignore the new people, despite your efforts to integrate them. Every once in a while, one breaks into the OG ranks and becomes an "honorary" OG, but this is rare.

There's another reason, though. You have a hole in your bucket.

Attrition happens.

Every month, a certain number of people are going to drop off. Your job is to keep that percentage as low as possible. So if you kept growing at say 10 people per month and losing 10% per month, then at some point, the growth and the attrition even out. And you get nowhere, Sisyphus.

The "pie" equation in the figure on the opposite page expresses the relationship between sign-ups and attrition mathematically. (I call it the pie equation because I was cutting one when I first thought of it, and when you draw a circle around the fraction, it kind of looks like a pie...or so I thought, because I was hungry.)

Understanding how this works is one of the keys to understanding how to grow your gym.

The problem simply stated is this:

> As your gym membership grew, your level of service delivery decreased, the difficulty for new members to assimilate and make new friends decreased (since cliques were already formed) and now, as you try and bring new people in, they don't get the same service

THE "PIE" EQUATION

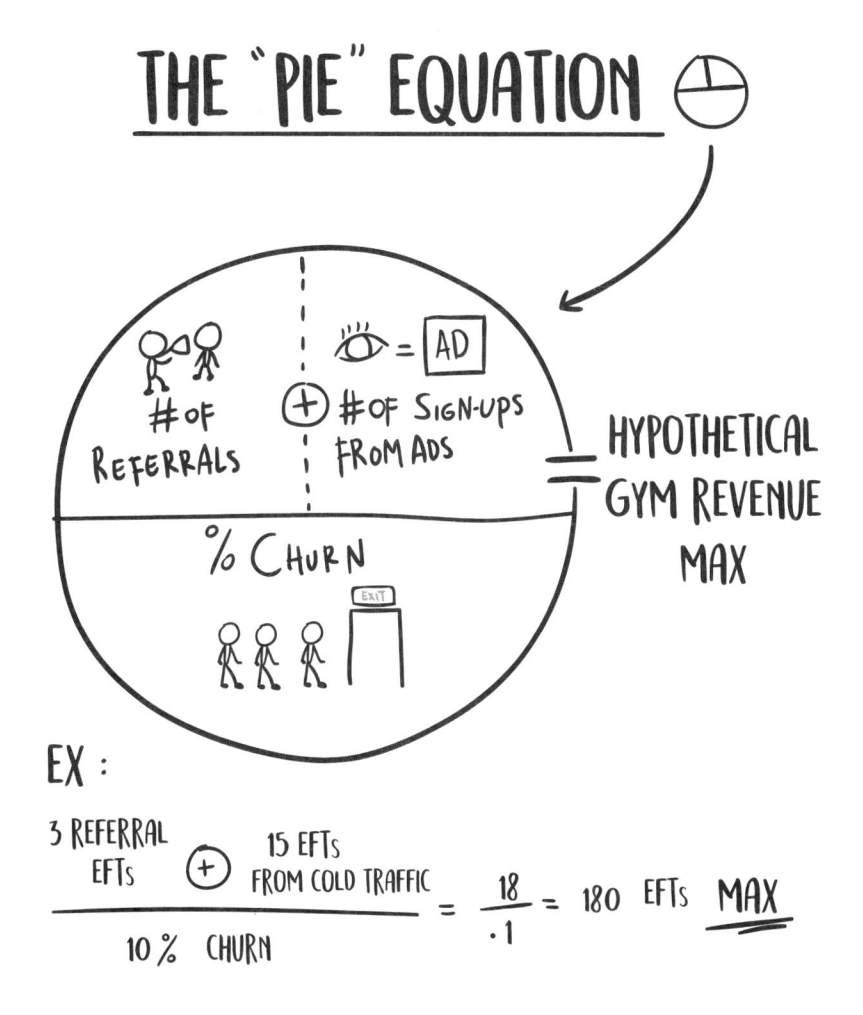

$$\frac{\text{\# of Referrals} + \text{\# of Sign-ups from Ads}}{\% \text{ Churn}} = \text{HYPOTHETICAL GYM REVENUE MAX}$$

EX:

$$\frac{3 \text{ REFERRAL EFTs} + 15 \text{ EFTs FROM COLD TRAFFIC}}{10\% \text{ CHURN}} = \frac{18}{.1} = 180 \text{ EFTs } \underline{\mathbf{MAX}}$$

they would've gotten when you only had 40 members or the level of community and welcome that the OGs had. And because of this, no matter what you put in the front end, they don't stick or stack up like they used to.

So how do you break this seemingly never-ending cycle and actually grow your gym and make a profit?

I promise there's a solution. Thank you for staying with me. Now let's get to the good stuff.

Let me set up this topic by telling you about a key characteristic of successful gym owners. It will help you understand the most important component of getting your clients to stay.

Weapons-Grade Compassion

How do you think about your employees and your customers?

When you employ this level of compassion with everyone you come in contact with, you can unlock a level of creativity and execution you never knew existed. You sort of move outside of yourself into your work and try to really understand it from the inside out. Then all of a sudden, solving a challenge becomes crystal clear, and you realize that what you were doing was 100% the wrong thing.

This mindset means taking full responsibility for another person's state, whether it be your employees or your clients, and taking action as a result. It comes from a place of intention to be someone who chooses to help, just because you can.

And whenever you help other people, you are by default operating from a place of abundance. You have enough of everything you need, so you don't need to focus on you, you can focus on them.

Because let's face it, as entrepreneurs when we think about ourselves, we post stupid, ego-driven Instagram pics. But whenever we think about someone or something outside of ourselves, we make some amazing stuff.

People can *feel* it when you are operating from this place.

The reason I am bringing up the importance of compassion is because, as a fitness professional and a gym owner, you are inherently caring and competent, but you may not know that your deep caring for others' well-being can be a huge competitive advantage, the way it has been for Gym Launch.

We tell everyone this, but most gym owners (or other small-business owners who attend our seminars) disregard it.

When we tell seminar attendees that we're obsessed with solving gym-owner problems and that our new release will continue to improve on everything, people nod then proceed to tell us how much money they think they can make in their market, because they're still only thinking of themselves.

They're simply not thinking about their customers.

They're the same people you hear saying things like this:

- My customers are so needy.
- My customers expect me to do everything for them.
- My customers can't figure out the simplest things.
- My employees are so stupid.

The truth is that you should be doing as much as possible for your customers and helping them solve their problems, whatever they are.

What your clients come in for initially (weight loss, fitness) is what they give you money to fix.

But what they come *back* for is everything else you gave them that they did not pay for—community, camaraderie, attention, and fixing problems they didn't know they had.

This is called abundant exchange. And it will take work, both for yourself and for your staff, to shift your mindset to one of abundance and compassion. But it's worth it. Trust me.

Here's an example: Gym Launch provides tech support for members of our programs. For a moment, I want you to think about how EASY it would be for our tech team to slide into this mindset of acting like all gym owners are non-techy idiots.

Imagine that after helping the four-hundredth gym owner who says their pixel isn't working and that they followed everything "exactly like it was in the video," the tech support team started slipping into thinking, "Gym owners are dumb, and I am smarter."

Do you have any trainers who operate like this?

Have *you* ever operated like this?

Imagine talking to yet another client who isn't seeing any progress toward their weight-loss goals. "I'm following everything exactly like it says in the meal plan," they say. And then five minutes later, after you've asked them exactly what they've been eating, they say, "Cheese isn't on the meal plan? Oh."

How easy would it be to roll your eyes and exclaim to one of your staff, "These people are SO dumb."

You get my point.

Because when you take full responsibility, the ball is in your court. It's your move, because when something is wrong with your business, it's your fault. As entrepreneurs, we MUST operate from a standpoint of 100% responsibility, because the only person we can control is ourselves.

Give when you don't feel like you have anything left. That first give is what unlocks some of our greatest inner strength and grows us more than anything. When you operate from this headspace, you never think, "I give them more than enough." Because that's your ego talking. And as long as your clients are humans and you want to help them, who cares if you give them more than you are charging for? (Provided you have an adequate margin.)

No one will ever give you the amount of credit you believe you deserve. Ever. So just get over it. Accept that life isn't fair, and choose to live in a world where you control the rules, because YOU control how much you give.

Compassion In Practice

So here is how this weapons-grade compassion idea massively impacts our bottom line.

For us, this level of love/dedication/obsession manifests in two ways that are measurable.

1. Lifetime value (retention)
2. Premium pricing (high-ticket offers)

It comes down to never settling and always providing value. And the key to this is either truly loving your customer or loving your business so much that you love your customer indirectly (for those of you who are "over" weight loss and fitness).

Because the reality is that I love gym owners—you are my people—so I don't need to push myself to want to solve all the problems associated with running a gym. It's just natural to me. Plus, I feel like I live vicariously through each owner. And with my success, I've come to realize that customers of any sort can feel that dedication toward growth and a drive to solve their problems.

And when a client truly believes you want them there and want to solve their problems, they will stay.

When that dedication is not there, people leave, because they feel like they have "gotten everything" and don't think they are going to grow anymore.

And if you feel like you have already given them "enough," then they're right. They have gotten everything you can provide. And they will leave.

I believe our reason for success is that we genuinely care. And we really want everyone to grow and make more money more easily.

The key for our business then is: how do we keep forcing ourselves to grow, and by extension, continue to innovate and learn and pass those learnings on to our clients?

The same is true of gyms. Dedication to your customers and a genuine caring environment will retain customers. Not only will people stay on at the same rate they've been paying, they're more likely to pay higher rates because they're getting so much out of their relationship with you, your trainers, and your gym.

Pretty simple.

I'll leave you with these questions to consider before we get into the tactical solutions to the hole-in-the-bucket problem:

- How much more can you serve?
- How many more problems can you solve that you haven't even asked yourself to solve yet?
- How can you blow people away and demonstrate your personal growth through business growth?

Chapter 14

How Retention Multiplies Revenue

It's fairly simple to get the first few people into your gym. You can use word of mouth, networks, and good old-fashioned shaking hands and kissing babies. And that works…for a while.

But then…DUN-DUN-DUN…it stops.
So what happens? What changes?
Why is it easier to grow in the beginning?
Why did I feel like I had more referrals then?
Why don't people stay as long anymore?
Why don't my marketing efforts work?
Why don't people become a part of the community like the OGs did?

These are the questions flooding our brains at night as we go to bed exhausted after yet another day of leading average class sizes followed by pleasant conversations afterward that end up taking 30 minutes too long. Another night where you only have enough time to get home, take a deep breath, and let the exhaustion drip off you as you fall into bed.

So let's fix it.

If you're tired of living off bread crumbs, let's get to the meat and potatoes.

As I explained in the previous chapter, when you started your gym, it grew at first but then it stopped growing because the number of people leaving was equal to the number of people coming in. Why? Because your business is maturing. Even though it feels like you're doing everything exactly the same, time has a way of changing things.

- Once, you were the underdog, the new kid on the block, and people were eager to give you a chance to prove yourself. Now you're just another business, and there may be a new underdog in the 'hood.
- Your service goes from new and exciting to "It's not like it used to be…" when you taught all the classes.
- Your members go from thinking, "No one will leave—we're all family here" to "I don't know everyone anymore—it's not as special as it once was." People get lost in the crowd, and the silent churn monster starts nibbling away.
- Your community goes from everyone being new and learning together to the OGs versus everyone else. Cliques form, and it's hard for outsiders to break in.
- Your inflow of people goes from immediate friends and referrals who say, "Come check out this new gym starting up" to cold traffic and total strangers saying, "Oh, they're running yet another promotion."

DETERIORATING SERVICE DELIVERY

	BEGINNING ⟶	NOW
SERVICE LEVEL	NEW, PERSONAL, UNDERDOG, DEALS ⟶	BROKEN-IN, HOURLY TEAMMATES, "OWNER", COMMODITIZED
CHURN BY %	SMALL ⟶	LARGE
COMMUNITY	OPEN, INVITING ⟶	OGs, CLIQUES
TYPE OF TRAFFIC	REFERRALS ⟶	LBOS, COLD TRAFFIC

One, two, maybe all of these resonate with you. And it can feel like there is no way out. Just realize it's not your fault. These things happen in just about every business. It's a function of time, not how much you care or how hard you work.

Fortunately, when you understand what's happening, you can take steps to get your gym back on a growth path. Let's spend a little time looking at the math behind churn and recurring revenue models.

This is the pie equation I referenced earlier. It's the formula we use to calculate the maximum number of EFTs you will have in a month. And it helps you see just how much your retention and number of sign-ups can increase your rate of growth.

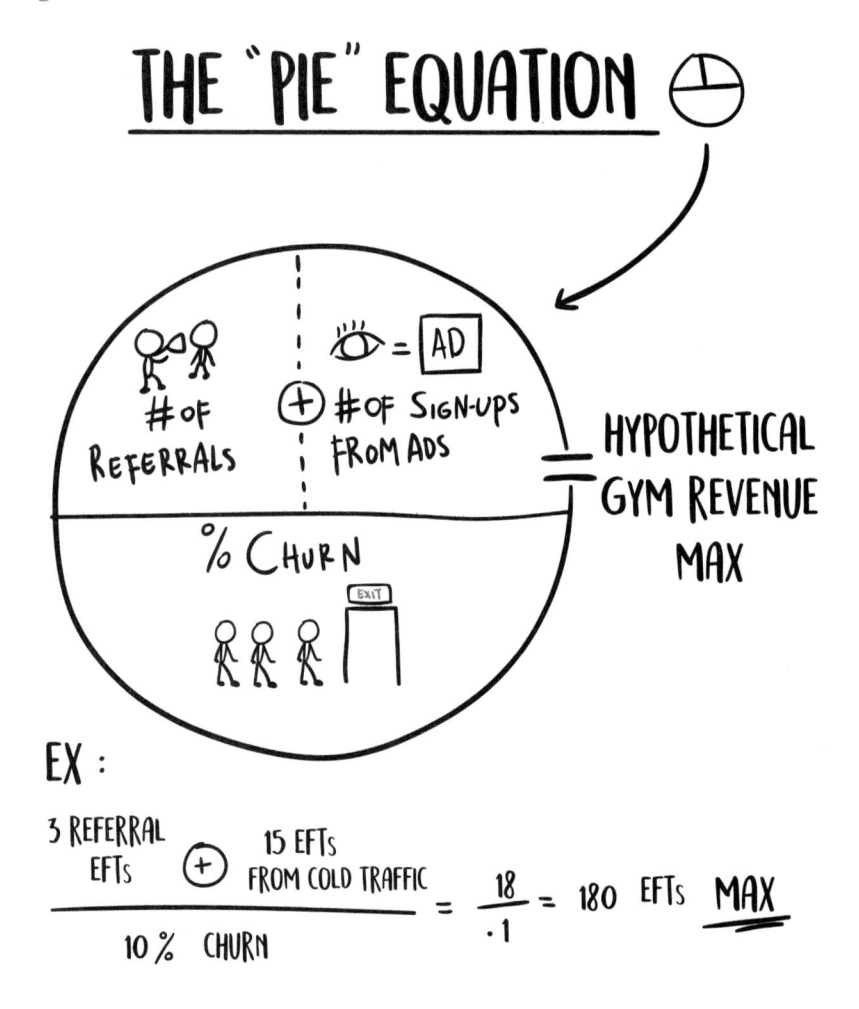

THE "PIE" EQUATION

Diagram: A pie chart divided into three sections — "# of Referrals" (stick figures), "# of Sign-ups from Ads" (eye = AD), and "% Churn" (stick figures walking out an exit). Labeled: HYPOTHETICAL GYM REVENUE MAX

EX:

$$\frac{3 \text{ REFERRAL EFTs} + 15 \text{ EFTs FROM COLD TRAFFIC}}{10\% \text{ CHURN}} = \frac{18}{.1} = 180 \text{ EFTs MAX}$$

When I go into a gym to help turn around a facility, we look at all three of these elements:

- Retaining existing customers
- Getting more referrals from existing clients
- Bringing more people in the door from marketing and advertising

If you know how many people you sign up on a monthly basis and what percentage of people leave, you can use those numbers to **predict how big your gym can grow** if nothing changes. And if you manipulate those numbers, you can also predict growth that could happen if you do make some improvements.

Say you have a bootcamp with 10 new sign-ups a month and 10% churn. Let's look at a few ways we can spin these two numbers.

Example #1: Calculate the hypothetical gym max (HGM) capacity with no changes.

Number of new sign-ups (from referrals and marketing) / % of people leaving = HGM

So say we had 10 sign-ups (2 from referrals + 8 from marketing) and 10% of our people were leaving the gym on average. (We'll need to change the percentage to a decimal point for calculation.)

$$10 / .1 = \textbf{100 MAX EFTs}$$

But we're gonna change some things to keep it interesting. Watch this.

Example #2: Calculate HGM capacity with increased sign-ups.

What happens when the number of sign-ups INCREASES from 10 per month to 20 per month because of badass marketing? Let's rerun the formula.

20 sign-ups (2 referrals + 18 marketing) / 10% churn = **200 MAX EFTs**

We just DOUBLED our max. Sweet.

What else can we do? How about reducing the churn rate?

Example #3: Calculate HGM capacity with decreased churn rate.

Let's say the churn rate goes from 10% to 5%, but the new sign-up number stays the same.

10 sign-ups (2 referrals + 8 marketing) / **5% churn = 200 MAX EFTs**

Again, we doubled the hypothetical max by just changing one piece of the equation.

Now here's what we do when we grow gyms: We manipulate *both* pieces of the equation. We raise the number of new sign-ups and reduce the churn rate at the same time.

Check it out…

Example #4: Calculate SUPAH GYM with better onboarding and accountability.

Number of new sign-ups goes from 10 to 20 per month with new marketing (using the client-financed acquisition model I described earlier).

Rate of churn goes from 10% to 5%.

20 sign-ups (2 referrals + 18 marketing) / 5% churn

20 / .05 = **400 MAX EFTs**

Kaboom. We just quadrupled that gym's EFTs.

But, as my dad always says, "Anyone can get rich on Excel."

I'm showing you these numbers because this is the game we're in. We're in a recurring revenue service model. And churn becomes the biggest issue a gym faces, especially as it grows.

What it took you to get to 100 members is not what it takes to get past 200 or past 400. It's a different set of skills. Don't worry, you'll learn how to master those shortly.

I like to show this because everyone I talk to wants to get more people in the door, but so few gyms even think about keeping those people over the long term. Few owners actively work on making their service remarkable and investing in their staff so the gym members actually want to stick around.

You can, and should, grow a gym by both increasing acquisition AND decreasing churn.

We've already covered acquisition in detail. So let's confront the churn part of the equation.

Problems That Affect Churn

To borrow from Marcus Lemonis from the show *The Profit*, there are three big components to any business: people, process, and product. I'm going to use the same three divisions when discussing churn and how to solve it, but I'm going to talk about them in a different order.

First, I'll talk about the **processes**, or the things you need to do to get your customers to have amazing experiences so you retain them.

Second, I'll cover the **people** who should do these processes, and how to structure the business from an organizational side.

Third, I'll detail the **product**—the actual session structure and coaches. I will not be talking about anything exercise-related. I will be focusing purely on the optimal structure of the sessions, based on what we've found that works.

The good news is that these things are 100% within your control. You are master of your own destiny. Implement the steps in each of these sections and watch your client outcomes improve and your EFTs and bank account stack up.

Here's a quick overview of how to solve the "hole in the bucket" aka retention, fulfillment, and staffing issues.

PROCESS > How To Treat Your Customers

- Define Ideal Customer Life Cycle
- Five Horsemen of Retention

PEOPLE > How To Treat Your Employees

- Define Organizational Structure and Compensation at Each Level
- Communication Structure to Keep It Agile
- The 5 Things Needed for Every Position

PRODUCT > How To Have Amazing Sessions

- How to Motivate Trainers Financially
- How to Motivate Trainers Personally
- How to Have Amazing Sessions

Read on to learn more.

Chapter 15

PROCESS:
How To Give Consistently Amazing Customer Experiences

All right, let's start sealing that bucket. One of the hardest things about running a gym is a lack of what we call "ideal scene." Basically, what it's supposed to look like when it's right. Of course, it's really hard to hit a target when you don't know where it is. So the first step is to define that ideal customer experience. Once we define it, we can try to hit it, and hit it consistently. All that takes is isolating key variables and executing a plan until the holes in the bucket have been plugged up and the churn rate drops.

If you don't have an ideal customer experience right now, it means new clients don't feel as integrated into the community as the original members did at the beginning. There are so many more demands on your time that you simply can't spend as much time nurturing relationships with each new person as you used to. These clients don't leave with a bang but with a whimper as they fade into the random-reason cancellation pile.

Gym members may sign up for your services because they dream of wearing that little black dress, but they stay for the relationships. So the biggest thing you can do to keep people engaged is to build an open, inviting community and have systems to keep them plugged in. But what does that look like?

At Gym Launch, we identified four customer milestones along the ideal path. We teach these same four milestones to all our gyms. These are the goals, what you want a customer to do.

- Connect
- Refer/Testify
- Testify/Refer
- Ascend

Note: Refer and Testify appear in different orders because some people refer friends who will work out WITH them, others only refer AFTER they've had a good experience. So the order can get flipped. Don't let it get you bent out of shape.

I'll break down each one briefly here, and in the next chapter, I'll outline the four tools we use to move people along this cycle and maximize lifetime value.

Connect

All milestones are important and, in general, build on one another. It makes logical sense that someone who doesn't feel connected to your business will not leave a testimonial. And someone who doesn't feel strongly enough about your business to leave a testimonial likely won't spend relational capital to refer a friend, and so forth. Connection, then, is the first and most necessary thing that needs to happen in order for the next three steps to work.

A new member's impression of a business during the first few weeks makes a significant difference in how they perceive it going forward. The first few weeks are also when they're deciding how they feel about this new experience. Once they feel they have a good relationship with your business, they'll be willing to cut you some slack if some things don't go perfectly. This is why your OGs may stay on while newer members leave. They got the best of you during those early weeks and are more willing to forgive.

We want to get this connected relationship formed as quickly as possible.

Refer/Testify

When people feel connected to you and your business, they will refer others to you. If you are doing something remarkable, they'll "remark" to others about you. On the other hand, if you are simply doing a good, average, or slightly above-average job, then you are unlikely to get many referrals except from influencer-type people who can't help themselves.

> **Fun Fact:** Despite how much I market my business, we are over 40% referral driven. It is our main key performance indicator (KPI) to show us how well we are serving our customers.

But if you want people to refer, and refer like crazy, then you need to accept that you have a 50% chance of being below average if you're reading this. Yep. Half the people reading this book are below average. (Actually, you're probably *above* average because you are reading a book.)

But mathematically, one out of two gyms is below average.

A decade ago, that might not have been such a big deal. You could still get by. But we live in a new world now, one ruled by something called "category economics." This basically means that all the money in a category naturally flows to a category king—the person who crushes it—leaving very little for anyone else. These days, being anything less than spectacular won't get you where you want to be. The big dog collects all the bones, and the rest are left fighting for scraps. That's no way to live.

So how do you get people to refer like crazy besides being amazing and employing weapons-grade compassion in your business?

Testify/Refer

Thanks to the technology at our fingertips, most people looking for a new item or service will check out reviews to see what other people have said. No one wants to risk making a bad decision because they didn't do some research. A great way to create a community feeling is to have a lot of testimonials that show how much people are talking about your business. They don't even have to be 100% positive. The key is that people care enough to put in the effort to talk about you. Here are a few ways to get your clients to give great testimonials.

> **Pro Tip:** A few bad reviews will make people feel like they are "real" instead of staged. So they can actually make your good reviews go further. Obviously, you don't want too many (duh). But some people are crazy. Or sometimes, you just F up. But if you had the option of going to a restaurant with 900 reviews and a 4.6-star rating and another with 29 reviews and a 5-star rating, which would you choose? Probably the first. There is certainty in "the herd," and if that many people went there, they can't be that bad. So it will be worth the risk.

- **Method #1: Inspiration**

    You get positive testimonials from doing a great job, but you also get them by complimenting your members and telling them how inspiring their progress would be to others. So you ask them to share their stories in order to give other people hope.

    Many people are uncomfortable posting to their public social media pages, but when you frame it in terms of helping others, they are more likely to agree. Simply ask everyone to post about their results (especially from a front-end program). When you ask, they will say yes. But then they might not do it, because people are forgetful.

    So when you ask them to post their results, have them take their phone out right then so you can take their "after" picture. And then suggest they post it immediately so they won't forget.

    Then you can screenshot that post and add it to the collection on your wall. Over time, this becomes an insanely powerful selling tool. You can see an example of ours at IDontHateMoney.com.

- **Method #2: Requirement**

    Yup. Make it straight-up required. This is how we did it for our gyms. In order to complete the program, your customers must review your gym on Yelp, Facebook, and Google. This will help you to get TONS of 5-star reviews. Make the irresistible offer contingent on them completing this piece.

    Note: you can't obligate people to leave a 5-star review. That is unethical trade practice and deceptive. But you

CAN make the review (whatever they see fit) a part of the program (which is optional by its very nature).

- **Method #3: Ethical Bribe**

    Give away free swag periodically for people who reviewed you on Yelp, Google, and Facebook. Just ask them to screenshot all three reviews and show them to the front desk when they come in. Dass it. A $5 t-shirt can make you thousands in positive referrals and reviews.

Ascend

This is basically a fancy way of saying "what you sell someone after you've already sold them something."

This can either be more or better service, an upsell. An example might be going from large-group training to semi-private training.

Another example of ascension is selling an adjacent service or need, a cross-sell. An example might be selling supplements to someone who came in for a membership.

So ascension is the last customer milestone. This is how we increase their lifetime value even further. The money is always in the back end. If you don't have a cross-sell, then you are missing out.

Now that you know what an ideal customer life cycle should look like, share it with your team and set that as the new standard. You now know what is supposed to happen.

The next question is how do you keep people long enough to actually achieve these milestones?

Glad you asked. In the next chapter, I'll introduce you to the five horsemen of retention.

Chapter 16

PROCESS:
The Five Horsemen Of Retention

We use multiple "weapons" at each point in the customer life cycle to increase engagement and lifetime value and to move customers along the path. That being said, the longer a customer stays, the more likely they are to accomplish each of the four milestones from the last chapter: Connect, Refer, Testify, and Ascend. Therefore, it is our goal to keep them as long as possible to increase the likelihood that all four happen, hopefully over and over again.

So to try and keep things organized, I'm going to break down each of the "retention weapons"—aka the five horsemen of retention—and show you how to tactically execute them within your gym.

Here are the five horsemen of retention:

1. Reach-Outs/Touch Points
2. Attendance Tracking
3. Handwritten Cards
4. Member Events
5. Exit Interviews

Look, there are a bazillion different things you can do to drive retention. Or at least, there are a bazillion things that people *claim* drive retention. The question is…do they work? In my experience, simple systems work best. Lots of golden BBs but only a few silver bullets. These five actions are your silver bullets, the key drivers of behavior. They are the small hinges that open up the vault door to lifetime value. I compiled this list by looking at what the best gyms had in common—not everything they do, but the few things that they ALL do.

If you only do these five things, especially the first two, you will be well on your way to reducing churn.

We have taken gyms at a 10%, 15%, and higher monthly churn rate and brought them down to under 5% within a month and under 3% within two to three months by just using these tactics.

And remember, a reduction in churn from 9% to 3% month over month is not an increase in business of 6%, but an increase in lifetime value of 300%. The devil is in the details. I have yet to see a gym with less than 3% churn that doesn't make good money. You need to master churn, or it will be your master.

So let's take a closer look at each of the horsemen.

Retention Tool #1: Reach-Outs

I could try and make this sound fancy, but all you need to do is PERSONALLY reach out via text or Messenger to each customer every 14 days. Someone on your team needs to reach out to every single person in your gym two times per month as a pulse check.

The goal is to offer praise and to commend the customer on their progress, then solve any small issues they may have. This line of communication is the cornerstone of the relationship. We need to keep it open to keep the relationship going.

You should keep notes about any customer life events or wins that are discussed during your daily team huddles. (I'll explain more about daily huddles in a bit.) But this way, everyone can share notes, and when you're scheduled to reach out, you can include the personalization. Do not underestimate the power of a personal touch. People crave attention. Give it to them.

If someone takes a long time (more than 24 hours) to respond to your correspondence or doesn't get back to you at all, they are likely to be on the cancellation route. This is what you might call a "leading indicator." You should escalate these clients to high priority and make multiple reach-out attempts or put a note in your CRM to pull them aside and engage individually the moment they come into the gym.

As long as everyone has been "touched" every 14 days minimum, then you can rest easy that you are taking the primary retention precaution.

Essentially, you can divide up all your customers into groups and assign each trainer to one. It depends on the size of your gym and infrastructure. Reaching out to 200 EFTs is a LOT different than reaching out to 600 or more. (I won't get into the systems for 400+ EFTs @ $200/month because most people reading this aren't there yet.)

Genuine Communication Attracts Attention

Do you know why personal training clients stay a bazillion times longer than other gym clients?

Relationships.

People yearn for connection. They crave attention. It's a basic human need. The moment someone realizes a piece of communication is automated, they stop paying attention, because attention is not being spent on them. It's an exchange.

"Communication is the best content." — Me

My recommendation is to SYSTEMATIZE communication, but never AUTOMATE it, especially with current customers.

Even with over 1,000 active clients (as with our Gym Lords), we still use Google Sheets and client concierge roles to ensure everyone is getting an abundance of attention from us. We send lots of "just because we love you" communication. Back before all this technology, we used clipboards with lists of all the gym members. It takes *effort*, but it's worth it. And it feels good to treat people like royalty.

Here are some things that have worked for us:

1. Get your new members to an event ASAP. They MUST attend the first meet-and-greet event.
2. Write them a handwritten card (more on that below) inviting them to the event the day they sign up, even if it is three weeks away. Write it immediately after they sign up, so their details are fresh in your mind.
3. Give them swag like a t-shirt or bumper sticker so they feel like part of the community, like they belong. This is especially effective if you give it to them publicly (like after class). They'll wear it or display it. Everyone wants to feel like a part of the "in" group. Swag works especially well if they wear it to five workouts. (That's the magic number of workouts in the first month to

> get someone to "stick" according to Orangetheory's stats from the 2017 MBO Conference.)
>
> 4. Introduce them to an OG buddy/mentor as soon as possible. And get them working with the OGs during warm-ups the first few weeks. Encourage them to exchange numbers and get to know one another's names.
> 5. Make sure an accountability coach reaches out to them regularly.
> 6. Create a no-show report (available on most CRM software platforms). New clients CANNOT miss workouts. That needs to be priority one. Reach out and connect with them.

Retention Tool #2: Attendance Tracking

Again, this is simple, but most gyms don't do it. Be exceptional by doing the boring stuff that no one else wants to.

This is a process you should do weekly at the very least, ideally by Wednesday of every week.

The #1 leading indicator that a customer is on the track to cancellation is when they make it to the gym two times or less in a week.

People in this situation should become a high priority and will need more aggressive reach-out attempts to establish communication. Once you connect with them, tell them you noticed they haven't been coming to the gym as often as they used to, and that you want them to get their butts in ASAP because you miss them and want them to reach their goals.

If they have an issue with you, the gym, or something in their lives that makes it harder for them to come to the gym, try to help them solve the problem and lower their resistance to working out. Even if it's not anything to do with you (for example, stress in their personal lives), you can remind them that working out will help relieve stress and give them a break from their problems.

Remember: compassion and connection are why customers will keep coming back to your gym.

Some gym owners run attendance reports monthly. That's way too late. You're leaving a lot of customers on the table. Weekly reports are good, but ideally you should know who hasn't shown up by Wednesday of every week.

Implementing this reach-out process for red-flag customers will cut your churn immediately.

Do it now. Seriously.

I have seen attendance go...

Week 1: 3 visits
Week 2: 2 visits
Week 3: 2 visits
Week 4: 1 visit
Week 5: CANCEL

The beauty is that by intercepting them at Week 2, you not only make the business more money, you are actually HELPING THEM STICK WITH FITNESS. And that's the whole point.

Retention Tool #3: Handwritten Cards

You'll want to send handwritten cards at multiple spots in the customer lifecycle.

The first time is right after they sign up. Send them a handwritten card welcoming them to the community. Include some swag and an invite to the next customer event (Retention Tool #4).

I recommend that you keep it simple. Complicated systems don't work, in my experience.

The second time handwritten notes are helpful is when you want to ask for a referral. Follow the system below and each trainer will be working 10 hot leads a week.

> Step 1: Divide customers into four groups—A, B, C, D.
>
> Step 2: Put their names, phone numbers, and addresses into an Excel spreadsheet. (Most CRMs can export this data.)
>
> Step 3: Give one column to each trainer.
>
> Step 4: Then divide each trainer list into four smaller groups (one for each week in the month).
>
> Step 5: The trainer writes a card to each person on the weekly list, with a P.S. that reads: "Take a picture of this card and text it to a friend of yours who is awesome, who you wish was here with you, and who lives close to the gym, and their first month is on us."
>
> Step 6: The same trainer follows up with that person when they come into the gym that week and asks, "Sandy, who did you send my card to?" (They probably forgot and didn't send it to anyone.)
>
> Step 7: In that moment, say, "Don't worry, I'm not heartbroken. But who *would* you have sent it to? Okay, awesome—go grab your phone right now."

Step 8: The trainer takes the client's phone, records a 20-second video together with the client. Say something like, "Hey, Sandy was just talking about you. If you're as awesome as she is, I want to get to know you. Come on in and say hi."

Step 9: Group message the text video to the prospect and include the trainer's cell number.

Step 10: The trainer then follows up from their own phone, adds the person as a lead, and schedules a time for them to come in.

The secret is not the card, it's what you do AFTER you send the card that matters. The card gives you the relational capital to make them feel a little guilty that they didn't send your free month to a friend. That's why it works.

The third way to use cards is to simply use them as a connection point. Send these at milestones—after three, six, and twelve months as a gym member—just to say thank you. The more cards you send NOT asking for something, the bigger the response you'll get when you do.

As far as ratios go, I recommend every other card be an ask. That being said, the main content of the card should be about praising the person, and only the P.S. should be the ask (for something like attending an event and bringing a referral or doing a new program).

Retention Tool #4: Member Events

The next pillar is holding regular social events for your clients, like an evening playing putt-putt golf or a pool party. They keep people connected and engaged in your community. After all, when people are working out or going to and from the gym, there's not a lot of time for chitchat, which is part of what bonds people together. Events help your members come together in a more relaxed, less goal-focused environment and just hang out.

Hold events at regular intervals. Don't announce the intervals, just hold the events. Every 21 days works well.

Here is my secret sauce for making client events a success:

1. We pay for the babysitter—members just bring their kids.
2. Members get in free (for putt-putt or BBQ, etc.) if they bring a friend.
3. We require all new customers to attend.
4. We send out handwritten invites, especially to new customers.

Why does this work so well? Because it gives people a reason to socialize. Most people don't have plans. Most people are boring. And now your gym is overdelivering by providing value outside of fitness.

Events make you money in several ways. You're lowering churn by developing deeper connections with your clients. The OGs and the new kids are also building relationships. You're getting a chance to sell to their friends by offering a bring-a-friend option. If you go play putt-putt golf, for example, you are paying for the babysitter, so they are already happy. But if they choose to bring a friend, you will also pay for both of their putt-putt games. This puts *reciprocity* on your side. If you meet your clients' friends at a gym-sponsored event, the likelihood is pretty high that they'll at least come check out your facility at some point.

> **Pro Tip:** If you decide to take your gym to a smaller establishment (even a chain), you can often negotiate a reduced rate or even an entirely complimentary evening because you are bringing them new business. This is how you can become mayor of your town. People love someone who brings them business, wouldn't you? Do it enough times, and they will refer people back your way, include a free XYZ card in their pamphlets, or some other form of payback.

Follow that up with being a generally nice person and pairing the friend with a trainer and/or yourself, so you can get to know them while you guys play putt-putt. If you asked them to come to the gym for a workout on Monday, what are the chances they'd turn you down? Pretty low.

How much would you pay to sit down with a warm referral? If you're anything like me, you'd pay a lot. And you'll have the capital to do that, because now you have pricing that will actually make you money and give your clients a great experience, as well as front-end offers that get results without giving your life away.

See how this is all coming together?

The most important thing is to make sure there's an activity where you can talk and mingle. A movie or concert is probably not a great idea, because everyone is expected to stay quiet and focus on the show. Here is a nonexhaustive list of ideas for gym-sponsored events to get you going.

- BBQ
- Bowling
- Charity Bootcamp & BBQ
- Charity Carwash

- Cheat Meal Night
- Dessert Potluck/Healthy Dish Potluck
- Farmers Market Tour
- Frisbee Golf
- Frozen Yogurt
- Grocery Store Tour
- Hike
- Ice Skating
- Iron Chef
- Paint & Wine
- Photo Shoot
- S'mores/Fire Pit
- Service Project
- Wiffle Ball

Retention Tool #5: Exit Interviews

The last of the retention horsemen is a simple one: exit interviews.

If you do these right, you can save half—yes HALF—of your cancellations. So imagine cutting your churn in half (or more realistically by 25%, since half of your cancellations will be people who don't call to give you new billing info (yeah, I've been there). Anyways, if the other half are true cancellations, you can save half of that half. It may not sound like much, but the feedback from these interviews can be invaluable to help you improve your service. And saving 25% of cancellations is a 33% increase in LTV (nothing to scoff at).

Now, in order for these to be effective, you're going to want to mention exit interviews on your contracts and have new members initial that upon signing up. This sets the expectation that you will want them to do this when and if they cancel.

And you need to SELL the benefits of doing so. Here is one way to approach that.

> We aren't the type of facility that's just going to bill your card or send you to collections; we actually want to know what went wrong or what went right that is causing you to leave…even if you were totally satisfied.
>
> Most gyms don't want to talk to customers who choose to leave, but they're our favorites because they help us make the best experience possible and serve everyone at a higher level.
>
> And, a lot of times, when we have these conversations, we find out that the issue was totally unrelated to the gym. Sometimes it's work or home life or kids. And luckily, once we know what the problem is, we can usually help solve it. So in the end, this is one more way we help people problem-solve and ultimately stick to their goals. Because if you are fit for eight weeks, it doesn't matter. We want you to be fit for life—and sometimes that requires creativity to figure out.

A script like that in the beginning works really well. And it is true: if you can help someone problem-solve, you can help them stick with it. Exit interviews show people you care and that you genuinely WANT them to stick with the goal they signed up for (which you should).

The script is essentially a re-sell. Think through the C-L-O-S-E-R framework.

C: "What brought you in when you originally signed up?"

L: "Okay, so you wanted to lose weight—got it."

O: "How much have you lost so far? What has been the main thing holding you back?"

Now, instead of going through PAST experiences, they're going to tell you about their CURRENT experience with you. And once you find out what the biggest obstacle is, you can solve it.

It might be attendance, in which case you need to dive in. Is it the session time? Is it the instructor? Is it the music? Is it the workouts? Just be blunt—there's no point in sugarcoating it at this point.

S: You want to dig to find the problem, then offer the solution.

E: And half the time, you haven't actually lost them. They just need to vent and be heard. A lot of times, they're just frustrated with themselves.

R: So offer encouragement and come up with a plan they can stick with and execute.

That is the essence of coaching.

Anyways, this is the last of the five key retention processes that you need to put in place immediately.

And even if people don't have a note about exit interviews in their contract, still ask them to come in and cancel in person. At the very least, get a phone call. You'll be surprised what a listening ear and a coaching cap can do for a conversation.

How do you keep it all organized? Great question. Spreadsheet walk-throughs and software demonstrations don't translate well to books. But in a nutshell, you simply need to make time. Set aside hours to get this stuff done. Think of these adjustments as being just as much your job as the other things you do to run your business.

You can track this information on a master spreadsheet or in whatever CRM you use. Either way, you need to have a 1,000-foot view of all your customers and what is going on with them.

This is how you scale personal touch. This is how you multiply your customers' lifetime value and measurably reduce your churn.

These five tools are the connecting dots that tie the four customer lifecycle milestones together.

$$\text{Connect} \rightarrow \text{Refer} \rightarrow \text{Testify} \rightarrow \text{Ascend}$$

Chapter 17

PEOPLE:
How To Build Your Dream Team

The second side of this community equation is the actual people running your business, not just the processes they are executing. Too often I see gym owners who treat their team like dog sh*t and wonder why their clients aren't happy.

Treat your team like gold, and they will treat your clients like gold.

Treat your team like sh*t, and they will treat your clients like sh*t.

Now that we have that out of the way, it's helpful to note that most gym owners lack CLARITY on a few fronts.

1. What should the organization look like both today and as we grow?
2. What communication structure needs to be in place to keep it running smoothly?
3. What does each position require to be successful?

This is what I'm going to try and clarify as simply as humanly possible, based on our experience with thousands of gyms.

So let's attack #1 together. I think visuals work well here, so I've made you a chart. The positions you need to hire for are in order from left to right. And as your gym grows, so will your team (the first column showing # of clients, aka recurring members or EFTs.)

# of Clients	Owner	Trainers/ Hourly $	Operations Manager	Challenge Manager	Retention Manager	Sales Manager	Admin
0–100	1	1–2	20 hrs	NA	NA	NA	NA
		$15–$20	$1,300/m	$0	$0	$0	$0
100–175	1	2–4	20 hrs	20 hrs	NA	NA	NA
		$15–$20	$1,700/m	$1,300/m	$0	$0	$0
175–250	1	4–6	40+ hrs	20 hrs	NA	NA	NA
		$15–$20	$3,400/m	$1,300/m	$0	$0	$0
250–325	1	6–8	40+ hrs	20 hrs	20 hrs	NA	NA
		$15–$20	$3,400/m	$1,300/m	$1,300/m	$0	$0
400+	1	6–8	40+ hrs	20 hrs	20 hrs	2 x 20 hrs	2 x 20 hrs
		$15–$20	$3.4K + 10% Profit Share	$1,300/m	$1,300/m	$1K+ Commission	$10/hr

I'm going to give a nod to Joey Huber, one of our Gym Lords whose gym has far surpassed the success of mine by using our systems.

He has managed to grow his EFT from 250 recurring members to over 800 EFTs. All out of one location, and at a premium price of $200+/month. This is also why I am a big advocate of having one super profitable gym rather than lots of break-even facilities (which is common in the industry).

Joey has run the four-minute mile. This is a hybrid adaptation of his org structure and mine.

Let's go through it in detail.

Each level shows you in 75-member increments what is needed. When the workload is small, one person can perform multiple roles, but as it grows, more and more attention goes to doing only one thing. That is why people at large corporations need to continue to subdivide and specialize, because they have so much business.

> **Pro Tip:** Hire BEFORE you need the position. It will give you time to find the right person, hire them, train them, and see if they work out. This may take a few tries. And you do not want to hire people hastily because you need them immediately. You want to choose wisely. When you do this, the business will continue to grow at a steady trajectory for a long time, with no need for plateaus. Plateaus happen when there is a missing person or process in the business that is causing a leak.

Why So Many People?

When we started Gym Launch, we had only one support rep. She did everything for everyone. Now we have over 37 support reps. Each rep is cross-trained initially so they understand everything and how it all works together. After their initial training, they are put into smaller more specialized roles like running ads, automation, and funnels.

On top of that, we layer strategic support from coaches of subject matter experts (SMEs), Gym Lords who have demonstrated extreme competence or mastery in a certain vertical. For example, we have operations SMEs, phone sales SMEs, high-ticket sales SMEs, retention SMEs, and automation SMEs.

This way, we have both the people and the tech side covered, and an expert specialized in each area.

This should explain why the organization grows as the membership grows.

Compensation

I am excluding the owner, but the first person you should put on payroll is YOU. You will notice that underneath each of the hour breakdowns is the compensation. This can vary SLIGHTLY by market but is a good benchmark.

You will also notice that sales manager(s) come at the very end. Why? Because it is one of the most expensive positions to hire, not from a PAY perspective but from a lost opportunity perspective. Rarely will someone sell as well as the owner/entrepreneur does. So the business loses money on lost opportunities.

This increases the cost of acquisition and decreases revenue. At some point, though, the owner simply won't have the bandwidth to keep selling. It is one of the last positions I recommend replacing, mostly because as you train someone, it takes time and effort—and sometimes it takes a few "errors"—before you find the right guy or gal for the job.

All the while, you lose out on revenue and opportunities. This is why we advise doing this last, and after you have a healthy profit margin and some decent money in the bank.

But that is part of business. It is an organic entity that comprises people. And people are not machines—they must be watered and tended to like a garden.

A Cautionary Tale: I see it all the time. We take a gym from almost closing its doors to full capacity within a couple months. The owner will reach out and say, "I'm opening a second location." But they will have forgotten one of the key goals of business—MAKE MONEY. They see their business finally working, but they haven't actually made real money from it yet. In fact, gym owners with multiple locations often make LESS money, because they scaled problems not processes.

There is a time for opening a second location, but often it is far later than most entrepreneurs are mentally prepared for.

1. You need to have consistently stacked cash ($20K/month profit) for six straight months.
2. Your staff should be handling all of the operations, including sales, during that period of time.
3. The gym should have grown during those six months.
4. You should have $200,000 MINIMUM in the bank before you begin looking.

That is the benchmark I give our gyms before they can even THINK about a second location. Most times, they end up having to stack more money than they thought they would and go in a few times to correct things and rehire and train people.

I often counsel owners about selling off locations to get their attention and focus back so we can fix their main location and make it super profitable with the systems I have outlined in this book. Only once they have reached the new benchmarks do we reopen the conversation about another location.

Real Talk: What happens most times is that an owner will take the advice, then start making $20K/month profit and realize they can do even more things at their existing gym to make profit. And then they do that, just like Joey did. Most owners will only open a second or third location because they don't know how to make more with their existing gym. They mistakenly believe that the only opportunity for growth is MORE instead of BETTER.

Use this organizational structure. Pay according to this scale. Do not skip steps or jump the gun. And don't think about a second location until you have all this in place.

Chapter 18

PEOPLE:
Communication Cycles
And Cadences

If you've been in my world at all, you'll know that I prefer to talk about business as a garden rather than a machine. It grows and dies. It must be watered and tended to. There are weeds that grow inside employees and members that must be cut off and thrown out. This is the pruning of the garden. It can sometimes be painful in the short term, but is necessary for the health of the overall organism.

The "water" of the business is your communication cycle. This is your irrigation system. This is how you keep your team on point, keep them growing, and by extension, keep your business growing.

If you don't have a defined communication cycle, you are leaving your growth to chance.

And if you are reading this book, I know that's not what you want.

So what should excellent communication look like?

There are three main communication practices you must start immediately. And if you already have some of these, put them in place with rigidity. These have to be as consistent as the sun rising. Your team should be expecting these and show up out of habit.

They are...

- Daily Huddles
- Weekly Team Meetings
- Weekly One-on-Ones

Simple enough, right? Join the top 5% of businesses that actually do them then.

Note: In the beginning, you will run these meetings. But over time, your operations manager should take point on this, and you should ride shotgun (in other words, shut up and let them run it). You want to not be needed? Then don't be needed.

Daily Huddles

Daily huddles are the lifeblood of the business. This is how you can keep a pulse on everything that is going on. It is BEST to include trainers in here. If you can't, then at the very least include all your non-trainer personnel.

Daily huddles should be no longer than 10 minutes. Oftentimes, they can be done in even less time. You only need to go over the previous day's numbers, such as number of sales, number of cancels. You could also talk about clients who missed sessions and current attendance records. Then discuss any client wins or losses and make any quick announcements you need to. Finish with a little spicy motivation and appreciation, and off you go.

These keep everyone focused on the main thing—GROWING THE BUSINESS. Huddles are super valuable and ensure everyone knows what's going on. You will also be able to spot anything that seems "off" and fix it immediately rather than letting it fester.

Weekly Team Meetings

This meeting should be incredibly scripted. Each person should have a defined period of time to talk. They will go over last week's goals, this week's goals, and anything they need from the rest of the team.

Here is a sample agenda.

> **9:00–9:12 am** > Trainers discuss vibe of community, client wins, and any losses that need to be addressed. Anyone missing or people who have been red-flagged (see the PROCESS chapters). Workout-related stuff, music, etc.
>
> **9:12–9:28 am** > Challenge manager goes over all challengers' progress as well as anyone who is experiencing issues and what they are planning to do to resolve.
>
> **9:28–9:41 am** > Operations manager goes over numbers from the past week and plans for this week. Billing issues, people who need to be pulled aside, supplement sales goal, etc.
>
> **9:41–10:00 am** > Owner goes over new internal promotion. Video and text release schedule promoting it. Reminder for handwritten card follow-ups. Praise for team members doing well.

If you are done talking before the allotted time, end early. No need to ever just talk because you have the floor. It will increase the efficiency of your meeting. And everyone loves meetings that end early. As more people join the team, each person's talking slot will shorten and become more focused.

And yes, you pay people to attend this meeting.

Weekly One-on-Ones

If you asked me what is the single thing that has grown our business so quickly, I would answer client-financed acquisition. But if you were to ask my wife, Leila (who ACTUALLY grew our business), she would say weekly one-on-ones.

Why?

Because to grow a business, you GROW PEOPLE. Especially in a service business.

As you develop and your time becomes more valuable, you will stop coaching clients. But you never really stop coaching. You simply coach people at a higher level.

Who else could give you a positive ROI for your coaching time?

Drum roll…

YOUR TEAM.

If you're trying to scale yourself, scale a culture, and make sure that no trainer steals all your clients, you need to pour into them. Yes, you need to invest your most precious asset (besides your attention) into them.

In fact, whenever we survey our team, their favorite thing is one-on-ones.

What do you talk about? In short, YOU talk about nothing. Instead, you listen for most of it and ask questions. If you want someone to come to a conclusion, you don't TELL; you ask leading questions. But THEY must figure it out—otherwise, you'll never scale yourself out of that role. The main questions to ask are...

- What's going well?
- What's not going well?
- How can I help you win more?

And if you ever feel like someone is not specific about what they're doing, it is usually NOT because they are some stealing, leech employee who wants to take your money. Instead, YOU usually didn't do a good job of defining the role or giving them clear outcomes, guidelines, or training.

Clear Outcomes = Motivated Employees

In time, your operations manager will take over these one-on-ones with the front-line staff, and you'll only do them with the managers.

If you have part-time employees, you can do this every other week, but I highly recommend you just do weekly with everyone.

These one-on-one sessions should last about 30 minutes. Put them back-to-back all on the same day if you can. I like them in the afternoons, but that is your call.

Use a phone call if you need to. Works just fine and may be more convenient for your staff.

These are the big three communication cycles you need to implement to make your gym business grow like a well-tended garden. This will reinforce all the processes you learned about in the process chapters. This is how you make sure everything was actually executed.

Actions to Take

1. Conduct daily huddles.
2. Conduct weekly team meetings.
3. Conduct weekly one-on-ones with all team members.
4. As the business grows, as CEO, you will only do one-on-ones with managers, and they will do one-on-ones with the front-line team members.

Chapter 19

PEOPLE:
Five Things Every Role
In Your Gym Needs

You can look at an org chart and understand the basic role for each person.

But what does that look like daily?

One of the things that will swamp any gym owner is continuously wasting time on new hires and people who are not a good fit.

Or worse yet, not being able to find the right people.

For each of the roles I just outlined in the organizational structure, you need FIVE processes.

These five things mirror a sales pipeline, except instead of being targeted at future customers, it's targeted at future employees.

The customer pipeline looks like this:

Lead Generation → Lead Nurture → Sales → Fulfillment → Retention/Ascension

The employee pipeline requires the same level of detail and attention if you desire to systematize your business. It looks like this:

Application → Applicant Nurture → Interviewing
→ Training → Management

Funny how they are mirror images, right?

Application

You always need to have an inflow for each position. This allows you to never be held "hostage" by any employee. This keeps the leverage in your pocket. Not to be used or hung over someone's head. But everyone should know—no one is irreplaceable.

The key here is having a reliable process for generating leads. This is where having ad copy is useful. Here are three of our best ads you can use for some of the hires you will likely need.

Operations Manager Ad

OPERATIONS MANAGER WANTED NOW

Our owners are CONSTANTLY buried with far too much to do, and I need to hire a detail-oriented, organized manager for them ASAP.

They own a rapidly growing gym out of [*location*] and I can no longer watch either of them get stuck working late again.

Because of how fast we are growing, they are buried in managing the day-to-day work, invoices, schedules, and client interactions that go with being in operations, but DANG—these things take way too much time for them. I need their superpowers directed elsewhere.

:P

Can you help me help them??

We are looking for a GSD (get-sh*t-done) type of person who is customer-focused but also knows how to get the job done and be a leader for the rest of the company.

- Superb at handling details and managing people
- Loyal & hardworking
- Always follows through and never misses a deadline
- So productive your last employer considered hiring two people to replace you after you left
- Strong communicator with good computer skills
- Comfortable in a fast-paced, small-biz environment where priorities can change quickly
- Loves working with business owners
- Able to "wear all hats"

If that sounds like you, READ THE REST OF THE DESCRIPTION and apply below!

Salesperson Ad

SALES ROCK STARS WANTED NOW!

If you haven't heard of [*YOUR GYM NAME*] by now, we are a FASTTT-growing company that is currently drowning in leads.

Seriously, our team is currently EACH taking 10+ sales calls a day because we are in dire need of more people to help us change this industry!

No cold calling

No paying for leads

No pushy referral asks

Just qualified prospects who need to chat with someone who can educate them on our company.

PLEASE DO NOT APPLY IF…

Your ego is bigger than Kim Kardashian's backside.

You aren't a team player.

You don't possess an OBSESSION to be excellent.

You don't care about WHAT you are selling.
(Only people with high morals, please.)

You are a fun-sucker with no sense of humor.

You hate money and gym owners.

IMPORTANT DISCLOSURE: If you loathe the person described above as much as us, apply USING THE LINK BELOW. (FB PMs will NOT be accepted.)

Simple instructions, y'all. To be frank, because of our reputation for high-ticket selling, we usually get more than 50 applications on the first day.

So if you're waiting for some mysterious sign to apply, I suggest you JUST DO IT before we fill up.

APPLY USING THIS LINK

Trainer Ad

[YOUR AREA] FITNESS ROCK STAR NEEDED

$30K–$60K/yr depending on work ethic

Overcrowded bootcamp/semi-private privately owned gym in need of trainers to train clients. Drowning in new people who want and need instruction, and we need YOU.

Must be a cheerleader at heart but a drill sergeant in execution.

Must love people.

Must love sweet beats and be able to come up with sweet playlists.

Must be comfortable giving sweaty high fives.

Must be comfortable in sweaty post-workout selfies.

Must be on time. Always.

Hours are early morning 5 am–10 am and evenings 4 pm–7 pm.

DO NOT APPLY IF…

You can't play in a team.

You are interested only in yourself.

You take yourself too seriously.

You're too cool for Wacky Sock Wednesday and themed events.

Your ego is bigger than Kim Kardashian's backside.

Over half your Instagram pics are shirtless bathroom selfies.

If you made it this far, then we are looking for you.

We need 6 to 16 sessions per week covered. If you crush it, there is a lot more where that came from.

We are growing fast, and there are many opportunities for growth inside the company.

Click the link and follow the instructions if this sounds like your brand of protein powder.

Those three ads should give you a good start.

Application Nurture

Do NOT let your ego get the better of you. Work these like you work leads. Don't think, "If they're the right type of person, they'll find me." That's dumb. People don't live to serve you. You need to remind them and give them a reason (money isn't enough) to come get on the phone with you. If their résumé looks good, show you care, follow up fast, and get on the phone.

Interviewing

When interviewing trainers, I get a feel for someone within the first 30 minutes. Then if they seem very upbeat, I put them on the floor to shadow a class. Then we let them lead a class. If it goes reasonably well, we give them feedback on ONE THING they can improve on. If they improve on it for their next class, I know I have someone who is coachable. If they don't improve, or the class they teach is god-awful, then we just cut it there.

When interviewing salespeople, you should look for five things.

- Work Ethic
    - Measured by fast response time once you've shown interest
- Past Success
- Curiosity
    - How many questions do they ask you?
    - Do they just talk the whole time?

- Coachability
  - Have them sell you, then give them feedback.
  - Provide a script before the interview.
- Energy
  - Are they upbeat and positive? (This is just a gut thing—you gotta like them.)

I evaluate candidates for Operations Manager and General Manager on their ability to make decisions and whether they're detail-oriented. They need to be able to take on the Mother Goose role within the gym and be a manager to the core.

Onboarding/Training

You should do these things with every new employee:

1. Introduce them to the team.
2. Introduce them to the customers.
3. Write out their first week's agenda.
4. Have them log in to your website and read about your core values and mission.
5. Prepare a growth path (including compensation details).
6. Let them know about your communication cycle.
7. Describe what a perfect day looks like for them.
8. Make sure they know the numbers they need to hit in order to succeed.

Management/Ascension

The communication cycle is where you should primarily manage and measure goals. You need to PRAISE people to success. Ingrain that in your brain. It's the only way.

Ascension within the context of employees is when you promote people. This is why you want to find people who understand and buy in to the vision of your business. Rock stars will quickly surface. And when they do, you want to be able to paint a picture of a growth path for them both as individuals and as professionals. For trainers, you describe how to grow their own semi-private client base. For admins and operations folks, you want to paint the picture of a shared revenue opportunity as the EFT grows. For salespeople, you want to help them imagine how many sales they could be making and what that will mean for them in terms of skill-set development and their paychecks.

Yowza, that was a long one.

So you now have the information you need for the first two parts of the retention system—process and people. Finally, we move on to product. This is where I'll go in-depth on the trainers and the sessions so you can provide consistently amazing experiences for your customers.

CHAPTER 20

PRODUCT: How To Motivate Unmotivated Trainers

The last retention process is product. In some ways, the training staff members exist out there on their own. Essentially, they are the widget that you are selling as a gym owner. Their time and expertise. So if you want to have a great gym, you need to have great training sessions, and by extension, great trainers.

There are two parts to product: trainers and the structure of sessions. In this chapter, I'll review some additional methods for motivating trainers. In the next chapter, I'll go over the most effective structure for sessions and some small tweaks that should improve the experience and make you some dollars.

The Unmotivated Trainer Problem

If people are leaving your gym, it's because your products or services are subpar.

It all comes down to the team. And if your team isn't performing, it's your fault. Period.

Don't get all depressed about it. Identify, improve, and overcome.

This section is also one of the most exciting for me because it's where I was lacking. Most of the skills and frameworks I needed to develop for my work with gym owners have been centered around this topic. And if I had known what I know

now back when I was starting out, I would have been able to improve on a lot of my older systems.

Lucky for you, I DO know what I know now, and so will you. And you'll be able to use these frameworks "from the future" to make you money now. Score.

Motivating Trainers

There are two ways to motivate people: extrinsically and intrinsically. Extrinsic means they are motivated by external or outside forces. The prime example would be money. Extrinsic is the way to start before they trust you.

Intrinsic is when someone is motivated by a higher cause or an internal purpose. A prime example is when people volunteer and donate their time and money to a charity they believe in. This is (hopefully) something they are intrinsically motivated to do. They take a loss of productive time and money in exchange for a feeling of fulfillment, purpose, and contribution. This is where you want to get to. This is where people would jump on a sword for you because they believe in what you and your business stand for.

So let's start with the easy stuff.

Extrinsic Motivators: Compensation

As you saw in the last section, gym trainers typically make between $15 and $20 per hour. That is their base pay. Where it gets interesting is the rev share and commission portion.

Within my gym model, there are three ways that trainers make money outside large-group sessions.

- Selling supplements
- Selling internal challenges (to existing members)
- Fulfilling and retaining semi-private clients (25% of gross revenue)

I ran my gyms without the third option. I paid the same rate for large-group sessions as I did for small-group ones.

But if I could do it all over again, I would have given up a little bit of the profit to make my trainers more comfortable. I was lucky—I found a lot of great people who were willing to work for the $15 per hour that I was offering. But many times, that can be more difficult or not worth the heavy time investment in recruiting trainers.

Side Note: Sales is the primary way they can make more money. Many gym owners ask me about having trainers make the sales. In my experience, they get torn between their love of training and sales. And many trainers want nothing to do with it. I prefer to bring someone in specifically for that. But sometimes you find a unicorn who enjoys both. And then you can give them 20 hours per week of sales and their training hours. (But as soon as someone starts making salesperson money, they usually don't want to do anything else.)

Every gym wants to take care of its trainers financially, but sometimes can't find the money to do so.

Here's how you find the money if they aren't selling. Let's do a teensy bit of math here. (It's been a while, right?)

Let's assume you have 100 EFTs and 30 people who sign up on average per month on a front-end program.

Let's also assume this trainer is training 20 hours per week of large group and does 9 sessions per week of small group with an average of 3 people in each session, for a total of 9 recurring, and is making $150/week.

Existing Members: 100

New Clients Signed Up on CFA Front-End Program: 30

Base Pay: 20 hours x $15/hr = $300/week = **$15,600/yr**

Semis: $150 x .25 x 9 = $337.50/week = **$17,550/yr**

So just from the added money from their nine semi-private clients, the trainer is now making two times what they were making before. A fundamentally sound $33,150 per year. Much better than just $15,600. For many trainers, this is all they want and need.

(Don't scoff. The average gym owner takes home less than that each year.)

But let's see what else is achievable by the entrepreneurial trainer.

If there are 30 new clients signing up each month, then that means they have the opportunity to sell them supplements as well.

Let's say they meet with half of the new clients and sell 80% of them into a supplement package, which is not uncommon. The average commission is about $15.

> 15 people means likely 12 people buying supplements (15 x .8)
>
> 12 people x $15 average commission per sale = $180 per month = **$2,160/year**

Okay. Now we're up to $35,310 per year. Now this trainer is getting paid about $10,000 a year more than beginning police officers and school teachers do.

But let's put in the last step: selling internal challenges to existing members. Let's say this trainer only works evenings. Then they'll only have the opportunity to sell 65 of the 130 active clients (100 recurring and 30 still in their front-end program).

Let's say they sell 25% of those 65 people into an internal play, which is $150, and they make between $25–$50 on the sale depending on the play. They have the opportunity to make an additional $600 per month.

This means an extra $7,200 in their pockets. Now, they're up to $42,510 per year in income. That's a good living for wearing shorts and short sleeves to the gym every day and hanging out with people you like.

Hopefully, this illustrates the earning potential and how your outcome and their outcome do not need to be mutually exclusive. In fact, they're intertwined.

And as a fun thought experiment, if you were to simply 2x the number of semi-private clients being managed by this one trainer from 9 to 18, then they would make over $60,000/year take-home.

Opportunities abound for those who aren't afraid of work.

When presenting a new pay structure, like the one I outlined, you want to sell the future of what is possible. What will end up happening is that trainers will WANT to do the large-group classes in order to recruit and upsell people into the high-ticket semi-private program. Win-win.

Now, let's move onto the even better stuff—intrinsic motivation.

Intrinsic Motivation

First off, you cannot lead what you do not live. If you feel like your trainers do not respect you, then there is no one to blame but yourself. The culture is your fault. Their performance is your fault. Their lack of belief is your fault. So just don't blame anyone else, okay? Because if you do, you give someone else the power over your business, which is not what you signed up for.

Now that we got that out of the way…how do we intrinsically motivate trainers?

We look to the six human needs. Mind you, this works for the other positions as well, it's just that most gyms struggle to motivate and manage their training staff, which is why I am specifically addressing trainers.

These six human needs are…

- Significance & Connection
- Variety & Certainty
- Growth & Contribution

Significance & Connection

For significance, always begin by praising trainers and publicly recognizing them.

You praise in the meetings, and you publicly recognize one trainer monthly as trainer of the month.

For connection, make sure they are involved in the events and the handwritten cards. This allows them to activate some empathy for the customers. They will start liking them more by default.

Variety & Certainty

In terms of variety, let them figure out the workouts. I distinctly remember how much my trainers hated when I took the session programming away from them. It was something they looked forward to putting together. Allow them to help create the variety of programming.

If you have a lazy trainer, then you can do what we ended up doing as a middle ground: dictate the movement patterns and rep schemes, but have them come up with the exercise and finishers. This allowed us a happy medium between structure and chaos.

As far as certainty goes, you pay them on time, every time. No exceptions. Ever. The moment you are late with a payment, that trust is broken forever. And it usually does not heal.

And show up the same way as a leader. No emotional swings. Ask questions and keep calm. Seek first to understand, and you will be amazed to discover that most times mistakes happen because of miscommunication, not from lack of character.

Growth & Contribution

Trainers are extremely growth-oriented. This is just something I've noticed over a career of managing them and helping others manage them. They like to work on personal development.

Ask this question in your one-on-ones: what book can I buy you that might make you better at your craft?

Or offer to pay for 30 minutes per week of personal development where they come in early and work on a certification or take a course on sales or training or nutrition.

These are small things, but they show a trainer that you're not only interested in what they can do for *you*, but that you are also willing to do something for them.

To encourage contribution, tie the trainers into the vision for the business. Involve them. Ask them what they think you could do to better serve people. You will be amazed at some of the ideas. And here's the crazy part—they will totally "own" any ideas they come up with themselves and see them through to completion.

This is also why it is good to start the meetings with client wins and testimonials. It gives perspective and context to the grind of the fitness industry. This is why we do it. It also reminds everyone that we all have the same goals.

To summarize, motivate your trainers extrinsically with income-earning opportunities such as…

- Selling supplements.
- Selling internal challenges (to existing members).

- Fulfilling and retaining semi-private clients (25% of gross revenue).

Motivate them intrinsically by…

- Reading off client wins in every meeting.
- Paying them to continue to learn and get new certifications.
- Asking them what else the company can do to serve your clients.
- Naming a trainer of the month publicly.
- Praising them individually in front of the team.
- Affirming them during one-on-ones and giving them three positives for every piece of corrective feedback.

Chapter 21

PRODUCT: How To Run An Amazing Session Every Time

Being an amazing trainer takes time and practice. It is as much art as science. To take a break from my tactic heaviness, let me tell you a funny story that might hit home with you.

Once upon a time, I had a trainer named Brian. (I changed the name to keep his identity private.)

Brian was the first trainer I hired. He was the son of one of my clients, and he didn't have any training experience.

I honestly felt like a big brother to Brian. He was 19, had just gotten out of high school, and wasn't sure what he wanted to do with his life. His mom thought I was a decent person for him to hang around (ambitious and such), so she encouraged the working relationship.

I loved him like a little brother.

And sometimes I wanted to smack him upside the head.

Brian loved gangster rap. He cranked it so loud at the gym I would get noise complaints from the city. He would always apologize and say the clients wanted it louder. (I'm smiling and shaking my head while typing this, because I let him get away with a lot.)

He was the type of person who would take a while to get something, but when he did, he would not change from it for a looooong time. Which made him consistent. Too consistent.

Before I had systems in place to get feedback from clients, a woman came up to me one day after class and asked, "You got a minute?" I nodded and she sat down at my desk.

"I hate to complain, because I love the gym and I love Brian…but we have done sleds every single day for the last thirty-eight days. I know because I counted."

I was mortified. Except for the small part of me that thought it was hilarious.

I remember when Brian had discovered that if you told people to do burpees while they waited for their partner to return with the sled, it was almost guaranteed vomit induction for anyone new. I was young, and I didn't know anything about "first impressions" or "tragic moments" or anything like that. Needless to say, I ended up having to clean the bathroom a lot from people's first days.

Sometimes I wonder how I even made it out alive from my first location.

Anyways, Brian was consistent. But whenever I wasn't there to make sure one of the approved playlists was on, he would plug in his phone and crank his gangster rap at my Orange County Huntington Beach 75% female gym (*facepalm*).

He really didn't get how anyone could not like the music he did. It was almost comical. I asked him to change up the music genre one time, and no joke, the next day he came in all fired up because he had a new mix that he KNEW I would like and approve.

"Totally different genre. I know you'll dig it."

He went from West Coast rappers to East Coast rappers. I couldn't make this up if I tried.

Anyways, I tell you that story to say that I've been there. I've made every mistake in the book. All of them. These days, I would quickly recognize that someone like Brian has the right attitude but not aptitude and he was not coachable, or not nearly coachable fast enough.

So let's get to business. How did I go from cranking gangster rap in a mostly female gym in Orange County and getting women to throw up on their first sessions at my gym to being able to scale my locations and now coach more gyms past seven figures than anyone in the industry?

The Hamburger Workout

Eventually, I would realize that each training session was my product. It was my hamburger. And the way ingredients were layered on top of one another would make it more likely for clients to have a great session experience.

These are the ingredients for an amazing session.

Prep Work

1. Make sure bathrooms are clean since that's where most people change.
2. Playlist should be fresh and new every day. Yes, every day. It should be FIRE, like amazing. Music matters and is a huge part of the experience. Do not shortcut. Playlist should also be clean with no profanity. (You can buy these versions.)

When They Walk In The Door

1. Greet the person by name within 10 seconds of entering building.
2. Check them in to the system.
3. Encourage them to check in on social media.
4. Introduce new clients to older ones for every workout of their first week. (You can do this with different color

name tags or by simply encouraging first-weekers to wear name tags. Wrist bands work too.)
5. Pair each new person with an OG as a workout partner for their first week.
6. Music should have two set volumes: one for between sessions, one for after session begins. Volume should never be higher than the preset level.
7. Use a mic. You may cringe at that concept. But in a big gym, no one can hear you, especially with background sounds and small talk and echoes. This was also a HUGE help for my trainers' endurance. They could train way more sessions when they didn't have to yell. Easier on their central nervous system too.
8. Make announcements DURING warm-up.
9. Use an automated timer. Trainers shouldn't have to count reps or track time. You want them to COACH.
10. Demonstrate no more than two exercises before telling people what to do. Otherwise, they'll forget and ask their trainer to come back around and repeat them again anyways.
11. Each session, call out each person two times by name for something good.
12. Give each person two correctional cues during the workout at some point so they feel like they're getting their money's worth.
13. At the conclusion of the workout, tell everyone to reset their last station or exercise then meet in the middle of the room.
14. Bring everyone together for a hands-in moment.

15. Repeat announcements and pass around clipboards for any internal promotions so participants can sign up. (These are easy sales to mop up that allow trainers to collect commissions from each session.)
16. Call out one or two people, especially new ones, for doing well. (These small recognitions go a long way to building loyalty.)
17. At the end, do a 3-2-1 cheer to wrap up the session.

This hamburger process can be used for whatever style of workout you have. The fundamentals will always be the same. And even a poor trainer who uses this and executes will still leave most people feeling better when they leave than when they came in.

Product Summary

The product category for gym owners is a combination of workout structure and the people executing them.

You've learned how to extrinsically and intrinsically motivate trainers. Their energy, vibe, and smiles will dramatically attract customers. A great trainer in a crappy structure will do better than a crappy trainer in a great structure. Satisfy your clients' needs and praise them to success.

That being said, you might as well have a great structure that is easy to follow so even mediocre trainers seem great, right?

You probably have most of the list above covered, but you may be missing a few pieces. Or maybe not all the steps are being done consistently. Having this structure in place can help make mediocre trainers become better ones and will ultimately allow you to provide a more consistent experience.

Keep in mind the process/people/product components of retention, including the five horsemen: reach-outs, attendance, handwritten cards, events, and exit interviews. Start those processes TODAY and watch your monthly attrition drop like a rock and your lifetime values soar.

Insert structure and communication cycles for your business. This will give you the pulse and ensure everything is being executed while you develop your team members. Show them the future of the business and what roles you will need to hire next. This will involve them in the gym's growth.

Treat trainers well and satisfy their financial and personal needs so they treat your clients well and give them the structure to succeed.

Do all these things and I promise you your hole-in-the-bucket problem will turn into a "What do I do with all these people?" problem.

Live What You Lead

As I said earlier, you cannot lead what you do not live. As a gym owner, if you are not the type of person who parks your car across the street to let your customers have the best parking spaces, then your employees won't be either. A business is always a reflection of the owner, and if you don't like what you see, you have no one to blame than the person staring back at you in the mirror.

So treat your employees as well as your customers. Heck, treat EVERYONE like royalty. And you'll live like royalty.

Conclusion Of The Three Main Problems

✓ Problem 1: The Broken Acquisition System → Client-Financed Acquisition

✓ Problem 2: The Broken Revenue Model → Profit Levers

✓ Problem 3: The Hole in the Bucket → Process/People/Product Retention System

You did it. You've learned how to solve the three main problems facing gym owners. You can exhale.

Now, in your mind, you know what you need to do to fix your current gym. That will bring you up to the present. But now, I want to take you into the future, and show you what our top Gym Lords are doing and the model that is minting $1 million+ facilities faster than any other model out there.

It's hard to know how long it will take until you figure out where you are and where you're going. Now you know where you are, the next section will tell you where you should be going.

You're gonna like the next part. It'll make you money. I promise.

Section IV

Baking The Cake

You are one of the few, the proud who made it past the three-quarter point in this book. In fact, most people don't make it past the first chapter in any book. So the fact that you are reading these words means you are a unicorn. Congrats.

As a reward, you'll get some extra gold nuggets in this section.

Reading this far also means you are much more likely to implement what I am about to lay out for you. Double kudos.

What I am about to outline is our most advanced model and understanding of the microgym business.

This is the model we are using to mint new $1 million+ facilities every quarter.

The concept is simple—a wedding cake. There are two main drivers to the profitability of the Wedding Cake Gym Model.

Main Driver #1: Accommodating Buying Curve

The first driver in this model is maximizing profit per customer. Every person spends money on a variety of things. What you want to do is maximize the amount of money you're able to extract from the customer given their priorities and spending power in a single vertical.

Earlier, I gave the fitness comparison of an accommodating strength curve, where the more mechanically advantaged you are in a lift, the heavier the resistance should ideally become. A simple example would be attaching bands to a leg press. You are stronger at the top of the movement and weaker at the bottom. If you train without bands, you are really only training the bottom of the movement, because the top is really not heavy enough in that range of motion to cause an adaptation.

In theory, using accommodating resistance allows you to maximally train a muscle through an entire range of motion. This would be in contrast to only being hard at one point and easier throughout the rest of the movement. An accommodating strength curve, in theory, gets you bigger and stronger faster.

I see customers spending in the same way. We need to create an accommodating buying curve. This encourages customers who are willing and able to spend more to do so, while also allowing the "weaker" customers to spend up to their limits.

Imagine we took a random sample of 10 customers at your gym. You are likely to have 8 who are lower spenders and 2 that are higher spenders, following a typical 80/20 split. Now, we want to give those higher spenders the opportunity to give us more money.

When we do this, since rich people tend to be A LOT richer than poor people are poor, a lot of times you can get 3x, 4x, 5x, or 10x the value from that customer. I am using easy numbers for demonstration only here.

EX: Normal Gym

10 customers treated identically

10 x $100 = $1,000 TOTAL

Monthly value per customer = $100

EX: Accommodating Buying Curve

8 weak customers x $100 = $800

2 strong customers x $600 = $1,200

$800 + $1,200 = $2,000

Average monthly per customer = $200 ($2,000 / 10)

So just adding this second level created 2x the revenue AND allowed you to serve people more aligned with the way they wanted to be served.

And this, in turn, allows you to increase your total LTV for ALL customers, because you allowed the people who want to spend more to do so. When you make 2x as much per customer, it also allows you to spend more aggressively in the acquisition, reach more people, and change your world. This is a good thing.

This is the first way we maximize profit per customer.

Main Driver #2: Maximize Buying Curves Per Customer

The second way we maximize profit per customer is by dipping into different "spending wallets" or verticals.

People have different priorities and different limits depending on what they are buying.

An example might be a client who spends $150/month on service at your gym but who also spends $200/month on supplements, $100/month on Lululemon gear, and $500/month on meal prep. It can be helpful to remind prospects that they spend money on all kinds of things they might not really NEED, and that money could be better spent to improve their health and fitness.

If you only offered ONE of these services, even when totally maxed out, you would only be capturing one aspect of that customer's true LTV.

The more of these value centers you can tap into, the more money you can make and, by extension, the more aggressively you can profitably spend and acquire customers.

This is how you change the world. You maximize your reach. And the way to do that is to serve people on as many levels and as high a level as you can. This is VALUE. This is how you win. And this is how our gyms are designed to become profit machines.

WARNING

Now before we get ahead of ourselves, the model I am about to lay out is NOT in any way an endorsement to go start five other companies. That would be idiocy for most.

Many facilities do not have the financial capacity, the bandwidth, the staff, or the infrastructure to actually DO more than their main service.

However, if you put your clever cap on, you can still use each of these revenue streams to feed your business and provide value to your customers. We have systems in place to do this without increasing the complexity of the business (and without risking a dollar out of pocket). All upside, no risk. That's the game we want to play.

Let's take a closer look at the Wedding Cake Model.

Chapter 22

The Wedding Cake Gym Profit Model

I will be the first to admit, the model I am about to break down for you is better and more successful than what I used at any of the six gyms I had. And that's because my gyms were the 1.0 model. They worked well, but there was still plenty to be improved.

The model I am going to outline for you here is the result of continuous iteration on best practices extracted from thousands of hours of calls, interviews, and roundtables with our best gyms and specialists to get to **the truth about what actually works**.

The beautiful (and also sad) part is that we continue to improve on the model, which means that it has improved since I wrote this book. This was the hardest section for me to write, because in the six months it took to make this book, the model continuously evolved and improved. But what you have here is better than what 99% of gyms run, so it will still give you a lot of room to grow. So if this gets you jacked up, just wait until you see what we're actually doing right now, in real time.

To give you a benchmark, the top gym in our program is on pace for $1.8 million in 2018 from one facility. (Though by the time you read this, we may have iterated on that model to improve it further.)

The process we use to innovate is simple.

1. Find an issue many gym owners are struggling with in one of the following categories: lead generation, lead nurture, sales, fulfillment, ascension/retention.
2. Grab 20 gyms in 20 markets experiencing the WORST of this problem.
3. Talk to the top 10 gyms who are CRUSHING this problem, and itemize their techniques into a teachable format.
4. Implement these techniques in the weaker gyms, and see if it works in at least 80% of them.
5. If it does, we systematize and simplify it for mass rollout, then we hand it over to our Gym Lords community. If it doesn't work, we take note of why and try to fix it, OR we try a different technique to solve the problem and repeat the steps.

This way, everyone adapts, implements, and grows at a much faster rate.

THAT is how we are staying ahead and continuing to provide value to our top gym owners. We sell them systems that we already know work, so they get to plug and play without bearing the cost of failure or wasted time and effort. It's also why so many go up the profit ladder so fast. If you have the right information, it doesn't take long to see massive changes.

We spend over $100,000 per month just testing things for our clients. (And probably more by the time you read this.) That's how we know our methods work…today… right now.

As a special side note, this is why information is the most valuable thing in the world. Because it buys you TIME. The better the information, the faster you can implement and see changes and literally leapfrog your old progress curve. That is how we can take a gym from barely making a couple hundred thousand a year to over a million within six months. It's not that the gym owner magically sprouted wings, they just acquired a new skill set based on better information.

Gym owners have a better work ethic than any other segment of people I have ever encountered. Standard 12-hour days are typical. So if your gym isn't growing, it's not that you need to work harder—you need to apply your work ethic to a better model. When you do, magic happens.

The Wedding Cake Model

So are you ready to dig into the good stuff?

What exactly is the Wedding Cake Gym Profit Model? And how is it making so many ordinary gym owners rich without opening more locations or working endless hours?

So let's just crack this egg open: why is this model called a cake?

Well, mostly because I thought the picture I made was pretty, and I was dieting when I put everything together.

In the Section IV introduction, you read about the two drivers of revenue in our model: 1) creating an accommodating buying curve by getting people with more money to spend more and 2) stacking curves on top of one another by having people buy different types of products/services through you.

The Wedding Cake Model fulfills both of these drivers. The layers and tiers of the cake allow customers to both spend more on fitness and to buy ancillary services.

At a granular level, there's another division that needs to be highlighted. This split in type of revenue is also what gave me the cake concept.

There are two main components to each tier in the Wedding Cake Gym Profit Model:

- Icing
- Cake

Any good cake should have both. (And if you're like my wife, you believe any good cake should have lots of icing.) But the point is, they work together synergistically, and neither can really exist without the other.

Icing

The icing represents front-end cash flow from new customers. This allows you to acquire customers profitably. It provides money to give them an amazing experience. And it allows you to afford virtually whatever media platforms you choose, because you can buy eyeballs with the cash they give you. This is how you never go hungry again.

On an emotional level, you feel like you are actually getting paid for a service, so even if someone doesn't convert into an

EFT, you still make a profit on the interaction and don't take the time and service as a loss.

But you cannot live entirely off of front-end cash flow. If you have a hiccup for whatever reason, like a salesperson going on vacation or an ad account getting shut down, you cannot afford for cash flow to stop.

So you cannot have a cake made entirely of icing, despite how awesome and delicious it is.

Cake

The cake represents recurring cash flow from existing customers who are ascending and buying again. This is your EFT. It is the backbone and stability of the business. Because when that hot day comes and the icing melts thin (and it inevitably will), you'll want to have a consistent group of paying regulars so you can get through it.

So you need both of these ingredients. And on each level, the icing and the cake (front-end cash and recurring revenue) work synergistically to create a tasty business model (if I may say so).

Understanding these two core concepts is what separates a lot of our gyms from those that are struggling. You need to master both sides to have a rocking microgym.

Of course, we're not settling for a nice little teacake here. We're building a full-on multitiered wedding cake. So what do the different tiers consist of?

Wedding Cake Overview

The main wedding cake has three tiers to it—each has layers of icing (front-end cash flow) and cake (recurring cash flow). This means that from these three tiers, you actually have six revenue streams. Beats just one, right?

You can see the three tiers outlined in the image below.

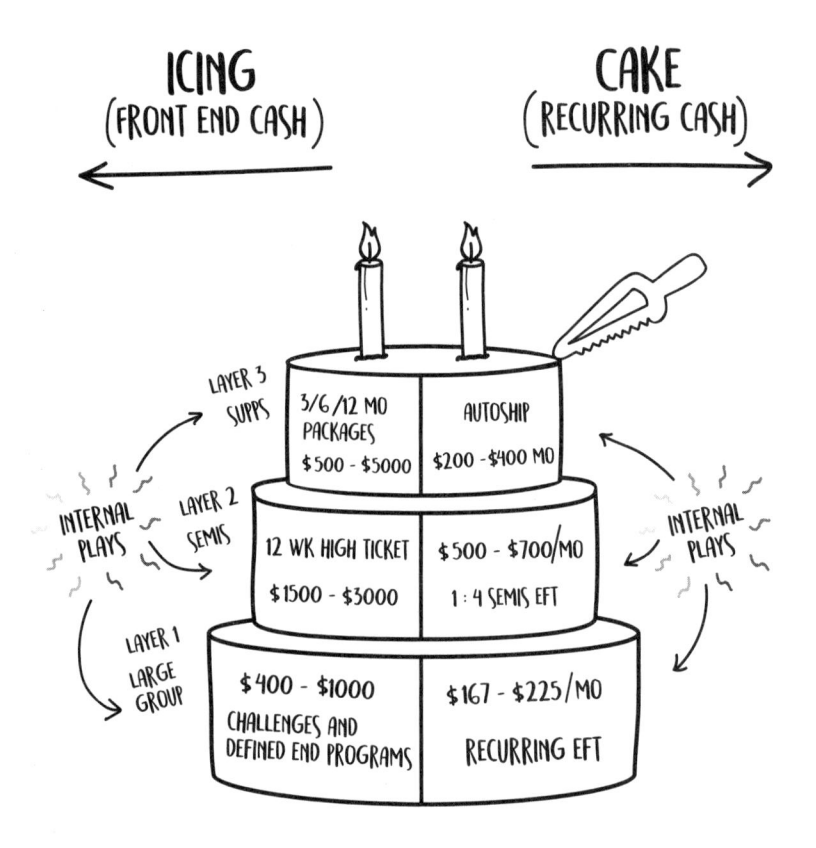

ICING (FRONT END CASH) ←

CAKE (RECURRING CASH) →

LAYER 3 SUPPS: 3/6/12 MO PACKAGES $500 - $5000 | AUTOSHIP $200 - $400 MO

LAYER 2 SEMIS: 12 WK HIGH TICKET $1500 - $3000 | $500 - $700/MO 1:4 SEMIS EFT

LAYER 1 LARGE GROUP: $400 - $1000 CHALLENGES AND DEFINED END PROGRAMS | $167 - $225/MO RECURRING EFT

INTERNAL PLAYS

You should have your large-group training, semi-privates, and supplements, in that order.

These are the trifecta that I think every gym should implement.

In this section, I'll talk about how we package and sell each of these things to generate both icing (front-end cash flow) and cake (recurring cash flow).

After that, I'll break down a concept called internal plays, which are one of the biggest secrets to our success. In an older version of the Wedding Cake Model, I considered them the fourth tier, but it's really a traffic source that feeds all the others. So now I call it the "sprinkles." No matter how you slice it, it's important and it affects the whole model. Don't skip that chapter.

After that, I'll break down the other easy profit centers you can pick up on and things you can do to provide more value to your customers and also to your employees. These give your team non-monetary benefits that really add up. These are all essentially "free money" layers that you should implement when you have the bandwidth to do so.

I can promise you that once you see all the different ways we make money with the gym, and how we do it with our increasing complexity to the business, you will dig it…a lot.

Real Numbers

The image above gives you an overall understanding of each cake tier. But I'd like to add some numbers to them to show you what is possible.

Mind you, the numbers are averages from a non-owner-operated facility, meaning that many of these have been TRIPLED OR MORE by a lot of our Gym Lords. And I bet you can blow these out of the water.

These are attainable numbers you can achieve with just normal folks following normal, boring business processes. If you have a team of rock stars, you can do even better.

Assumptions

- 30 new customers per month from client-financed acquisition
- 4 new high-ticket clients per month from client-financed acquisition

- 65% conversion from front-end offers into recurring
- 8% attrition rate for both semis and large group
- 23% attrition for recurring supplement orders (this is the actual number)

A note about the numbers above: 8% attrition and 65% conversion are pretty mediocre. And getting only 30 new sign-ups a month for a defined front-end program is also fairly average. (You can see 800+ testimonials from gyms who do wayyy more than that here: IDontHateMoney.com.)

And one person per week for high-ticket is not much. Realistically, most gyms only run their high-ticket front end a few times a year, because they will sign up 10 people in 14 days then turn it off for a while. So the one person per week is a mathematical average, not a real-life one. In reality, the distribution is clumpier.

All this is to say, I am purposely using ridiculously achievable numbers so you can see the power of the model.

Tier #1 Large Group

ICING: Front-End Revenue Layer: 30 x $500 = $15,000/month

CAKE: Recurring Revenue Layer

> 30 new customers x .65 conversion into recurring / .08 attrition = 243
>
> 243 recurring customers x $167 = $40,581/month

TOTAL FOR TIER #1 = $55,581

Tier #2 Semi-Privates

ICING: Front-End Revenue Layer: 4 x $2,500 = $10,000/month

CAKE: Recurring Revenue Layer

> 4 new customers x .65 conversions /.08 = 32 recurring clients
>
> 32 x $550/month = $17,600/month

TOTAL FOR TIER #2 = $27,600

Tier #3 Supplements

ICING: Front-End Revenue Layer

> 34 (30 large group + 4 small group) x .85 take rate = 29 buyers
>
> 29 buyers x $200 average ticket price = $5,800

There is no conversion here, so it all feeds into the recurring. This will not be added to the total for the layer, since the recurring covers this first sale in the equation below, but I thought it would be useful to see how you make money for the acquisition immediately.

CAKE: Recurring Revenue Layer

> 29 new sign-ups / .23 attrition = 126 recurring supplement buyers per month
>
> 126 x $200 = $25,200

TOTAL FOR TIER #3 = $25,200

Total Revenue For Wedding Cake (first 3 tiers only, no sprinkles) = **$108,381/month**

I'm asking you to just trust me. And hopefully your curiosity is still piqued to see how each of these cake tiers work in more detail.

So let's start with the base of the cake: large-group training.

Chapter 23

Tier 1: Large-Group Training

The base tier of the wedding cake represents your large-group training. For some facilities, this is 40+ people per session; for others it's only 20. Either way, this is your larger of your two groups.

Large Group Icing: Front-End Cash

Remember, the icing is the front-end cash, which means you need to be selling something here for a high-ticket price. Honestly, I don't consider $400–$1,000 to be high-ticket, but many gym owners we speak with in the beginning consider it to be.

This is the front-end, defined-end program you will offer in order to acquire customers from your marketing. (That irresistible offer you learned about in the beginning of the book.) In other words, a 42-day, 6-week, or 28-day challenge, or whatever you decide to create to entice people to come to your gym.

It also serves as your indoctrination get-them-to-love-you program. So even if someone comes in through a referral, you should put them through this defined-end program first. Here's why:

- Once the systems are in place, it's automated.
- They begin with a cohort, which fosters camaraderie.
- It allows you to get a big cash commitment up front, which makes them less likely to fall off, lose commitment, or switch facilities.

What do the numbers look like?

The average facility we work with signs up about 30–40 of these a month, so about 7–10 per week. This seems to be a very sustainable number for most and doesn't overwhelm the staff or the existing client base. If you're keeping track from home, that's about $15,000 to $20,000/month on front-end revenue, and we're just getting started.

Sure, some of our sales-y Gym Lords sign up 200 people in like 3 weeks at $600 and go nuts telling everyone about it. But most people can't handle that kind of volume, even if they did make the sales. And the people who hit those numbers oftentimes end up scaling down until they can dial in their delivery (hole-in-the-bucket systems). More gyms than I can count have gotten out of tough spots, experienced a huge cash-flow injection, and been able to catch their breath in order to put the rest of the systems in place in their gyms using this front-end high-ticket model.

In fact, here's a picture that was sent to me by Robyn Thrasher, who was able to pay her landlord $28,000 in back rent within three weeks as a result of using these practices.

That pretty much sums it up. Pretty simple. The icing is the program you market. At the time of this writing, our top-converting offer is a 6-Week Challenge. Why? Who knows?

My theory is that a 6-Week Challenge (42 days) is just enough time for people to believe that a significant outcome or result can occur, but short enough that they think they can actually accomplish it. We've spent a literal million in cash testing offers, and it is hands down the best one. So we don't mess with it. When it stops converting, there will always be another offer and another platform to market it on. So don't sweat it. And once you have an acquisition system that is super profitable, buying traffic is the easy part, thanks to client-financed acquisition.

But now that we have our icing, what about our cakey back end?

Large Group Cakiness: The EFT

The great marketer Frank Kern once said, "The amount of money you make is directly proportional to the amount of goodwill you have in the marketplace times the number of offers you make." But making offers tends to decrease the amount of goodwill you have, which means that you really need to be CRUSHING that part. And at the end of the day, that's what it's all about.

So how do we bake the cakey goodness? How do we sell the EFT recurring membership? We make THREE attempts to convert people during a member's first six-week period.

Wha...? Yeah, three.

First Conversion Attempt: Bribe

This is targeted to the hyper-responsive buyers. Some people come into the gym and fall instantly in love and talk about it as though they are going to be there until they die. You can convert these people at the first opportunity.

We use a bribe. What that means is we price position the offer nice and high, like $599, and we say, "This is the offer. Loads of people have done it and love it. But if you want, we'll give you the entire program for FREE if you just become a member today." At that point, we get them to prepay their first six weeks or whatever duration of time we sold them, but put them straight into recurring.

So if someone said, "Yeah sure, I'll take that offer," then you would have them pay $49/week for six weeks ($294) up front and set up their next payment six weeks from then. They would then have made the mental shift from being a front-end customer into a full member. Very important psychologically.

> **Pro Tip:** If you really want to go all-in on this offer, which I highly recommend if you know your EFT lifetime value is greater than five months, then you should raise the price anchor even higher. Present the front-end program at $799 or higher. This will make the membership option seem even more appealing, and 90% will take that offer. Mind you, some people will still take the $799 offer. Those are great customers who will buy EVERYTHING. So keep an eye out.

Anyways, this offer is absolute fire. It's an easier sale. It has goodwill. It feels like a gift. And it accomplishes the once incomprehensible—it gets new people to sign up for a membership on Day 1.

Kaboom.

Now, if you need more front-end cash because you are in a hard spot or just want more padding in your bank account, skip straight to EFT conversion sale #2. This is what MOST of the gyms we start out with do, because they need the cash injection for the variety of reasons I outlined earlier.

Second Conversion Attempt: Abandon Hope Sale

So if you were one of the people who needed more cash (totally cool), then you would take the $500 or $600 up front for the program, and this sale (the Abandon Hope Sale) would be your first attempt at closing the recurring EFT. This SHOULD be your biggest conversion point, if you opted to skip #1.

This sale happens at Week 3, or the halfway point of the program if you have a different duration. Why do I call it the Abandon Hope Sale? I used it in a staff meeting as a joke once, and the name has stuck ever since.)

To sell the EFT, you are trying to get the client to see that it's very unlikely that they'll be creating or sustaining any long-term effects for their fitness within only six weeks. Ironically, you are sort of "unselling" what you sold on the front end.

The basic structure of this sale is as follows:

1. Schedule a halfway meet-up with the client to talk about their progress. This should be called a "mandatory halfway meeting." (Of course, no one HAS TO do anything, but it sure helps the response.)
2. Once you meet with them, provide tips and nutrition help. You must provide VALUE.
3. Provide encouragement. A lot of people need affirmation that they're doing everything right. Sometimes, people are CRUSHING it but don't know whether to celebrate until you tell them to. People need permission to feel

good sometimes. And you need to grant it to them. No joke. Give them a high five for ANY level of win (weight loss, energy, lifestyle, clothing fit, exercise performance). And make it a big deal—because it is. That is what good coaching is all about.

4. Once you have them in the right state of mind, re-ask the major sales questions that you asked them in the beginning about their a) long-term goals, b) sustainable results, and c) permanent weight loss. Asking these questions reframes the conversation you will have.
5. Now you simply make an irresistible offer again: "Hey, I think you may be a good fit for our ongoing transformation program. If I could save you some money by staying, would you want to hear about it?" Almost everyone says yes here.
6. They lean in, and you explain this offer: "If you sign up today, I'll give you all the money you paid for this front-end program as credit off of a year membership, and on top of that, I'll let you finish the program—on me—at no extra charge. So you get your first six weeks free, and you get a lifetime lower rate for staying."
7. Then you take out the paperwork, fill it out for them, and have them sign to claim their lifetime lower rate.

This is an assumed close. If you do this right, you can close 95% of people at this halfway point. Most salespeople average around 50% their first time and float in the 70%–80% range after they get used to this model of conversion. But the killers can close just about everyone. The key is taking control and directing the person on what they should do as a fitness consultant, not as a salesperson.

Here's an example:

Abandon Hope Sales Math

When: Week 3/halfway through a 6-Week Challenge

Challenge Cost: $600

Offer: Remaining 3 weeks at no extra charge if they sign up for a 12-month EFT contract

Desired EFT (what you want them to actually pay): $49/week, but you will do your math using months when explaining it, because it's easier for most people to follow, so you will say $199/month.

Inflated EFT: $249/month

Here is a script you can use:

> If you sign up today, I'm gonna personally credit your $600 toward our year-long transformation program, which includes everything you are currently receiving except you pay less. Cool? So instead of paying our normal rate of $249/month, we're gonna knock off $50/month, bringing you down to about $200 a month. And we bill on a weekly cycle here, so you'll actually only have to pay $49/week. As a second gift to you, we'll honor that rate for the duration of the time you are with us. But this will be the only time you get this offer. Do you want to just use the card we already have on file? Great. Just sign the bottom here, and initial here next to the price and terms, and I'll fill in your card number later.

It's that simple. You get to your desired number by just doing the math ahead of time. Everyone feels like they're getting the six weeks for free and a discount, but if you follow the money, all that really happened was they signed up for $600 and, three weeks later, signed up for a recurring weekly EFT beginning at the end of their promotional period for the full price. It's all how you position it.

It's important to understand that we're manipulating numbers here, not people. It's in their best interest to sign up with you and to stick around, because you're going to take care of them and help them reach their goals, right? So you have to sell the plan in a way that makes sense to them and helps them feel confident in their decision. That's all you're doing when you work the numbers to come out the way you want. Sometimes people need to hear things presented in different ways before they will sign on.

About 90% of our EFTs are structured off the halfway point sale, so get familiar with the math here, and back into whatever number you desire your EFT to be.

Warning: You cannot offer different prices for different people for the same service. That is price discrimination. That is a no-no. This is why every person should go through the defined front-end program first. That way, everyone's price is unified. Even referrals. Everyone gets the same indoctrination process. It helps keep things automated and consistent and keeps you out of the doghouse.

Third Conversion Attempt: Last Chance

Most people are converted by this point in the process. But if we have any stragglers, we close them on the back end in our "last chance" offer.

Here we give people some type of credit toward a membership based on how much weight or how much body fat they've lost. Why? Because either you give them some money off of a random amount or you lose them. And everyone likes to get a deal. So it's up to us as business owners to structure the offer in such a way that even when people get a "deal," they are still well within our profit range.

This sale is more flexible, since everyone has different credit amounts and buying thresholds. You can't change your prices—that's illegal and price discrimination, a big no-no, like I said. But you CAN change the terms—which, in reality, is everything. You can quote me on that.

Last Chance Sales Math

Now let's say that you or your sales team aren't as good at the Abandon Hope Sale. Or you forgot. Or for whatever other reason, you didn't close the person. Now you only have ONE SHOT left.

Despite what some people feel about hard closing, sometimes you just gotta sell. The weigh-out, or the last day of someone's front-end promotion, is about as hard of a sale as you will ever make. Not in difficulty, but in terms of the finality of the decision. Mind you, it's usually no more than 15 minutes long, so just get in the groove and start stacking EFTs.

> **Pro Tip:** After doing this a bajillion times, we've found something interesting—people who haven't hit their goal are MORE likely to sign up for the EFT than people who have but haven't converted by this point. It's really odd. But I think it has something to do with the psychology of success. They've seen progress but didn't reach their goal. So they are almost shoo-ins if you can get them to come in for their weigh-out, which is the actual challenge. Making them feel good about their progress, even if they are falling short of

> their goal, is key to getting the people who are close but not quite there to come in. But if you get them in, you'll probably close them. So don't skip the follow-ups and reminders. These weigh-out appointments are just as important as your weigh-ins (if not more so).

No Excuses

Now, a quick mindset shift for the Last Chance Sale. You need to believe what I am telling you right now about some of the excuses people tend to give at this point.

- No one needs to "think about it."
- No one needs to talk to their spouse.
- No one needs to check their finances and budget.

Why?

Because there is nothing left to think about. They just had six weeks of the service, and they know what the food tastes like. If they don't say yes immediately, they just don't want to make a decision, because people hate making mistakes. So just help them make the decision that will best serve them: STAYING. That way they don't fall off. If they don't stay, we both know they will go back to doing exactly what they were doing before.

There is probably nothing they need to talk about with their spouse, because they already signed up once, so that person was clearly okay with them working out and the results they are getting. There are a million ways to make $49/week, and they were already able to afford $100/week for the last six weeks, so there is no reason they shouldn't be able to stay for half that price.

So there are no excuses. Make people confront the decision. And if they walk, they walk. But don't let anyone walk out undecided, because this is very much a sale—do not think otherwise.

Now, another EFT math example.

Challenge Cost: $600

Desired EFT: $49/week

Inflated EFT: $250/month

Weight Lost: 13 pounds

Credit Given: $25/lb.

Total Credit: $325

So let's say one young man lost 13 pounds so far. As an irresistible offer for staying, we might give him $25 per pound lost as credit toward his membership, sort of like a reward for his effort. The question is, how do you get him to use this credit without him saying, "Cool, I'll take the next month and a half for free."

Got to give credit to Justin Blum of Raw Fitness in Las Vegas for this one. I drove out to his facility in my first or second year as a gym owner, and I saw him doing this extended credit thing and loved it. When I was there, the answer smacked me upside the head—terms.

If you can control the terms around the credit, then you can back into whatever number you want.

In this example, we would spread this over six months, equal to a $54/month discount ($325/6). $250 - $54 equals… *drum roll…*

$196/month

You get right back to where you started and the same ideal EFT.

All we're doing here is making it 6 months instead of 12 months to make the math work. After their 6 months, you can choose to bump them up, but I just like to let people stay as added goodwill during the sale.

Here's a few more examples to show this concept of changing the terms to back into your ideal EFT price:

- Teenage girl loses 18 pounds. That is $450 of credit (18 lbs. x $25/lb.), which means I would spread it over 9 months and take off $50/month for the next 9 months. That would take the price from $250/month to $200/month.
- Woman loses 10 pounds. That's $250 of credit (10 lbs. x $25/lb.), which means I would spread it over 5 months and take off $50/month for the next 5 months. That would take her from $250/month to $200/month.
- Guy loses 6 pounds. That's $150 of credit (6 lbs. x $25/lb.), which means I would spread $50 per month over 3 months. That would take him from $250/month to $200/month.

So hopefully this shows you that no matter what comes in, you can always back it into whatever price you want it to be.

Mind you, I always tried to "sell to goal," which means that the duration of their membership was entirely up to me. And I would just work backward to where I needed the EFT to be. I recommend you do the same. This is how we can give reasons for the different terms we are offering.

Here's how the sales conversation might go:

> So...you need to lose another 15 pounds to hit your lifetime goal, then once you're at your goal weight,

you eventually want to go from 28% body fat to 18%. So 15 pounds at your current rate of loss will take you 4 months, then we'll begin the recomposition phase, which typically takes another 2 ½ to 3 months—let's say 3 months to be safe. That means that in 7 months, we can get you to where you want to be.

But you want to stay there, right? Right. So I prefer to have people do at least the same amount of time they dieted as maintenance to let their body's set points reset, so that becomes your everyday weight, not your "light" weight. Make sense?

Great, so it's looking like 14 months and we can get you into perma-bikini body at your high school weight, and likely with a little more muscle and metabolism to boot. Sound good?

I am purposely using different numbers here to show all the variables you can use.

I hope from this little example you see how malleable everything can be. Maintenance or "stabilization phase" is something I got from my good friend Cris Cawley, who owned Thinique, a very successful weight-loss franchise. I did not invent it, but the first time I heard of maintenance as an actual sales phase, I loved it. It basically gave me free rein to adjust membership as needed, which allowed me to always back into whatever price I wanted (which is usually just what I want everyone to pay), and I adjust the terms to get to that number.

Back-End Cakiness Conclusion

So let's wrap this layer up. If you sign up 30 clients a month on these front-end promotions (ICING) and you keep 65%, then it means you are growing by about 20 EFTs a month (CAKE). If your attrition is the industry average of 8%, you can still grow your EFT to 250 people (20/.08 = 250). That means that you can get your EFT to around $40,700/month, plus $15,000 (30 x $500) on the front end.

Of course, you could charge $600 on the front end and make yourself another $3,000 if you wanted to. I use $500 and $600 interchangeably. So don't get lost in it.

Pretty sweet, right? So this back-end money plus the front-end money takes us to about $55K/month so far.

These numbers are real and happen every single day to gym owners just like you in all kinds of markets. So if it's a lot higher than you are accustomed to, that's okay. That's why it's called breaking beliefs. It's my job to show you what's possible.

Let's get to our next tier of the gym profit wedding cake.

Chapter 24

Tier 2: Semi-Privates (1-on-4)

This may be my favorite part of the entire business model (but I probably say that for every part). I genuinely love the gym business. There so much individuality an owner can express within the confines of this structure, it's awesome. It works with boxes, bootcamps, semi-private studios, martial arts, kickboxing—the whole gamut.

But anyways, let's get jiggy.

We call this layer HTP, which stands for two things:

- To clients, it means **h**ybrid **t**raining **p**rotocol (or program).
- To you and your trainers, it means **h**igh-**t**icket **p**rogram.

I like having dual meanings so everyone can call it the same thing, though it means different things. Clients are like, "I LOVE HTP," and we as owners are like, "I love HTP too."

So let's break down why I love these programs.

The price points for semi-private, if you recall, are $500 to $700/month, which works out to between $125/week and $175/week, for three sessions. As a reminder, I prefer one-on-four here, because you can sell them at the same prices as personal training sessions, except you get 4x the revenue per session with the same costs. Solid.

It's one of the most profitable services you can offer in your gym—a business that has historically low margins by design. Finally, getting a gym owner to start selling high-ticket offers is an awesome experience. They see REAL margins and quickly fall in love with them. I've had so many owners ask me after their first high-ticket campaign, "Can I just sell this for the rest of my life?"

The answer is yes, of course. But it's good to have both offers firing at the right time, which I'll explain.

Creating Demand

The reason you start semis second is because you need to fill up your large group first. Once your large group is full, it naturally "flows over" into the next level of service. So you create demand for a service before you need it (aka "digging your well before you're thirsty").

Offering an "exclusive" one-on-four experience doesn't mean too much if your average class size is 1-on-8 in a room that can take 25 people, right? So you have to fill up your larger group sessions first, to increase the demand for a higher level of service among people who desire it and can afford it.

What is "full" for the large-group base-level service? For me, it's when sessions are 85% filled. That usually means your packed times are full and your off-peak hours are around 60%–70%. It's not science, just use your gut here. Make sure you don't add complexity to your life until you have your bases covered.

If you start your semi-private after your large-group program is full and you already have 200+ EFTs, then you will easily get 10% (or 20 people) to upgrade from just a small internal campaign.

And though 20 may not sound like much, at $600/month, it's a nice pop and an added $8,000/month of new revenue. It's

$8,000 of added revenue instead of $12,000 because you have to take out the money that these people were already paying you. So if they were all paying $200/month prior to launching your semi-private program, then as soon as they signed up, they would go from $200 to $600 per month. That is a net increase of $400/month per client (20 upgrades x $400/month = $8,000 revenue increase).

Cost-wise, you're only looking at 15 sessions a week (5 each on MWF). And for each of those sessions, you're making $186 ($139 weekly cost/3 sessions x 4 people per session). And you have the same fulfillment cost ($20 to the trainer, or if you've started profit sharing, then 25% goes to them).

For math's sake, I'm going to just assume you are doing the 25% profit share on semis that I referenced in the hole-in-the-bucket section. So now you are making $139 of profit on each session x 15, which is an extra $2,085/week in your pocket, for recurring clients. Not bad at all for an extra 15 sessions a week and some happy trainers.

For those paying attention, I am fine with semi-privates operating at a 75% margin instead of 80% or more like we do with large-group.

I won't go into too much detail on how to fulfill here, but this should essentially be your highest level of service. Check in with these people and write them cards (which you should be doing anyways for everyone). In terms of what kind of fitness to provide, it typically makes sense to have a higher emphasis on barbell moves, as you are now in an environment where you can teach them with sufficient attention. But the main selling point is the trainer-to-client ratio. Don't get it twisted. ALL of your levels of training should get results; HTP should just make them happen faster and in a more personalized and enjoyable format.

Don't stress about this. If you've never done semi-private training before, going from large group to small group automatically makes everyone feel special, and it's not nearly as hard as you may think.

Now on to how we fill these sessions up.

Layer 2: Semi-Privates (Icing) Front-End Cash

We sell HTP as a front-end 12-week transformation program for between $2,000 and $3,000.

There are two primary differences between the HTP front-end program and the large-group front-end program. The first is the targeting. Your actual targeting and the copy you use for your ad should call out wealthier folks. The second is the sales process.

With the original sales process I outlined, you are getting people to show up for an appointment without any real qualification step. And at a $500–$1,000 price point, you can pretty much do that. People will spend in that neighborhood on fitness on their first visit.

But in order to get someone to drop from $2,000 to $3,000 on their first visit, you need to do some more selling before they come in the door.

A great saying to commit to memory for selling is "The longer the runway, the bigger the takeoff." In other words, the more time and effort you invest in selling to someone, the bigger the potential payoff.

So to accomplish more selling before the person comes in, we use a two-step sales process.

This means that before coming in to meet with a "closer" (which can be you or someone else), the person talks on the phone to someone who is a "setter."

If you don't have a deep enough bench to pull this off with the staff you have, you can set and close by yourself. I have done it. (Sometimes, you just gotta do whatcha gotta do.)

This is the script we use.

Consult/Sales Script For High-Ticket Fitness Sale

Small Talk: Build rapport and make the prospect comfortable. Find something you have in common, if it seems natural to mention.

> Okay, let's get started. I only have [#] minutes, and I really want to make sure that by the end of the call you've gotten clarity and value. Is that okay? So I have a few questions for you. It might sound like I'm interrogating you, but really we're just going to dive in and get to know where you're at, what you need help with. And at the end, all I want to know is if it makes sense and whether we can help you or not. Sound good?

Get a yes from them before you continue. (Yes or no questions are purposefully injected into the convo.)

> Great. So what is it that motivated you to take time out of your day to schedule a call with us? Why me and why now?

Get them to explain why they wanted to talk, why they wanted to talk to YOU, and why now, then get the ball rolling on identifying their pain.

Goals & Diagnostics

> Awesome…thanks for sharing that. Definitely going to be able to help with that and give you some steps

> to get there. So take me 12 months into the future and describe in detail what your perfect life looks like. In other words, what would have to happen in the next 12 months for you to feel like you've truly made progress?

Future pace…get them to tell you their ideal destination.

> Got it, so you want to be a size X and lose Y pounds. That sounds good. Why is that important to you? What is it you are hoping that will bring you? How will that affect other areas of your life?

Get deeper on the details. You don't care about the amount of weight they want to lose; you want to know what it actually means to them. Let them talk, pause, and let what they say sink into themselves. Let the moment sit. Let them hear themselves say impactful things.

> Okay, so you want to really be able to keep up with your kids and also be an example of health for them. That's great. And what's important about that to you? Are they doing fine now, or what's the goal that you being an example for them would accomplish?

Deeper still…you're looking for that WHY that packs emotion.

> Wow, okay that makes sense. So right now, your kids are not eating right either, and they're adapting the same behavior you had when you were a child. So if they keep on this current path, you're not confident in their ability to become healthy adults.

Boom. Obviously this is a specific scenario, but you will often get answers like this. Then you move on to questions like…

- Okay, so what have you done to work toward this goal?
- What are you currently doing to get to your goal?
- How much weight loss or what kind of results have you gotten thus far?
- What changes would you like to see over the next 12 weeks?
- What's your motivation for that?
- What's stopping you from getting there on your own?

You're going to home in on WHY they need you.

> You tried X, but that didn't work out. Why?
>
> Okay great, thanks. So given everything you've told me, if it were possible that I could take you very quickly to losing that weight and having the energy so that your kids would then have an example to live up to and be healthy adults, how long would you want to wait to start making this happen?

If they say anything besides "Right freaking now," give them one extra chance because they may not have understood you.

> Hmmm…so you're saying, even if it could take 12 weeks, that you'd be willing to wait 8 more months before this starts being handled? I was under the impression you wanted this to happen quickly because it's affecting your family. Did I misunderstand?

Most of the time, they'll say, "Oh no. I want it now, I thought you were asking how long I THOUGHT it would take."

If they still don't get it, say, "Unfortunately, I don't think I can help you then. Thanks for your time. Goodbye." (At that point, they have disqualified themselves.)

If you feel good about the prospect, recap what you can do for them, have them imagine it, and ask what it would be worth to them (as a monetary value).

Once they've told you "I want to start NOW," move to the close.

> Great. Okay, well, I have something that I think might do just that for you. Let me know if you'd like me to tell you about it.

Then, SHUT UP. Don't say anything. Let there be silence. The prospect should ASK you to tell them.

If they aren't clear in asking you, rephrase the question.

"Okay, so you want me to tell you about it?"

"Awesome, so here's what this program is about…"

Fill in the details about what the prospect told you they want. In this case, it'd sound like this:

> This program is designed to get you LEAN and TONED in 12 weeks. The average person can lose up to 30 pounds of fat, which is more than your goal, but that means even if you only nail part of it, you'll hit your goal no problem. And it's designed to take you there FAST—within 12 weeks—so you can reach your goals as soon as possible and get your family and kids on the right track like we talked about. We'll work together [*insert brief details about the program*]. Sound good?

Wait for them to say yes. If they have questions, answer them.

Do NOT tell them the price. If they don't say anything, just add, "Cool, so where would you like to go from here?" Make them ask you what it costs. Once they do, you may tell them.

> So here's the deal. Your goal is to lose 20 pounds, right? That's awesome, and we can get you there, but obviously what you've been doing isn't working, so we're going to need to work with you closely. And we are 100% committed to getting you to that goal, which will be completely life-altering, right? So I need a 100% commitment from you as well. Sound good? So the total investment is $2,497, but because you showed up for our call today and sound like such a good fit, I can do it for $1,997.

Let them talk. They'll either have questions about the program or they'll say "HECK YEAH," in which case you simply say, "Awesome. How do you want to make that investment?"

Make sure that if you are setting, you have all these things covered at the end of the call:

- Credit card details and $50–$100 deposit for consultation
  - At the very least, hold the card and bill $50 for a no-show.
- They must have a decision-maker with them or preapproval by the decision-maker.
- Payment method—make sure they bring whatever they want to pay with when they come in to the gym.
- Special Note: Optional depending on strength of setter: mention total price or minimum investment of $500.

- "So when you meet with Brad, our master trainer, on Wednesday, would you be able to put down $500 toward the program if he finds you to be a good fit?"
- A weaker setter would only close the consult fee and say it is up to Brad to determine the price.

Do not schedule them unless they say yes to all of the above.

Offer a deposit of $50–$100 to hold the (discounted) price if they need to talk to their spouse first.

Listen, when you have objections, that's normal. Just repeat back to them what they've told you they want and remind them that they wanted to start fixing it immediately.

> **Pro Tip:** We actually use the same script for setting and closing. The only difference is that once you get to the close, you would alter the last portion to "The price will ultimately be up to Brad, but in order for you to meet with him, we charge a [*$50–$100*] deposit, since his schedule is so busy." At that point, you would close the exploratory meeting and it would be up to Brad to see if he *wants* to take them on as a client. Now, you have established premium positioning and can drop a $3,000 ticket on their first visit.

> **Pro Tip:** The setter has to edify the closer the whole way through. They need to act like a gatekeeper, like "Brad" is truly a demigod. I say this half-jokingly, but you need to give off this vibe. The most important part though is closing the consult fee. That is everything. You can give the price over the phone if you choose, or you can say it is up to Brad. It depends on the strength of the setter. But what we know for sure is that the set is the close.

If you close the $100 for the consultation, you will close them when they come in the door. If you do NOT close the $100 over the phone, there's a 90% chance you will not close them in person. So don't waste your time. If you don't get the credit card info, don't try and schedule them anyways. We've done this with hundreds of gyms. Every once in a while, someone tries to reinvent the wheel. Don't. Close the $50–$100 consult fee or don't bother.

The set is the close. Keep saying it in your sleep...*the set is the close...the set is the close*...and it will sink in.

So you may wonder, why do we at Gym Launch use so many different sales processes? Because the sales PROCESS always has to match the PROMOTION and the PROSPECT.

But now that you have the script, how does this work out by the numbers?

Money Math

Typically, lead cost will be in the $10–$50 range. Why the big range? Different markets.

Does it matter? Nope. Not one bit.

One of the first gym owners to run HTP exactly as outlined was Ryan Karas. He paid about $42/lead, closed 50% of leads onto a $2,500 program, and made $135K within three weeks. That is not a misprint. The next time he ran it, he made over $300K in three weeks.

Do you think he cared about the $40 leads? Yeah, me neither.

You'll also note that for these types of leads, you can close a much higher percentage, because they are simply better-quality leads. They're responding to copy clearly geared toward the affluent AND to a promotion that does not say "free" anywhere. So they're expecting to pay money.

But if you want to see some cool math...

Pay $4,000 for 100 leads.

Sell 55 of them on a $100 nonrefundable appointment fee (ad cost is now covered).

Then sell 50/55 on a $2,500 package, and you get pretty much the exact number Ryan got.

Pretty neat, right?

But if you want to work with the numbers I promised—an outsourced facility with a sales manager—the front-end icing would look more like this:

1 sale/week at $2,500 = 4 sales/month = $10,000/month

In reality, as I said earlier, the actual process is clumpier, so you may only need to run it a few times a year. So the $10,000 of front-end money is an average. You may in fact do an extra $30K the month you run it, then $0 the next two months, averaging out to $10,000 per month in front-end.

For example, in Ryan's first year with us, he only ran the promotion twice. Why? He didn't need to run it more, because he filled up his semis on the first shot.

So that pretty much sums up the ICING.

Semi-Private Tier, Layer 2: Cake

Now, if you were following along with the numbers, you may have noticed that the $2,500 is actually about $200/week and $3,000 is $250/week.

Why do we set it up that way?

Because it makes it easier to DOWNSELL YOUR UPSELL.

After someone does 12 weeks of semis with a trainer they love while getting an exceptional experience, what's the likelihood that they'll want to stay for almost half price? Pretty high.

So you "downsell" them into a $125/week ongoing or a 12-month contract.

Again, you can use the credit-the-money concept here, but in our experience, it isn't necessary. These people are the highest-quality customers in your business. Just treat them right, and they will never leave.

Ironically, they are also the lowest maintenance, despite paying the most. Crazy, I know, hence the virtuous cycle of price. Back-end retention on your highest level should be near 100%. In the cake layer examples, I use ridiculously below-average numbers. Most people retain close to 100% on the back end for semis.

And what's extra nifty about this is, when you start doing the LTV numbers on these clients, it's incredible. I've got gyms who have only run one HTP campaign, filled up their program with 20 clients, and basically never needed to run it again because that's all they wanted to fulfill.

What are average numbers though?

Most salespeople will sign up between 15 and 30 people on their first go-round, with about half coming from internal upgrades and half from cold traffic. I'm giving you these numbers so you don't get discouraged if you only sign up 12 from outside ads. You'll get better.

The experienced gym owners only run these every quarter or every six months, because the stick rate is so high. So ironically, the most experienced guys I work with have maybe only run it three or four times max, and they're the ones closing 50% of leads, because they've got the process down to a science.

Conclusions For Semi-Privates

Icing: 12 x $2,500 = $30,000 (but spread it over several months = about $10,000/month)

Cake: Grows to around 50 members at $550/month = $27,500/month

Total second level = $37,500/month in revenue once HTP program is at 40-person capacity

We're already clocking in a chill $55,000/month from our large group and $37,500 from our small group. That brings us to a whopping $92,500/month from the first four revenue streams (front- and back-end cash from tier #1 and tier #2).

Now we get to the third tier of the foundational Wedding Cake Model: supplements.

Chapter 25

Tier 3: Supplement Sales

I've worked harder at figuring out how to sell supplements than anything else in my business In fact, this section was so in-depth that I'll be writing my next book about it, *Supplement Selling Secrets*.

It's a process we run in every new facility that comes in with us. Within 14 to 21 days, we can add an average $1,000 in sales on recurring for every 7 EFTs. So if you have 100 EFTs, then you would be able to generate around $14,000 in sales on recurring within the next 14 to 21 days. It's stupid.

And yes, I am aware that my claims are insanely high. And if I were in your shoes, I wouldn't believe them. But we have helped literally hundreds of gyms to accomplish this using the systems in this book.

If it's so easy, why isn't everyone doing it?

A. Everyone *is* doing it as soon as they find out how to.
B. If they aren't, they don't know about it yet but will… soon.
C. If they have heard about it and haven't done it, it's because of some weird limiting beliefs around money that we won't get into.

Now, before you get yourself worked up, I'm not pitching some multilevel marketing scheme. And if you have issues that surround selling supplements, such as…

- Not believing in the products
- Not wanting it to detract from your membership sales
- Not thinking there is enough margin
- Not wanting to take money out of pocket for inventory
- Price matching with Amazon
- Not wanting people to think supplements are going to replace diet and exercise

…I suggest that you take my section overview regarding maximizing the customers' LTV to heart. I'm going to assume you are aligned with the concept of selling more services to clients who already want them and are going to buy them anyways. And I also assume you want to have money left over to serve your customers at the highest level possible.

My main point is they might as well buy supplements from you, because you can at least point them in the right direction and make sure they get good-quality stuff. You can also use this money to turn around and acquire more customers or reinvest it into providing even more amazing service.

Now, because the selling system is a work of art and because there is a lot more I want to get to before we wrap up our time together, I'm just going to do a brief overview about selling supplements in this book. (However, you can find the "do this, then do that" tactical outlook in my 90-minute video at SupplementSellingSecrets.com.)

Here's how you do supplements right.

First, you need to use a supplement company that does all of the following:

- Uses a drop-ship model so you have no inventory or up-front costs and never run out of flavors
- Provides 3-, 6-, and 12-month packages you can sell up front as high-ticket
- Provides 0% financing for these high-ticket $2,000 to $5,000 packages so clients only need to pay $200 to $400 per month, but you get paid immediately

(These add up INSANELY fast.)

- Has a solid autoship functionality so you can get recurring cash flow
- Uses sticky commissions so that if a client buys more or other stuff from that company, you still get paid for it
- Tracks data down to the sales rep level so your trainers can get recurring sub-commissions and are incentivized to keep the clients on recurring
- Advertises a price on the site 40% higher than what you are able to sell it at, so that you never get price-shopped, and it always looks like a smoking deal to order through you
- Offers premium price positioning so that you can capture the most margin
- Provides celebrity endorsements you can use like PhDs, Olympians, and professional athletes so you can use them to further reinforce this premium positioning

- Uses proprietary blends for common ingredients and lists precise amounts on the expensive ones, so you can highlight the fact that no other product has the same amounts of the expensive ingredients, which again reinforces the superiority of your product
- Only sells high-margin products, so you don't waste a consumer's budget on items with less of a margin, and you get paid more on average per customer
- Provides a beautiful retail selection without you having to put up money for 100+ bottles of product, so you can maximize the massive retail opportunity in your gym lobby
- Actually has the best product on the market, one that is formulated by PhD biochemists for Olympic teams, so you can sell with conviction rather than lying or feeling like you are tricking people
- Provides follow-up marketing for every customer to increase the average ticket by another 30%, so you can make even more without additional work
- Pays out on a bimonthly timetable, so you can pay payroll or commissions with the sales of the product and not have to wait 30 or 60 days like virtually every other dropship company

Since there wasn't a company that did all that stuff I wanted, I made my own and called it Prestige Labs. We put almost eight figures into it to get it off the ground, and we bought at economies of scale to maximize profit to the gym owner without sacrificing product quality. That was the biggest challenge. Having to buy more than 50,000 items was the key. In other words, we bought 50,000 of just one flavor of one product, another 50,000 of another flavor, etc.

These are things I could never have done as a gym owner, even with six locations. Nor would I have had the capital to contract PhDs to formulate the best product.

That's the advantage of the position we are in now: we can provide solutions we couldn't before.

But the point isn't to push our company. It's to show you how you can add another tier to your wedding cake.

So let's dive into how supplements fit into the cake and become a massive profit center for a gym business.

There are four primary ways we sell supplements to our customers.

- Existing client base launch: we run a commemorative internal campaign to your existing customer base; this works whether or not you currently sell supplements
- Bolt-on sale for new customers coming in the door
- As a part of internal plays on an ongoing basis
- Sampling sprees

The reason all this stuff works is that supplements represent the first of multiple "stacking" buying curves. Put differently, selling supplements is the first of the tiers that represents a new wallet of the customer we are dipping into. We've already gone into their "fitness classes" wallet; now it's time for them to open their "supplement" wallet. The more of their needs we can fulfill, the more wallets we can access, and ultimately the more money we can make from the same customer.

I said it earlier, but I wanted to make sure you didn't miss it: **The business owner who makes his prospect more valuable to his business than to that of his competition wins.** It is a more tactical take on the classic "He who can spend the most to acquire a customer will win." The answer to "But how?" is in the first quote: you make them more valuable. And you do that by encouraging them to spend more with high-ticket service AND by satisfying as many of that person's needs as possible.

I consider supplement selling one of the core offerings for every gym, because it's so easy to do that it's nonsense not to.

Supplement Sales Icing

Supplement sales icing is the front-end cash flow generated. The primary way we implement this is by selling to new customers.

The way we do this is by selling them as a part of the nutrition plan that we recommend in their front-end program.

Since these customers are new, they won't know any differently and will assume you have been offering supplements all along, even if you are new at it.

These sales are so easy, it's scary.

From a numbers standpoint, we will typically close more than 85% of new customers on a supplement package. That's an average. Some of our Gym Lords close nearly 100%. The percentage is so high because these are no longer prospects, they are *customers*. And customers are very different than prospects. They have already given you money and therefore intrinsically trust you more than a prospect would.

This is how these sales percentage numbers are so high. It's not a traditional sale; it's an *upsell*. There's a big difference. And on top of that, it is a prescriptive assumed close upsell, the most powerful kind of sale. That's what pharmaceutical companies have been using since the dawn of time: a person of authority *prescribes* pills and you go buy them. Price doesn't matter. You just do. We use the same process. That's why it's so scarily effective.

Furthermore, we do not sell these as part of the first visit. That never works well. You need to give people time to cool off after the first sale (the fitness service package).

The way we sell them is on the second meeting we have with them. This is the nutrition orientation, where we amaze them with a beautifully choreographed experience and then finish with an assumed close and prescription of the supplements they are going to need for the program they bought a few days earlier.

Icing (Front-End Cash) Money Math

You bring 30 customers a month into large group and 4 per month into high-ticket and sell 85% of them on a $200 supplement subscription. If you use the companies we recommend (Prestige Labs…*cough*) you should have between a 40% and 50% margin on that. Note: That's two to three times better than most people get at their gym. And the beauty is, there is no fulfillment. No sessions. No measurements. No counting reps. No attendance. Nothing. Just money for a few extra words.

But this means you will get **between $80 and $100 immediate profit** on average for every new customer who walks in your door. If that is ALL you sold, even if you didn't make money on your service, you'd be able to spend an additional $20/lead (assuming you sold to 20%–25% of them). For most of our guys, the supplement sales more than cover their ad spend, and everything else becomes gravy.

Note: There is also an entire process of selling $2,000–$5,000 supplement packages, which I mentioned earlier. I got the exact sales process from my friend Cris Cawley (former owner of Thinique weight-loss franchise) and her top sales rep. It is pure fire. So the numbers I'm giving you with average ticket does not include these high-ticket packages.

You won't believe me until you see the selling system in action. So for now, we'll just focus on the simple recurring subscription and the money math behind it.

Back to it.

So if you sold to 29 people per month (30 large-group people + 4 high-ticket people as new customers x 85% take rate) at $200/month, you would already have added nearly $70,000 year to your revenue.

34 x .85 = 29

29 x $200 x 12 months = $69,600

But that is only the beginning. The real magic happens with the stacking of the recurring sales.

Supplement Cakiness (Recurring)

Besides having the ability to sell high-ticket supplement packages up front, you must have recurring payouts.

At the time of this writing (December 2018), the average attrition or churn from Prestige Labs was 23%.

That means for every $200 subscription, you're actually making an $869 sale of lifetime value ($200 / .23).

So if you're selling 29 people an $869 product, you'll be making $25,201 per month from supplements.

The other way of looking at this equation is how it would actually show up in reality, by having more people buying each month until you achieved maximum capacity given inflow and outflow equilibrium (that is, you sign up as many as drop out).

Month 1

29 sign up/0 drop > 29 new subscribers

You sign up 29 people on subscription. Zero people drop off, because you didn't have anyone from the month before. So you are left with **29 subscribers**.

Month 2

29 sign up/7 drop > 29 new this month + 22 from last month's remaining subscribers

In the second month, you sign up another 29 people on subscription. You should expect about 7 people to drop off because you lost 23% of the initial 29 sign-ups. So you are left with 22 subscribers from the month before.

$$29 + 22 = \textbf{51 total subscribers}$$

Month 3

29 sign up/11 drop > 29 (new) + 22 (Month 2) + 18 (Month 1)

You sign up another 29 people on subscription. Then 11 people drop off, because you lost 23% of the last two months' 51 subscribers. So you are left with 40 subscribers from the first two months (22 + 18). Then you add in your 29 new subscribers for a total of **69 at the end of Month 3**.

Month 4

29 sign up/16 drop > 29 (new) + 22 (Month 3) + 18 (Month 2) + 13 (Month 1)

Hopefully, you can see how the math works out from an attrition standpoint.

But you would eventually even out, when the drop-off rate becomes equal to your sign-up rate. That is when you hit your hypothetical max. In the example, that's when 23% of your total number of subscribers is equal to the amount of people you signed up new each month. For us, that means 126 subscribers x 23% loss = 29. At 126, you should gain and lose at the same rate (29 customers), meaning your supplements recurring amount has stabilized.

And at $200/month, this gets us back to the $25,201/month in sales we calculated initially.

Note: This is the pie equation I showed earlier.

So this one little revenue stream stacks up to $25,201 per month in revenue, which equates to an **additional $120,000/year in profit** (when you factor in a 40% margin).

That's more than a lot of gyms make net total, and even more than some make in gross profit.

This is the final of the three tiers of the Wedding Cake Gym Profit Model. Now, I want to walk you through one final piece—the sprinkles.

(Your wedding cake might have roses—I like sprinkles.)

Chapter 26

Sprinkles: Internal Plays

An internal play is a marketing campaign you target to your existing customers. The play is typically some sort of added service or benefit beyond their current level of membership. The hardest part about making a successful internal play—that is, one that a lot of your existing clients sign up for—is a good HOOK.

A marketing hook is something NEW OR DIFFERENT that invokes curiosity or desire in the prospect or customer.

I use three types of internal play hooks.

- Nutrition-Based
- Fitness-Based
- Community/Experience

Nutrition-Based Hooks: These are the hardest and most in-depth to make and manage, but can typically be sold at the highest price. If I had to choose, this would be my favorite, because these hooks lend themselves so well to upselling other ancillary services. (I'll cover that in the next chapter.) Mind you, you WILL use all three. You have to, or things get stale.

Examples

- Lose Weight While Drinking Alcohol → Lose While You Booze/Slim Down For Santa
- Lose Weight While Eating Candy & Chocolate → Lean By Halloween
- Detox/Reboot/Cleanse → 21-Day Detox
- Eat All Your Food At Night (Intermittent Fasting) → Late-Night Weight Loss/Fourth Meal Challenge/Eat More To Lose More Challenge
- Keto → Eat Fat To Lose Fat Challenge
- High-Carb/Low-Fat → Eat Sugar & Look Sweet Challenge

Fitness-Based Hooks: These are typically based on a particular body part or area and are super easy to sell and execute on. Usually, the price point will be a little lower since they are less involved, and you are more or less teaching someone execution, form, and new movements. It's hard to make a life-changing difference in muscle within just six weeks, whereas with a nutrition-based challenge, you can make a much bigger difference.

Examples

- Big Booty Bootcamp
- Cellulite Dynamite
- 6-Week 6-Pack
- Stubborn Belly Fat Challenge
- Buns & Guns
- Sexy Back

Community/Experience Hooks: These are the easiest to fulfill but the hardest to demonstrate value with. You're creating teams and competition. That's the main value: creating external motivation for your clients. These also pair well with charitable causes and referral pushes. Stacking these with an event at the end or a party makes them more effective, in my experience. The charitable causes also make people take out their wallets and allow for hilarious ad copy. For example, for an internal play where you donate half the proceeds to Toys for Tots, you could jokingly say, "The only reason you wouldn't sign up for this is because you hate children."

Examples

- Bring-A-Friend Challenge
- Accountability Challenge
- Team Challenge*
- Spouse Challenge
- Battle Of The Sexes
- Coworker Challenge

*Allow the trainers to sell this and make their own teams.

Advanced Notes

You don't need to keep the internal play exclusive to one of these categories. You can combine things. If you are doing a stubborn belly-fat challenge, you should probably include a nutrition component. But the nutrition isn't the hook. You'll be showing them lots of ab exercises and they'll be eating a deficit. Nothing crazy.

Seasons can be a big boost here. If you can tie a challenge to an upcoming holiday, you get bonus points. It also answers the "why" question. Prospects often ask themselves, "But why are they doing this?" And having a holiday to wrap it around answers that question easily.

Holiday Examples

- Slim Down For Summer
- Lean By Halloween
- Turkey Tone-Up
- Slim Down For Santa
- Holidays Accountability Challenge
- Holiday Hangover Detox

Manufacturing events and deadlines are some of the most powerful tools to use in conjunction with an internal play. It's also a great way to stack value. An example would be holding a members-only event that is AWESOME…but only the people who take part in the internal play are invited. Photo shoots at the end are a great motivator for people to get in shape, and you can usually trade with a photographer in exchange for introducing them to a bunch of potential prospects if they like the photos. These work great for things like a Little Black Dress Challenge.

A lot of people will want to go to these events. FOMO (fear of missing out) is real. Use these opportunities to make more money while also giving people fun events to look forward to. If someone just bought tickets to an event you are holding in eight weeks, what do you think is the chance they will cancel their membership between now and then? Food for thought.

I really like to add silly prizes at the end and a little fake podium for the winners to stand on. This stuff matters. I also like to have them make their own jerseys and team banners to hang in the lobby to further increase FOMO. You can buy pinnies (vests) for nothing online. Buy some spray paint and let them go nuts. People really dig this stuff.

Make sure to post videos of people doing the extra workouts that are reserved exclusively for people who buy these internal plays. And, like any good social media post, it should show everyone having a great time as if life is perfect.

Ask clients to take "sweaty selfies" to post when they check in on social media and to tag your business to enhance your free marketing opportunities.

Also, always have a different price for visitors. Or make it free for a friend, or free for the member if they bring a friend. There are lots of cool things you can do. If you execute these well, you can get about a third of your total sign-ups from outside. FREE sign-ups—that is a good thing.

You can fulfill on these with extra sessions. I prefer to add these during off hours, primarily weekends. You don't need to add a lot here. A TON of our Gym Lords have success giving at-home workouts and just giving them a way to track clients like the sweaty selfies and other ways I mentioned. That means you are effectively getting money for $0 added overhead. Pretty sweet.

(I personally never did it this way, but this is one of the things our community has innovated and executed on. I always liked to do in-person sessions, for reasons I will outline in a moment.)

I could keep going with these, but this should give you a good start.

Why Do Internal Plays Affect The Whole Cake?

The reason internal plays are not a tier unto themselves is because they are really more of a traffic source.

They feed the rest of the tiers but aren't another distinct profit center. But when combined with the other ingredients, these plays only serve to make them stronger. The sprinkles make our cake that much more delicious!

Internal plays are some of the major secrets to our success.

A lack of these is usually the biggest gaping hole that I come across in gym businesses. I'm talking maybe 5% of gyms I know actually do this right.

The beauty of internal plays is that they take almost zero effort to fulfill, they're all profit, they increase member engagement by bringing in more outside prospects, AND they serve as a second funnel into your programs. Oh, and you could do this tomorrow, with zero prep.

That, in my mind, is a grand slam.

Monetization

There are numerous ways to monetize these internal plays. But here are three I will focus on:

- Increasing average large-group customer value (retention and blended EFT)
- Funnel into HTP (semi-privates)
- Conversion point for supplements

Do you recall the graphic with the three circles—Acquire, Ascend, Resell—from Chapter 2? Get more customers, increase average ticket, get them to buy more times. Internal plays satisfy all three.

Increasing Average Large-Group Customer Value (Retention & Blended EFT)

Most gyms will average between $3K and $10K every six weeks from internal plays. So let's just average it to about $4,500/month. Nothing to scoff at, and it's like a 90% margin.

Even though it's not the huge cash pop of an external play or challenge, it's still money, and it helps the business. And it will be the EASIEST MONEY you'll make aside from selling supplements.

Internal plays are simply stuff you market to your existing customers.

You learned about this earlier as a way to build connection and community. And guess what? They're also a great way to increase your profit.

Internal plays are upsells that allow people who want a temporary boost to satisfy their buying needs or get extra attention. This might occur when they put a higher priority on fitness, like before a vacation or a wedding.

For the less "economically advantaged" folks, this gives them a taste of the good life (HTP). For those with a bit more money, it serves as a way to try before they buy.

Either way, we serve more and we make more. Win-win.

So the numbers usually work like this…

Let's say you are an average gym and have 120 EFTs.

From those, typically about 25% take internal offers. (Our best gyms hit about 60% member engagement with internal plays.) It's also a good way to measure the amount of goodwill you have and the strength of your culture and community. A great barometer of gym health.

As an example, let's use the Big Booty Bootcamp.

Why is it called that? Because my 6-Week Deadlift and Squat Seminar really doesn't convert well with the primary audience—women. Marketing matters. You can be a purist or a realist. I choose the latter, and I suggest you do too.

We market these bootcamps by flooding our customers with hilarious emails, Facebook posts, posters, and SMS/text blasts during a 10-day countdown before the start date.

Each day, I'll have a trainer make some funny video (humor is key with these) and post it in the group, then push the email and the texts telling them to watch the video. That way, no one feels like you are annoying them—it's "advertainment." And it works…big-time.

Because you typically get 25% of 120 to take the offer, that would be 30 people in this example. (But we've seen gyms with 100+ clients signing up to take an internal play routinely. Sky is the limit.)

Price is typically between $150 and $199. These are low-ticket because there are no marketing costs. You already own these contacts, so you don't need to liquidate acquisition costs. So if you do the math, you pay $0 and you get 30 x $150 = $4,500 (aka free money).

Fulfillment: One "specialty" session per week for 60 minutes with a trainer in a 1-on-10 setting on Saturday or Sunday morning (whichever is easier for your staff).

This works out to 3 sessions x 6 weeks = 18 sessions of 10 people each.

So you just made $4,500 on an 18-session pack at $250 per session. This is the ICING. You actually made money in the acquisition of a potential HTP customer.

Pay your trainer $25, and you keep $225 for each session, meaning a 90% margin on the service.

Would you be happy with an extra $4,000 every six weeks and building a more engaged customer base?

Most of our Gym Lords are.

To satisfy the Growth Path #2: Increase average ticket component here's the math:

120 EFTs

$4,500 over 6 weeks = ~$3,000/mo

If you add $3,000/month to your revenue, that is an additional $25 per customer per month and virtually all profit. Easy peasy.

Feeding Internal Plays Into HTP

This is an important way to continuously maintain that great profit center of one-on-four semi-privates. You can also now see how the first monetization mechanism increased the average EFT of your large group. This allows you to feed into the second tier of cake and increase your semi-private customer base (ascension).

It's really simple. At the end of one of these internal plays, you'll be surprised how many people will love it and ask if they can continue. That's when you say, "Of course. And you can actually do three of these every week for almost the same price you just paid." (This equals their membership and the internal play cost.)

Off the back end though, you'll usually get about 25%–35% into HTP, which is about 8–10 people.

This inflow all but maintains the HTP program without needing a big external pop. And you don't need to have HTP set up to start doing these plays; it's just a bonus since a lot of people will want to continue. Plenty of gyms we worked with who weren't ready for HTP yet ran an internal play and ended up repeating the times and dates and just changing the hook or emphasis. The possibilities are endless.

The point is, there are a million and one ways to market to your existing customers. Just be sure to do it, to keep them engaged, to show that you care by making fun new things, and to take home some extra money in the meantime.

Conversion Point For Supplements

One of the primary advantages of internal plays is that they allow you to set yourself a paid-for sales consultation.

Essentially, someone will pay to start your program. You can then choose to overdeliver in value and meet with them individually to talk about how the program will help them with their goals. This is called a sales consultation.

Now, the key here is to DELIVER VALUE. You have to keep your first promise. So whatever hook you sold on the front end, this is where you outline and overview what is going to happen next. What's cool about this is it allows you or your staff to increase your engagement with current clientele and give them a little love.

And you are able to do this because you can make up the cost by selling supplements.

Imagine you are meeting with clients for a 30-day cleanse. Wouldn't it make sense to sell them a detox product or bundle in addition to the meal plan you will provide? Boom. Second monetization. And this one you can do even if you don't have HTP set up at your facility yet.

Hopefully, you are seeing the power of stacking revenue streams.

What was once a single play that you make $99 on could transform into this:

Take Rate by % / Cost $ / Category of Spending Vertical, Product, or Service / Added Ticket Value

> 100% / $99 / Large-Group Service / Cleanse Workouts and Meal Plan Program / **$99**
>
> 90% / $167 / Supplements / Cleanse Bundle / **$150** Added Ticket Value

25% / $550 / Semi Private Service / **$137** Added Ticket Value (just from Month 1)

Total Customer Average: $99 + $150 + $137 = $386

So if you signed up 30 people and you stacked these additional ancillary services, you would go from making 30 x $99 = $2,970 to 30 x $386 = **$11,580**. And I'm only including the first month of semi-private billing so as not to increase the number into the realm of non-believability.

Now that might be something to write home about.

Please believe me when I say you can make an insane amount of money with your gym, without working endless hours or opening more locations. You just need to treat it like a business.

Sprinkles: Internal Play Summary

- About 25% of your members should take an internal offer.
- Set the price point between $150 and $199.
- Run 90% margins on the play.
- Run every six weeks. The promo should be four to six weeks long
- If you have an HTP program, upsell 25%–35% into it on the back end.
- Fulfill these sessions on weekends during off hours.
- Sell ancillary services and products like supplements to maximize value.

Conclusion

Whew...you made it.

I'm sure you feel overwhelmed with information right now, but don't worry. The concepts in this book have taken me six years to flesh out, but they have been tested to work in my business, in other people's gyms, and in hundreds of different markets. Acquiring this information has cost me more than $500,000 in coaching and mentoring, and millions in trial and error (mostly error). Knowing that, you can move forward confident that these techniques will work.

My hope is that you see this as your giant shortcut to getting the gym you want and—as long as your intention is pure in helping others—the gym you deserve. I wish I'd had access to this information when I started out. It would have saved me a lot of time and money, as I hope it does for you. Selfishly, I've really enjoyed writing this book, because I feel like I am paying it forward to an industry that has treated me very well.

The infographics I included in each chapter will also help you quickly remember the information when you implement the steps outlined in this book.

Summary

Here is a quick recap of what you learned:

- The Broken Acquisition System
    - Client-Financed Acquisition
    - Irresistible Offers

- Lead Nurture
- Sales
- The Impossible Profit Model
  - Pricing Levers
  - Capacity Levers
  - Overhead Levers
  - Communicating the Change
- The Hole-In-The-Bucket Problem
  - Process
  - People
  - Product
- The Perfect Gym: Icing & Cake
  - Large Group
  - Small Group
  - Supplements
  - Internal Plays

In the beginning of this book, I promised you a good return on investment in exchange for your most valuable asset—your attention. I hope you feel that I have delivered on that promise. I also said I was aiming to gain your trust. Now, I know that reading a book doesn't mean you suddenly want to become best friends with the author, but I hope it served as a good introduction to us meeting one another.

If you are anything like me, you feel like you deserve an award for actually finishing something. So I hope you will allow me to give you a few bonuses.

Here are eight more FREE ways I can help you make more money with your gym.

IF YOU WANT FREE TRAINING...

If you'd like to learn about selling supplements and how we use them in any size fitness business to make its owner more money and get their clients better results with zero risk, you can register for free training here: SupplementSellingSecrets.com.

IF YOU WANT CASE STUDIES...

To download some extensive case studies on how we use the client-financed acquisition process to turn gyms around fast, click here: GymLaunchSecrets.com/quiz.

IF YOU LIKE TO ASK QUESTIONS & WATCH VIDEOS...

If you would like access to cool videos and our community of 10,000+ gym owners, join our Facebook group for FREE at AlexsGroup.com.

IF YOU LIKE PRETTIER VIDEOS...

You can check out our YouTube channel, which has more in-depth videos for binge consumption at AlexsYouTube.com.

IF YOU LIKE TO LISTEN TO PODCASTS...

Check out AlexsPodcast.com.

IF YOU WANT TO TALK TO A HUMAN BEING...

If you would like help implementing any of the steps you saw in this book, you can schedule a free call with someone on my team at IReadAlexsBook.com.

IF YOU WANT TO CHECK OUT OUR COMPANY AND OUR BLOG...

Just check out our ever-growing team and what we are all about at GymLaunch.com.

IF YOU JUST LIKE PRETTY PICTURES...

Go to the Appendix to see all the infographics together in one place.

I hope you enjoyed this book as much as I enjoyed putting it together for you. This was a labor of love in the truest sense.

And even though we don't know one another, if you are a gym owner, you are one of my people, and I hope the content of these pages serves you well.

Thanks for spending time with me. Talk to you soon.

Alex Hormozi
P.S. Gym owners rule.
P.P.S. #gymlords

BONUS: Obstacle Overcomes

You want more?? Cool. Well I've got some more. This was originally in the sales section, but my editor thought people would get lost. And besides, I like the idea of having an obstacle overcome bonus section. So that's exactly what this is.

In this section, I'm going to review specific objections you may encounter when you're closing with a potential customer. I have grouped them into the four primary types I mentioned in the sales portion of the book:

- Stalls/Delays
- Decision-Maker
- Price
- Fitness/Program-Related

That's literally it. If you internalize how to overcome these four primary objections, you will become very proficient at sales and give yourself a skill that will feed you for life.

Closes tend to work well when stacked together, meaning the more you can effortlessly go between them and use one after the other, the more effective they will be. Each one dents the prospect's apprehension, hesitation, and self-doubt. When used together, like a punching combination, they can be devastatingly effective.

So for the advanced closers out there, I stacked the ones that have worked best in combination (Jab–Jab–Uppercut–Hook). You should be able to hear them flow together in your mind.

Sales is a lot like tennis, in that the more times you can hit the ball back, the more likely you are to win. Having a few great shots can take you far, but so can having a lot of countermoves. You can wear out an opponent just as well as you can go for the overhead smash. There's a place for both, and your skill will be predicated on how well you know when to use which, when to push up to the net, and when to stay at the baseline.

I organized all the closes into groups, first by which obstacle they overcome, then into smaller subsets for which ones work best in combination with which others.

> **Pro Tip:** If you grab the audiobook, listening to these will help you out a lot. Tonality is so much of selling, but is often lost in text. And it's what separates the best sellers from those who are so-so, even if the words are identical.

> **Pro Tip:** ALWAYS AGREE with the prospect. Transition every close with "I agree" or "I totally understand." Then move to "Let me ask you a question…" or just ask them. Don't say "but" or "I disagree." That's a surefire way to put someone on the defensive. They need to conclude on their own that they should do this; otherwise they will feel pressured.

With that being said, let's rock and roll.

① ⧖ DELAY

You've probably come across some very common stalls and decision-delay tactics, including a prospective customer saying, "I need to think about it" or "I'll call you tomorrow with my card."

What do you say in response to that? I've tried and tested the following overcome sentences and phrases in over 100 sales. You only need a few that you feel comfortable with.

Now, what's important is understanding the argument that you are making. They all fundamentally say the same thing: "You should make the decision NOW." But each of these overcomes gives a different reason. Some help your customer understand important criteria for making decisions, others highlight the pros and cons of waiting, and some are simply exploratory to find out more information so you can figure out what they are unclear on.

People hate making decisions because they hate making mistakes. So your responsibility is to convince them that the REAL mistake is NOT making a decision. And that not making a decision is, in fact, a decision—one that leads to them staying unhealthy.

Here are some of my favorite responses to stalls and delays.

Prospect Excuse: "I left my wallet at home."

> No problem. Do you have your phone on you? Great. Just pull up your banking app, go to statements, and you can find the account number on the top right. I'll google the routing number while you do that.

(If you don't currently take automated clearing house [ACH] payments, you should. Besides the lower costs, fewer expirations and account changes, and decreased risk of chargebacks, you can always sign up a new client, even if they don't have their wallet. We used to save a ton of sales with this. Very useful.)

Prospect Excuse: [says anything but yes when you ask whether they are ready to start]

Ask, "What's your main concern?"

This gets a lot of the placeholders and fluff out of the way. It also prevents them from leaving with the "I need to think about it" excuse, because you're encouraging a discussion. It's probably my #1 most used overcome to move the sale forward. It doesn't close anything on its own, but it moves the conversation forward to something you CAN overcome.

Then I continue by saying, "Let's consider the options," and elaborating like this:

> If you walk out the door/hang up now, you'll be actively choosing to stay in the same place you were when you came in/called, which we know you don't want, because that's why you came in/called in the first place. And when people leave, they don't come back—it's hard enough even walking in the door. So let's make the decision now, while I'm here to answer your questions.
>
> Option 1: You decide not to go with us and think that you are going to use your 24 Hour Fitness pass. The thing is, we both know you won't do that, because you just told me that you haven't gone in a year. And when you do go, you don't get any results, because you don't want to hurt yourself, you don't push yourself, and you don't know many new exercises.
>
> Option 2: You hire a personal trainer to keep you motivated and accountable. But that costs between $600 and $1,000/month, and you would still only be getting maybe two or three workouts a week at $60

each. Most people don't have the cash for that. Do you? Me neither.

Option 3: You could do another diet-only intervention like Weight Watchers or Nutrisystem. But for the reasons I just mentioned, you know that Weight Watchers won't work in the long run, because you need to gain muscle to keep weight off so you can keep eating like a normal person and NOT gain weight. And you know that with Nutrisystem or any done-for-you program, you won't learn how to do it, so you'll eventually gain most or all of the weight back.

Last Option: You have all the accountability you said you needed. You get a nutrition plan that *teaches* you how to eat healthy instead of *telling* you, one that's flexible so you can do it for life. You get a personal trainer with you at each workout. You get a cookbook that helps you actually ENJOY eating healthy so you never go back, because you'll like it. You have a community of people just like you who are happy, normal people just trying to prioritize their weight loss and health. You have an online health hacks portal with a path to permanent body health and freedom.

Let us help you get the DREAM GOAL you came in here for. And if for some reason you don't like us and think we stink, we will happily give you your money back. Besides, you get to see ME every day, and that alone has to be worth it. Let us do what we do best and help you. Let's do this.

Rocking Chair Close

And let's be honest, when we say, "I'm going to think about it," we don't go home, sit in our rocking chairs, and stare at the wall, do we? I mean, you're not going to do that, are you? Of course not. You're going to leave here, then your mind is going to get filled with buying groceries and cooking dinner and doing laundry and picking the kids up and the millions of other things that fill up our lives.

And then, four days from now, maybe you'll catch a glimpse in the mirror or some pants won't fit you right, and the whole reason you came here to begin with will pop into your mind. But in that moment, you'll just think, "Oh well, I'm too busy to do that right now anyways." And that will be it. In those two seconds, you will have made the decision.

So I'd rather we just take the decision here for what it is—whether you're going to actively do something about what you came in here for or not. And can I tell you a secret? It seems like no one has time for anything, but that's a faulty mindset. We MAKE time for the things we desire most. And you said earlier you were really motivated to do something about this, right? Well this is where we find out whether or not you meant it. Do you want to let us do what we do best and help you get the body you've been wanting all these years?

The honest truth is that decisions don't take time, they take information, because thinking is instantaneous. So we can confront it together and save you time in the future. There are only three reasons people don't do this: they don't like the program, the person, or the price. Which of the three is the main issue? What's your biggest fear about signing up?

The only time I don't buy something is when I am afraid of making a mistake. Are you like that too? So I like to think to myself, what's the best case and worst case of what can happen? What's the worst thing that could happen if you do this? Let's just confront it—you invest $600 and we run off with your money, right? The thing is, I don't think that is really the worst-case scenario, because if you get the level of service I'm promising you, don't you think you'll lose weight?

The other scenario is that you don't get the level of service I am promising you, and then we'll just give you your money back. So the real best case is that we totally change your life forever like all the people in the gym right now and on the wall behind me, and the worst case is that you get six weeks with my team to help you and if we don't, you get your money back. So there's no risk, but you have the opportunity to get exactly what you want. But if you walk out the door you are guaranteed NOT to get what you walked in for.

Prospect Excuse: "I don't make fast decisions."/"I need to sleep on it."

I totally agree, and saying yes now would never be considered a fast decision because you've needed this for years. Doing it now is reasonable (you even came in because now is the right time, despite thinking about it for years). So if anything, signing up now is the most logical decision you can make given your years of wanting this.

OR

I totally understand, but you have been making this decision for the last three years, which is why you have tried X, Y, Z. You have already made the decision that you want to lose weight—all we're doing now is exploring the way you're going to do it. And now we know the reason you failed in the past, because of the lack of fitness, nutrition, or accountability. But now we have all three of those problems covered and an awesome opportunity for you that is going to go away. So let's do it.

Prospect Excuse: "I'm probably gonna be too busy."

There's never gonna be a good time. You're always going to be busy. Now it's XYZ, next month it'll be Halloween, then after that it'll be Thanksgiving, then Christmas, then it'll be a birthday, then your friend's birthday, then you realize you're getting doughnuts because it's a Tuesday. There will always be something.

But here's the question: is looking the way you want to look more important than cake? If you're going to get into the shape you always wanted, you're going to have to realize that life will never make it convenient—that's why so few people are where they want to be. It's about whether or not you actually want to solve what you walked in to solve. Because I can tell you, if you want to make it a lifestyle, the BEST time to figure it out is when you're busy, because if you figure it out when you're busy, then when life gets easy, it'll be a breeze. But if you're always wishing for life to be not busy, then the moment it gets busy again, you'll fall off. So we gotta figure this out now, so we can get this problem solved for good.

The truth is that either way, you're making a decision. You'll either decide to continue with what you have or to get what you deserve. The question is whether you're going to reward yourself with something you need and want or continue with something you don't want, don't need, and no longer solves your problems.

Prospect Excuse: "I have my kids and soccer practice, so it will be hard."

Totally understand, and that's why we have a group of moms here who are dedicated to helping one another out. In fact, Jessica is a single mom with four kids and works an extra shift to afford coming here, but she says, "If I don't take care of myself, I can't take care of them. I don't have the energy or the stamina."

So right now, if you're exhausted and spread thin, it's not because you have too much to do, but because we need to increase your capacity to do things. That's why people start exercising and eating right, because their family situation isn't going to change anytime soon. So expecting that to change is silly. We need to make this work with the schedule you've got, not the one you'd like, because that ain't never gonna come.

On a scale from 1 to 10—1 being you want to go home, eat cake and ice cream forever, get diabetes, die 15 years earlier, pass on bad habits to your kids…

and 10 being you want to totally transform your life, live forever, and become super mom and take action today—where are you? Awesome.

Why is it a 7 instead of a 2? Why isn't it a 10 with all those reasons you just told me?

The discussion might continue like this…

Prospect: "Well, I have my kids, and I can't make this a high priority without them suffering."

You: "What if doing this one thing will help you be better at all those other things, so you could be the best wife, mother, friend, and daughter. Wouldn't that make this a 10?"

Prospect: "Yes, I suppose so."

You: "Well, if this is a 10, that means it's a priority, so let's do it."

Prospect Excuse: "I need time to think about it."

Not a problem. Do you need two or three days or two or three months to think about it? (*They will of course look at you weird when you say two to three months.*) The reason I ask that is because it doesn't really matter how long you have—either way, you're just going to have to confront the decision and answer three questions. Can I tell you what they are?

After each question, ask, "Yes or no?" and wait for their response.

1. Do you think this program is going to help you lose weight?

2. Do you have $X in your bank account or available on a credit card right now or access to someone who does, or are you going to get paid within the next 30 days?
3. Am I the person and is this the business you would like supporting you throughout this process?

> Awesome. Then we have the answers we need. Let's do it.

The reason this works so well is that people are afraid of making mistakes and don't know how to make decisions, so you're just leading them through the decision-making process. Don't underestimate how a little guidance goes a long way to help people make decisions.

> You're not going to stay like this forever, right? You're going to sign up to do something about this sooner or later, right? So you might as well do it sooner and start enjoying the results now, because it will never be a perfect time.
>
> OR
>
> Totally understand. If this program were absolutely perfect and you knew when you signed up that in six weeks you would be walking around in your dream body, would you sign up for it? Cool. So then what is this program missing that makes it not perfect? Is it the program, is it the price, is it me, is it the gym? Which is it?
>
> Asking prospects to think of valid reasons is typically a great move, since most people don't know what to look for, which means they're probably just afraid of making the decision to help themselves. And if they

do name something as the problem, then you can specifically address that obstacle.

OR

Totally understand. So give me an estimate, on a scale from 1 to 10, if 1 meant "No way in hell, Alex. You suck and your gym sucks and I hate you," and 10 being "Yes, I am totally in. I am putting money down and signing up right now." Where are you? (*Response doesn't matter.*) Great, so what would it take you to get from a 6 to a 10?

Then they will tell you, and all you have to do is address that one thing.

The only people who fail the program are ones who had to think about it, because they weren't committed enough in the beginning to make a decision.

This is actually a preset. During the explanation, before you begin, you can throw this line down—especially in group pitches, this works insanely well…

We have one rule about people who do this program: they must make a decision same-day. And the only reason we have that is because we did it in the past without that, and what happens is that the people who delay the decision tend to be more wishy-washy—they say they want something, but they don't really, so they sign up, but then they fall off.

And after having enough people "think about it" then come back, then fall off, we now know that those are the people who aren't successful. But when people come in and sign up straight off the bat, they do really well. So now, we simply ask people to make the decision—for their own good and for our own good—so we don't have members who have one foot out the door.

The only people who fail the program are ones who had to think about it because they weren't committed enough in the beginning to make a decision.

OR

Totally understand. We actually don't allow people to come into this program after seeing it only once. We used to do that, but after we got better at tracking our metrics, we realized that 78% of our failures were people who were unsure upon signing up. Since we've enforced this policy, those success percentages have gone up tremendously. Now when people sign up, we know—and they know—that they're ready to go and stack the chips in their favor.

OR (What If)

I totally understand your apprehension. One thing a lot of people are afraid of is that if they sign up, they're going to actually lose weight and do all the things necessary for that change. And sometimes coming to grips with that is hard.

All I can tell you is that after responding to an ad, making time in your schedule, and coming in today, to fall off when you are so close would be such a setback for your goals. I sometimes think, "What if I had decided not to start on the program that changed my life? Where would I be right now?"

If you leave now, it may be a long time before you hit another point where your health becomes a priority again. And you're going to make a decision either way—one way will get you a lot further from your goal, and the other will take you toward it. Why not take the one that makes a positive difference in your life?

OR (Unicorn Close)

You need to think about it. I totally understand. So if you're going to do another program, what would it have that we're missing? Like, what kind of unicorn program are you looking for? Because you're gonna need all these things:

- A personalized meal plan
- A personal grocery list
- A personal eating-out guide
- Recipes specifically matched to your meal plan
- A super shake guide
- Bomb-ass breakfasts
- Lick-your-fingers lunches
- Delectable dinners
- Workouts with a trainer up to three times a week
- Your own personal accountability coach

So what is this program missing? I just gotta know. If you don't have any reason not to do this program and it has everything you need to reach your goals, the only thing getting in the way is YOU.

So let's do this and take that first step. Otherwise, it'll always be something you struggle with, something where you knock on the door then run away, then knock again, then run away. But we're standing here with our arms wide open, ready to help.

Okay, so there you have a whole bunch of responses for delay tactics. The next set of responses is for folks who say they need to talk to someone else before they can make a decision.

② DECISION - MAKER

Prospect Excuse: "I need to talk to my husband," or "I never make decisions alone."

There are really only three main ways to go about this one:

1. Explain that their spouse would surely say yes and approve of the decision. This relies on past agreements. So we are trying to bring up things that their spouse already approved of to make the argument that this is just like those, and to close the gap with the assumption that they would approve of this as well.
2. Get around them making the decision and ask what the spouse would object to. This diverts focus back to a different obstacle that you can overcome.
3. Remind them that they are their own person and should make the decision for themselves.

Now, this is my LEAST favorite obstacle because someone is saying they are not in control of their circumstances, which I hate. It's also nearly impossible to overcome, if someone says they can't make a buying decision. That being said, I will stack each one of these closes together seamlessly. They flow smoothly, and even if you forget a few, it's still a hammer. Check it out.

I like to start with the following agreements:

> Does your husband know you're here right now?
>
> Does he know that you're not happy with how you look?
>
> Does he want you to be healthy and feel better?
>
> Then is there any reason he'd say no to this, given the fact that he already knows you're here, that you're unhappy with how you look, and he supports you in getting healthy?

If that doesn't work, I stack on the following obstacle overcomes.

Response Stack #1: What if your spouse says no?

Response 1: "I'd do it anyways."

> Awesome. Then let me get your ID so I can save you a spot.

Response 2: "Then I wouldn't do it."

> Totally makes sense. What is it that you think your spouse wouldn't approve of? What do you think their main concern would be? The price? The program? Or me? (ha ha).

At that point, you pivot to overcome whatever new obstacle they have.

Response Stack #2: Does your spouse approve of your current situation?

> Does your spouse approve of your current situation? Do they think you're happy with your weight? Do they know you're not happy about it? Okay, so if they know you're NOT happy about it, then they DON'T approve of your current situation. So then why would they be against you improving your circumstances?
>
> I'll tell you what. Let's get your spot saved so you don't miss out, and if you go home and tell your spouse you've done something to fix a situation they already don't approve of and they say, "No, honey, I want you to be a bad example to our kids, have less drive, less energy, feel less confident about yourself, and live 10 years less," then I'll be happy to refund your deposit.

OR

> Well, quick question for you—is this something you really want to do? Because if not, the last thing I want to do is convince you to get healthy if you would prefer not to be. Okay cool, so you DO want to do this? Great. Well, I know that my spouse would never tell me no for something I really want, just like I wouldn't tell her no for something she really wants, because I know she deserves it. In the end, if I need to cut spending from somewhere else, then I will. But we always make it work in the end.

You could also tack on, "It's better to ask for forgiveness than permission. And sometimes that makes more sense when it's regarding our health."

Delayed Payment Close

Okay, so worst-case scenario, if I could reserve your spot without you putting money down, would you still want it? Yes. Okay cool. Let me get your ID. Great, let me swap you for the card you want to use. I'm just gonna reserve a spot for you and delay your deposit date to the day it starts. That way, if between now and then your spouse says they want you to stay unhealthy forever and not get the help you need, I can tear this up. Then I'll give your spouse a call about how much they should support you. (*I say this jokingly.*)

I've covered delay tactics and decision-maker objections so far. Now let's go over objections about the price of the program.

③ $ PRICE / VALUE

Prospect Excuse: "I can't afford it," "I don't have the money," "It's not in my budget."

I want you to really let this sink in: people DIE from bad habits. They don't get to see their grandkids, they miss out on years of life. They walk around in a sullen fog, unconfident and waiting for the other shoe to drop. What people with this objection fundamentally don't understand is the value of transforming their lives and bodies.

If you were to offer them a $500,000 house for $2,000, they would surely find a way to get that money. People will ALWAYS find a way to get money if they see sufficient value. What you need to help them realize is that the life they want and the satisfaction they crave will be even more pronounced from a transformation of lifestyle than from a $500,000 house.

This is a question of priorities and values. If you can break their beliefs here, you can see massive transformations. These are probably my favorite ones to overcome (if you can have a favorite obstacle).

Best Case/Worst Case

Yes, it totally IS a lot of money. But whenever I'm afraid to spend a good deal of money, I always think, "What's the best case/worst case?" So best-case scenario, you start the program and in 6 weeks you lose 26 pounds and you get 100% of your money as credit toward staying on with us. Would you be happy about that?

Okay cool. So that's best case, and if that happens, you're good.

Even if you're not using that irresistible offer, you can still say, "If you get your dream goal, you would be happy, right?"

Now let's cover the worst case. What's the worst that could happen? We take all your money and send it to Algeria to put toward work in diamond mines and you lose no weight. The thing is, that's not the real worst-case scenario. The worst case would be if we

> don't deliver the quality of service I'm promising you. But in that case, I'll personally write you a check for what you paid. Why do I do that? Because out of the thousands of people who have gone through this program, only two have taken me up on my refund offer. So I can give you a 100% service guarantee that you will get service far in excess of what you are paying. And if on the last day, you think we sucked, I'll give that money all back to you.

This is 100% true. I have given a personal service guarantee on everything I've sold at my gyms and, out of the five years I ran these offers, I only had two people take me up on it. (Phrasing it as "I'll write you a check" really tends to hit home.) And they were people I shouldn't have sold on the front end in the first place. As a business owner, you don't need to be afraid of guarantees unless you're not providing good service. I promise you'll make a LOT more money by offering this guarantee than not doing it. It also positions you as kind of a badass.

Alternate Best Case/Worst Case

> I totally understand, it IS a lot of money. But the good news is that you remind me of Rosie who came in a few months ago. She said the same thing, and she ended up doing it. You know why? Because I told her, "If you care this much about the money, then I KNOW you're going to be successful, because it means so much to you. We put our money where our mouth is. And in this case, you shouldn't put your money in your mouth. So what's the worst that could happen?

Prospect: "I lose $600."

> Right, so $600 means a lot to you? I don't think you would pay for it and not get results, because I think you would be really dedicated to the program if you put that much down. So the real worst-case scenario is that you walk out the door right now and get no results.

You can tack this on next…

> Well, you've got two options. They're both risk-free, but only one of them will get you the body you want. The other one is guaranteed to leave you exactly as you came in…or potentially heavier. So which door would you prefer: the one with no risk where you get the body you want, or the one with no risk where you're guaranteed NOT to get the body you want?

> **Expensive Clothing**
>
> What's the most expensive piece of clothing, accessory, or shoe that you bought in the last three years (not including your wedding dress)? Thousand-dollar heels. Got it. And how long have you had these heels? Two years. Okay. How many times have you worn them? About 4 times a year, so 8 times total. And for how many hours? Four hours each time? Okay, great. So you spent $1,000 to wear those heels 8 times, for a total of 32 hours. So you spent $33 per hour to wear those shoes. Right? So if you spend $2,500 on this program, how many times are you going to walk out wearing your body?

Ruh-roh. Truth bombs, here they come. So we're talking about $2,500 and you're going to spend 24 hours a day—not just when you're out, but also with your husband, with your kids, with your friends, in every picture for the rest of your life. And every piece of clothing you wear will be affected by the body you're carrying around. Isn't that worth it? Don't you think it would be a much better investment to have your dream body?

Identity Swap

I totally understand. I had a woman just like you, same [*job, number of kids, life challenges*]. She came to the same conclusion, which was that she didn't have the money to do the program. So I told her a story about two girls at a makeup store and how it changed my life forever. Mind if I share it with you?

Cool, so we tend to vote with our dollars about the things we care about, right? Because we can SAY we care about X, Y, and Z, but what REALLY matters at the end of the day is where we spend our money. The things we really care about, we spend our dollars on. So if we want to change the things we care about, we have to change the way we vote with our dollars.

So this story really breaks down the same perception shift that this other person went through, which you'll also have to go through at some point in order to actually achieve these health goals that your soul craves.

This 14-year-old girl went to Sephora or Mac or one of the makeup stores with one of her friends.

The makeup lady said, "You need one of these pencils...one of these lipsticks...some mascara..." Basically a makeup starter kit. She was like, "Okay, I want you to understand that moving forward, you are a grown-up now, so you'll need to start budgeting for things like this, because this is something you're going to start spending money on regularly now, okay?"

And I thought that was SO interesting because that expenditure got the girl super excited, like "Yes—I'm ALL-IN," because it marked the transition from being a girl to accepting her new identity as a woman. And with that new identity came new priorities.

And so right now what we're talking about is you going from a woman who's unsatisfied with how she looks, whose day-to-day habits got her where she is right now...to a woman who IS satisfied with how she looks and feels and one who has better habits, right? You wanna have that fit identity, and part of that new identity comes with new priorities for where you spend your money.

And if you really break it down, we're only talking about $8 per day. On top of that, here's the thing most women don't see but eventually discover after committing to the challenge: with that new identity comes new savings. You're not going to go out to drink as much, you're not going to spend as much money on junk food or on doctor's visits. A lot of other things come with this new identity that will save you money.

What we need to do for you is bring these new priorities along with you so that we can solidify that identity shift...so that you CAN get what you're looking for and you're not just "trying to lose weight" but you're actually becoming that new identity, that fitter, better woman. Because THAT woman spends money on health, on supplements, on coaching so she can become the best version of herself.

The great news is you only have to budget for this once, and if you really want to become that new person, then at some point you're going to have to vote YES. So you might as well do it now. Let's get started.

Gonna Spend It Anyways

Over the next three months, you're going to spend this money anyways. So the question is, do you want to spend it on a few dinners out that won't make you healthier, a shirt that you'll put in your closet and forget about, or nails that will chip off two weeks later? Or do you want to invest it in yourself to make a change that will make every night out better, every piece of clothing you have fit better, and make you look so good that no one will even see your nails or your hairstyle because of the glow from your new amazing body and your renewed energy and confidence?

Have You Ever Bought Something You Couldn't Afford?

Totally understand. It IS a lot. So let me ask you a question: have you ever bought something you couldn't afford?

If they respond yes…

> So I assume you didn't go homeless or run out of food to eat, right? (Although, for a weight-loss diet, if you run out of money for food, that would actually help you hit your goal faster.) But you get what I'm saying—we often worry, but we make it work in the end.
>
> You're here, right? Let's just space it out with your paydays and do this. I even have a single mom who drives Uber one day on the weekends to afford this. It's just a question of priorities. Is this important to you? Great. Then let's make it work.

If they respond no…

> Then for how hard you work, you deserve to invest in yourself. And this is something you need. At the end of the day, if you could have done it without assistance, you would have already done it 10 years ago.
>
> **Delayed Payment Close**
>
> If you can't afford the entire thing today, it's not a problem. In fact, 95% of our clients break it up into payments. Actually, did you see Becky walk out the door before you came in? No? Oh, well I swear you guys could be life twins. She is the same age, has a son, and she's a nurse too. And she wanted to do the program but wasn't able to pay it all today, so what we did for her was split it up. When do you get paid? Every other Friday? Great, that's how Becky was too. What we did with her was do half today

and half on her next payday, next Friday. Does that work for you?

If This Means A Lot To You, I Know You Will Succeed

It totally is expensive. And believe it or not, this being out of your budget makes you like 95% of the people who do this program. The reason we have the success rates we do is that it's such a big investment. People take it seriously. So do you have any doubt that if you followed the meal plan, worked out with a trainer, and had an accountability coach that you wouldn't succeed? Of course not—the money is there to hold you accountable. If this were $10, you wouldn't care about it, just like the other things you have done in the past. This is an investment, and that's why I can look you in the eyes and tell you that you ARE going to succeed.

Cheap Comparison Close: "I could go to LA Fitness for $29."

If all else were equal, and you had six weeks of gym access or you could do our six-week program, which one would you do? 6-Week Challenge. Great. Why? (*Keep asking why to get multiple reasons so they convince themselves.*) Now you see why our program costs more, because you're actually going to see results.

You'll Pay Either Way

I agree it's a significant amount of money, but you will pay either way. You wouldn't be here if you had made this investment earlier, and the amount of money and time it will take will only increase if you keep delaying. So let's get this done.

Two Choices: Cheap Or What You Need

At the end of the day, you have two choices: you can get yet another thing that doesn't hurt to buy because you and I both know it won't do anything, or you can invest in yourself and solve this problem for good. If you look at the value of your time and what being in amazing shape for every picture, event, summer with the kids, and other events in your life, don't you think this would be worth it?

Don't Let Past Mistakes Burn You Twice

I totally understand that you spent a lot of money on this XYZ program in the past and it didn't work for you, but the worst thing you can let happen is for that experience to burn you twice. Because not only did it not work for you then, but now you're allowing that one bad experience to prevent you from ever getting what you want, and you already said you need this. It would be like swearing off dating in junior high because you had one bad date. That would be ridiculous, so don't let that sort of logic get in the way of getting what you need.

It's Expensive Because Of The Amount Of Time It Will Save You

It totally is a lot of money, but that's because of the amount of time it will save you. How long have you been wanting this? As long as you can remember, right? If 10 years ago, you could have made a decision that would have made the last 10 years of your life the fittest and best, would that be worth what we're asking? Of course, right? So then let's do Future You a favor and have her look back on these next 10 years really excited about having made the decision that changed it for good.

OR

It totally is a lot of money. But it costs that much because of the amount of time it will save you. For the past 10 years, how much have you spent on fitness? And you aren't any further than when you started. The reason those were cheap is because they weren't going to get you to where you need to go. But this program will, and that's why it costs more. It's the investment that will solve this for good.

You can tack this last stack on to push someone over the edge when they are teetering.

How Much Would It Be Worth If All This Did Was...

At the end of the day, if all this did was get you back into your smallest clothes, would it be worth it? I mean, how many clothes do you have right now that you'd like to wear but can't because they don't fit like you want them to? Well, how much would it be if you add them all together? Well, unless we do that, it would be like throwing all that money away. So you might as well pay this small amount today and get all that money back out of the trash.

The alternative would be potentially even having to throw away the stuff you are wearing now on top of the stuff you've already had to toss out. The cost will only go up with time, but we can reverse all that right now. Seriously, if we could get you back into those clothes, would that be worth it? Awesome—let's get you started.

For Men Who Say "I Can't Afford It"

Really?? I wouldn't have taken you as someone who'd be financially stressed about this. Can you not afford it, or is it something else?

This works SUPER well with guys, because they don't want to admit that they don't have money. So they will then mention a different obstacle, which you can overcome.

Phew. Are you still with me? Good. So we've covered responses for delays, decision-makers, and price. Now let's get into fitness-specific objections.

④ FITNESS SPECIFIC OBSTACLES

These are usually questions or complaints, not obstacles. Things like "I have a bad back" or "I don't like waking up early" or "I hate broccoli. Do I have to eat broccoli?" You just want to have answers prepared so your conversation seems fluid and natural.

Script for Workout-Related Concerns

Before every session, we ask that you let our trainers know of any pains or issues you are having so they can give you modifications for your session. They will also recommend some stretches for you to do to hopefully improve the issue. These injuries should be one of the main reasons you sign up for a facility with a trainer, because you want to be with a professional when you're learning something new, especially if you have an injury. We've found that a lot of these nagging injuries come from strength imbalances or lack of strength in the musculature around the joint, which puts more stress on it. So when we strengthen the muscle, many times the joint stabilizes and the pain goes away.

Note: This also works with the "I'm too old" or "I have a previous injury" arguments.

"What if I get hurt?"

It is very unlikely that you will get hurt. And the probability is much lower than if you were to work out unsupervised on your own. That being said, if you were to somehow get injured, we would work around it, so you wouldn't skip a beat.

"What if I don't like the workouts?"

Well, I can tell you it is not going to be Zumba or running on the beach with the wind in your hair, but it is going to be EXACTLY what your body needs in order to look the way you want it to look. And I can tell you that people like the workouts. Otherwise, we wouldn't have a business, because no one would come back. So I wouldn't worry too much about it.

"What if I get bored?"

We vary the workouts constantly. And typically, boredom comes from lack of progression. If you are getting better, faster, and stronger every time you come to the gym, do you think that would bore you or motivate you? Most people get bored because they just don't know how to progress. Progress is how workouts get addictive, and that's what this is all about.

"Can I try a workout first?"

We actually don't let people who come in for the program you are signing up for do workouts first. The main reason is, it doesn't matter. You're going to do some cardio to burn maximal calories, and you're going to do some resistance training to tone your muscle and rebuild your metabolism. But at the end of the day, you already know that's what you gotta do. It's not gonna be Zumba. You're gonna sweat. You're gonna get sore. But you're also gonna get what you walked in here for—the number on the scale we talked about and your dream body.

"What if I get too sore?"

We actually have protocols to deal with this exact situation. So when you come in for your nutrition orientation, we will talk about this in depth. If anything, it's one of the reasons people do this program over others.

Note: This also works for the "I don't want to get bulky" argument.

Start-Date Concerns

"I can't start until next week."

No problem. We have a new group starting that date, so you'll be just in time.

Note: This also works for the "I'm busy until next Friday" argument.

"Can't I start right now?"

You can absolutely start now, but after having seen this literally hundreds of times, I can tell you the best thing to do is give yourself a week of mental preparation. This is going to be much harder emotionally than it will be physically. So we have found it works best if you relax for a week. Get those last cravings out of your system. Realize that they're only food, and then come in next week so you can start with the group all together, ready to rock.

"What if I move away during the program?"

Then we will happily refund you half your money.

"What if I fall off?"

That's what we're here for—to make sure you don't.

"What if I no-show?"

That's why you pay us for accountability. If we had a gym model like LA Fitness, which only works on the assumption that 90% of people won't show up, we wouldn't offer accountability. But lucky for your body (and our souls), we actually care, so we'll follow up with you until you tell us to go screw ourselves… then a few more times after that. So don't worry about it. We got you.

"What certifications do you have?"

Which ones were you looking for? (*They never know.*) Well, I'll tell you what. The reason I ask is because most people don't know this, but the entire industry is a farce. A certification is just $500 and a weekend. So instead, we have our own in-house certification that we put our trainers through to make sure they coach at the highest levels. We also require that our trainers coach over a thousand sessions before getting the title Master Trainer. And all of our staff but one are Master Trainers. So you have nothing to worry about.

Concerns About Specific Conditions

"I'm currently breastfeeding. Is losing weight okay?"

It is okay and natural. That being said, you should not have a specific weight-loss goal in mind if you are going through this right now. We don't want you to cut calories too drastically and decrease your milk production, so we're going to focus more on the training side and building up your muscle tone and metabolism, and the weight will come off more naturally. The last thing we want to do is have you lose milk. I'd also recommend you add in oats as one of your primary carb sources, since it tends to help with lactation.

"I have low thyroid."

When was the last time you got it tested? And what were your numbers? What medication are you taking? The good news is, this works very well with people who have slower metabolisms and low thyroid. Nothing can cure that, but we have lots of people who have been able to stop their medications entirely as a result of diet and exercise.

Caution: Be careful about saying anything related to curing or treating disease. The goal here is simply to make them feel okay about signing up.

This also works with the "I have a slow metabolism" argument.

"I have XYZ condition."

I'm so sorry—that must be a big burden. The good news is that eating nutritious food and moving your body will be approved by any physician you talk to. (And if they don't, then run the other way.) So I wouldn't worry about that too much. Just let the trainer know if you have any issues, and we can always make modifications for you. Regardless, if you're trying to get healthy and lose weight, then eating better and moving is going to be the way to get there.

Concerns About Modifications

"The goal seems unattainable/unrealistic."

Most things do seem unrealistic until you have context. If you worked at a facility that had 10–15 people a week weighing out and hitting XYZ goal, do you think you would still say it's unrealistic? Of course not. And besides, we don't make our money from the program—we make our money off memberships. The investment is only there to motivate you and hold you accountable. Believe it or not, we actually offered this program in the past without a deposit and we had over 100 people signed up for it, and guess what happened? No one finished, because they had no skin in the game.

So like I said, if we could just sign people up straight as members we would, but this seems to be the best first step to get people results fast and get them the momentum they need to change their lives. Just check out the wall behind me.

"Can I drink alcohol?"

No, but you can do as many drugs as you want (joke). Unfortunately, what got you here isn't going to get you to your end goal. But later we will provide you with an ongoing diet that will allow a far more expansive food list. The list of acceptable foods for now is meant to simplify this process for you in the beginning. We eliminate before we moderate, because in our experience there aren't a lot of people who can have "just one," so we don't like to tempt fate.

"Are there cheat days?"

After the six weeks is over, absolutely. But we like to eliminate before we moderate, and oftentimes these cheat days give you more cravings instead of fewer. We do sometimes use strategic re-feeds, but that is on a case-by-case basis. That's one of the advantages of coming to a facility that specializes in this sort of thing—we can make adjustments as needed in real time, so you never need to worry about getting stuck, which is where most people fail. We do this all day, so breaking through plateaus is just a part of what we do here.

"This diet seems really restrictive."

Well, if it were all-inclusive, it wouldn't really be a change. My dad always used to say, "You gotta change to change," and this is no exception. But you already knew that. Don't worry—people with less motivation than you have come in with less confidence and smashed their goal. You'll be fine.

That's it. Think you have enough responses to handle anything that comes your way?
Me too.

Appendix

PROBLEM #2: THE "SELL YOUR SOUL" PROBLEM

LOW BARRIER OFFER
(21 DAYS FOR $21)

SOFTWARE	-$199	
FACEBOOK ADS	-$1000	MONEY IN VS MONEY OUT
LEADS	$100	(+) (-)
COST PER LEAD	$10/LEAD	
% OF LEADS CLOSED	30%	
NUMBER OF 21 LBO SALES	30	
PRICE	$21	
REVENUE	+$630	
COMMISSION ???	$21 × 30 = -$630	
NET	-$1199	

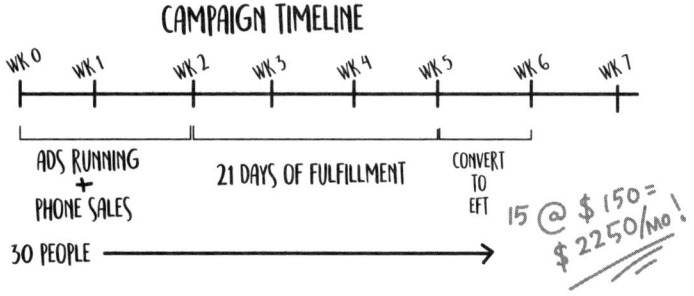

CAMPAIGN TIMELINE

WK 0 — WK 1 — WK 2 — WK 3 — WK 4 — WK 5 — WK 6 — WK 7

- ADS RUNNING + PHONE SALES (WK 0–WK 2)
- 21 DAYS OF FULFILLMENT (WK 2–WK 5)
- CONVERT TO EFT (WK 5–WK 6)

15 @ $150 = $2250/MO!

30 PEOPLE ⟶

BUT WAIT... DURING THOSE 6 WEEKS YOU ALSO LOST THE INDUSTRY AVERAGE OF 10% PER MO WHICH MEANS IF YOU HAD 100 EFTS TO START... YOU LOST 15 DURING 1.5 MONTHS BRINGING YOUR NET GROWTH TO <u>ZERO</u> AND COSTING YOU $1199 TO STAY THERE.

THE ONLY 3 WAYS TO GROW YOUR BUSINESS

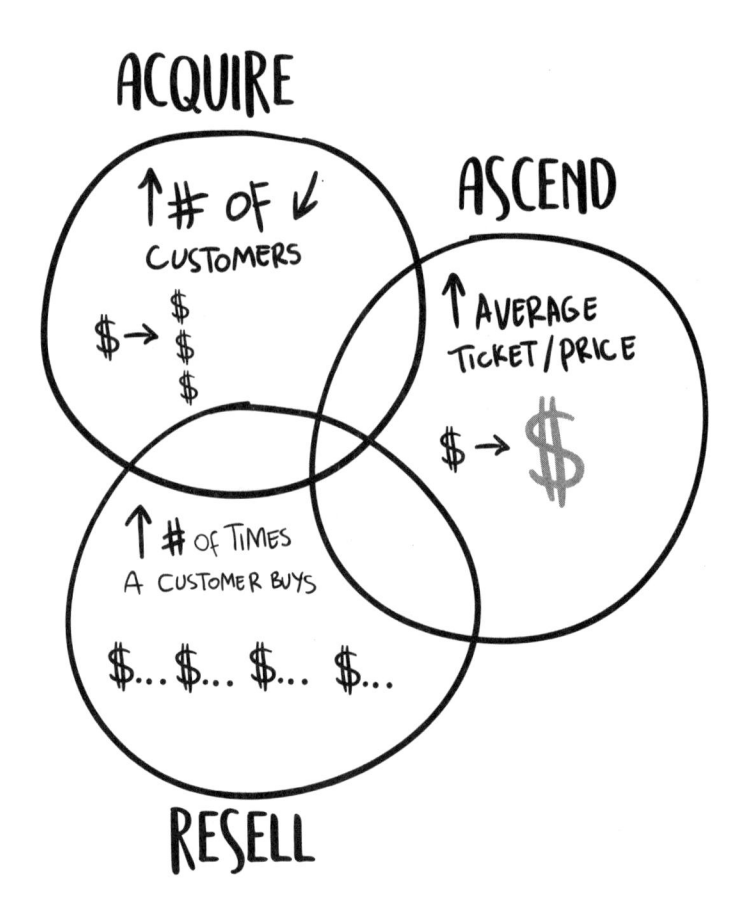

ACQUIRE
↑ # OF ↙ CUSTOMERS
$ → $
$
$

ASCEND
↑ AVERAGE TICKET / PRICE
$ → $

RESELL
↑ # OF TIMES A CUSTOMER BUYS
$... $... $... $...

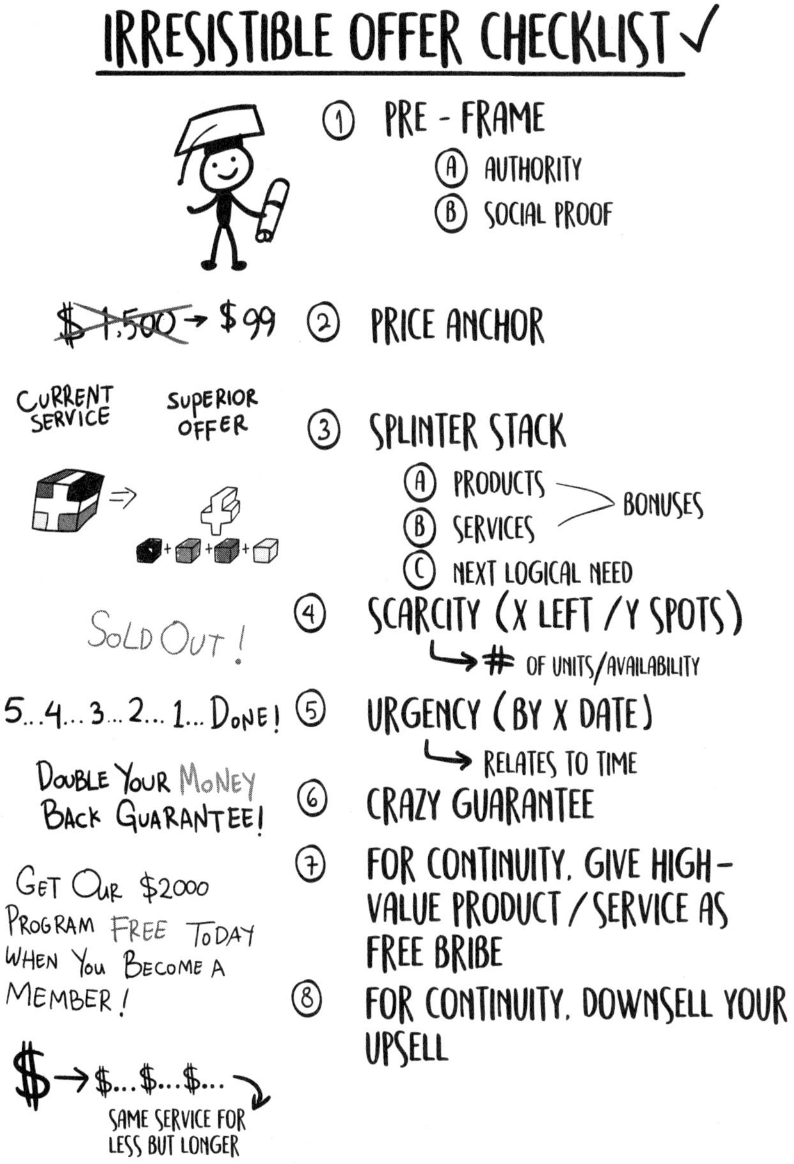

IRRESISTIBLE OFFER CHECKLIST ✓

1. **PRE - FRAME**
   - (A) AUTHORITY
   - (B) SOCIAL PROOF

2. **PRICE ANCHOR**

3. **SPLINTER STACK**
   - (A) PRODUCTS ⎫
   - (B) SERVICES ⎬ BONUSES
   - (C) NEXT LOGICAL NEED

4. **SCARCITY (X LEFT / Y SPOTS)**
   ↳ # OF UNITS/AVAILABILITY

5. **URGENCY (BY X DATE)**
   ↳ RELATES TO TIME

6. **CRAZY GUARANTEE**

7. **FOR CONTINUITY, GIVE HIGH-VALUE PRODUCT/SERVICE AS FREE BRIBE**

8. **FOR CONTINUITY, DOWNSELL YOUR UPSELL**

CLIENT-FINANCED ACQUISITION®

① CREATE HIGH-TICKET FRONT-END PRODUCT
② MAKE MORE MONEY ON FRONT-END SALES THAN YOU DO ON LEAD COST/ADS
③ NEVER NEED A MKTG BUDGET EVER AGAIN

EX:

100% PROFIT →

	DAY 1	DAY 2	DAY 3	DAY 4	DAY 5
SPEND	$100	$100	$100	$100	$100
LEADS	10	10	10	10	10
SALES %	20%	20%	20%	20%	20%
SALES	2	2	2	2	2
PRICE	$600	$600	$600	$600	$600
REV	$1200	$1200	$1200	$1200	$1200
DEPOSIT	$0	$0	$0	$2400	$3600
BANK ACCT	-$100	-$200	-$300	$2000	$3100

NOTE*: I SHOW A DELAY BECAUSE MOST PROCESSORS TAKE 72 HRS TO RELEASE FUNDS. SO THIS GIVES YOU REAL CASH FLOW #s.

LEAD GEN SCRAMBLER
NEVER STRUGGLE TO MAKE "FRESH" ADS AGAIN

① **HEADLINE:** -DURATION -GENDER -BENEFIT/STATUS ↑
-CURIOSITY -AGAINST FEAR -NEGATIVE -CHALLENGE

② **COPY:** -SHORT -LONG -FREE -NEW
-REASON WHY -BENEFITS -STATUS
-SO THAT YOU CAN -DESCRIBE, DONT TELL
-SCARCITY -URGENCY -IMPLIED AUTHORITY

③ **PAGE NAME/BUSINESS NAME:**
-HAVE MULTIPLE VERSIONS
-DESCRIPTIVE -3rd PARTY

④ **IMAGE:** -↑CONTRAST -BLACK/WHITE -BANNERS -DIAGONAL
-GROUP PICS -SELFIE -WORKOUT PICS -PEOPLE IN CLASS
-PEOPLE SWEATING POST CLASS -MEME -DOO-DADS

⑤ **VIDEO:** -FLASH CARDS -BACKGROUND -SCENERY
-PRO U. IPHONE -SUBTITLES -PITCHING -FACILITY TOUR -WHITEBOARD
-GROUP TESTIMONIAL -AVG JOE TESTIMONIAL -SELFIE TESTIMONIAL
-GROUP EXERCISE IN UNISON -GET CLIENTS TO SAY HOW GREAT YOU ARE

ENTER
PROSPECT
1
TEAM
GREET WITHIN
10 SECONDS BY NAME
2 SIGN-IN
FITNESS CHALLENGE
SIGN UPS
3 TESTIMONIAL
"WAITING" ROOM/AREA
WOW!
DETAILS :
A OVERWHELMING
SOCIAL PROOF
DETAILS : A PAGE SHOULD BE ¾ FULL
B TITLE SHOULD
ASSUME THE CLOSE
C HAVE MANY USED UP
SIGN-IN SHEETS
UNDERNEATH
4 FILL OUT PRE-SELL
QUESTIONNAIRE
5 EXPERT COMES OUT OF OFFICE
TO ESCORT BACK ...
6 SALES OFFICE SETUP
I NEED HELP
I WILL TRY
I AM SERIOUS
PROSPECT
YOU
A STACK OF
SIGNED CONTRACTS
B HAVE LOTS OF
CHAIRS
C NEVER SIT
ACROSS A TABLE
D TRY TO BE
ADJACENT

THE CLOSER FORMULA

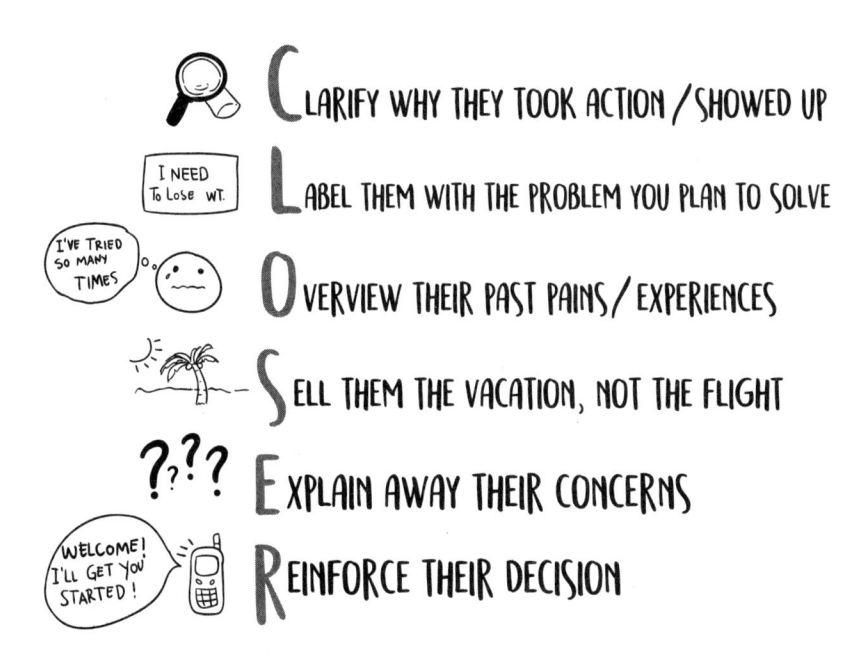

CLARIFY WHY THEY TOOK ACTION / SHOWED UP

LABEL THEM WITH THE PROBLEM YOU PLAN TO SOLVE

OVERVIEW THEIR PAST PAINS / EXPERIENCES

SELL THEM THE VACATION, NOT THE FLIGHT

EXPLAIN AWAY THEIR CONCERNS

REINFORCE THEIR DECISION

PROBLEM PAIN CYCLE:
OVERVIEW OF PAST EXPERIENCES

① WHAT HAVE YOU DONE? ←────────────┐
② HOW LONG DID YOU DO IT FOR? HOW LONG AGO?
③ HOW DID THAT WORK FOR YOU?

CATEGORIZE: ALIGN SELF WITH POSITIVES, REPEL SELF FROM NEGATIVES/GAPS

	FITNESS	NUTRITION	ACCOUNTABILITY
BIG BOX GYM	X		
PERSONAL TRAINER	X		X
WEIGHT WATCHERS JENNY CRAIG FOOD-BASED SYSTEMS		X	X
PILLS, SHAKES, SUPPLEMENT-ONLY		X	
WORKOUT FROM HOME	X		

④ WHAT ELSE HAVE YOU DONE? ────────┘

BELIEF-BREAKING FORMULA

EXAMPLE:

1. "SO YOU BELIEVE CHEAP FRONT-END OFFERS WORK?"
2. "THIS DOESN'T PROVIDE CASH FLOW TO MARKET OR ACQUIRE CUSTOMERS"
3. "USE A HIGH-TICKET FRONT END ACQUISITION"
4. "IT'LL ALLOW YOU TO SPEND WHATEVER YOU NEED TO GET PEOPLE IN PROFITABLY"
5. "DON'T BELIEVE ME OR THE MATH?... BELIEVE 1000+ OTHER GYMS"

FORMULA

1. SAY WHAT THEY BELIEVE
2. SAY WHY IT IS WRONG
3. SAY WHAT IT IS RIGHT
4. SAY **WHY** IT IS RIGHT
5. SHOW **PROOF** (3rd PARTY STATS + TESTIMONIALS)

idonthatemoney.com

THE PROBLEM

INDUSTRY AVG : $118/MO UNLIMITED SESSIONS

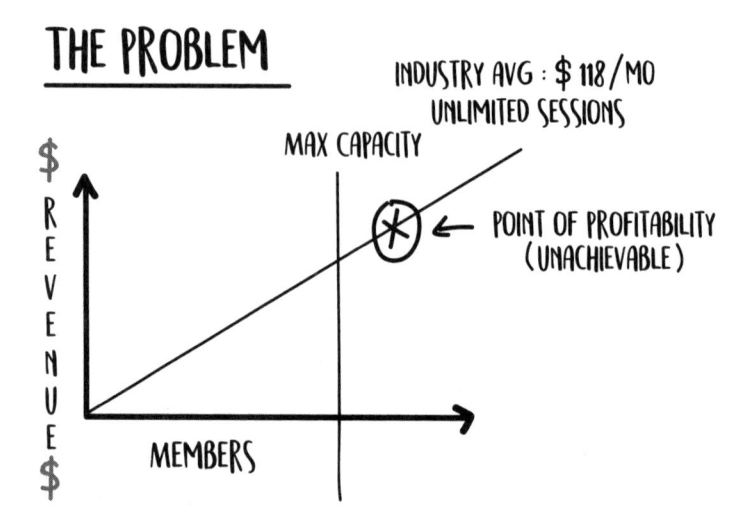

MAX CAPACITY

$ REVENUE $

MEMBERS

POINT OF PROFITABILITY (UNACHIEVABLE)

EX : A LARGE GROUP TRAINING FACILITY HAS A CAP OF
16 PEOPLE / SESSION
AVG EFT = $120/MO
CURRENT = 100 MEMBERS
DAILY SESSIONS = 7
MAX CAP_1 = 114 (ASSUMING 100% COME DAILY)
MAX CAP_2 = 134 (ASSUMING 85% INDUSTRY AVG ATTENDANCE)
MAX REV = $16.000/MO (134 x $120)

$14,500
- RENT = $4250
- PAYROLL = $4000 (163 SESSIONS x $25) + $2750 ADMIN
- MKTG = $1000
- UTILITIES/SOFTWARE/CLEANING = $1750
- MISC = $750

OWNER PAY = $1500
PROFIT = $0

VIRTUOUS VS. VICIOUS CYCLE OF PRICE $

⬇ PRICE	YOUR CLIENTS	PRICE ⬆
DECREASE	EMOTIONAL INVESTMENT	INCREASE
DECREASE	PERCEIVED VALUE	INCREASE
DECREASE	RESULTS	INCREASE
INCREASE	DEMANDINGNESS	DECREASE
DECREASE	REVENUE FOR FULFILLMENT PER CUSTOMER	INCREASE

⬇ PRICE	YOUR BUSINESS	PRICE ⬆
DECREASE	PROFIT	INCREASE
DECREASE	PERCEIVED VALUE OF SELF	INCREASE
DECREASE	PERCEPTION OF IMPACT (RESULTS)	INCREASE
DECREASE	SERVICE LEVELS	INCREASE
DECREASE	SALES TEAM CONVICTION	INCREASE

MEMBERSHIP PRICE BUYING CURVE

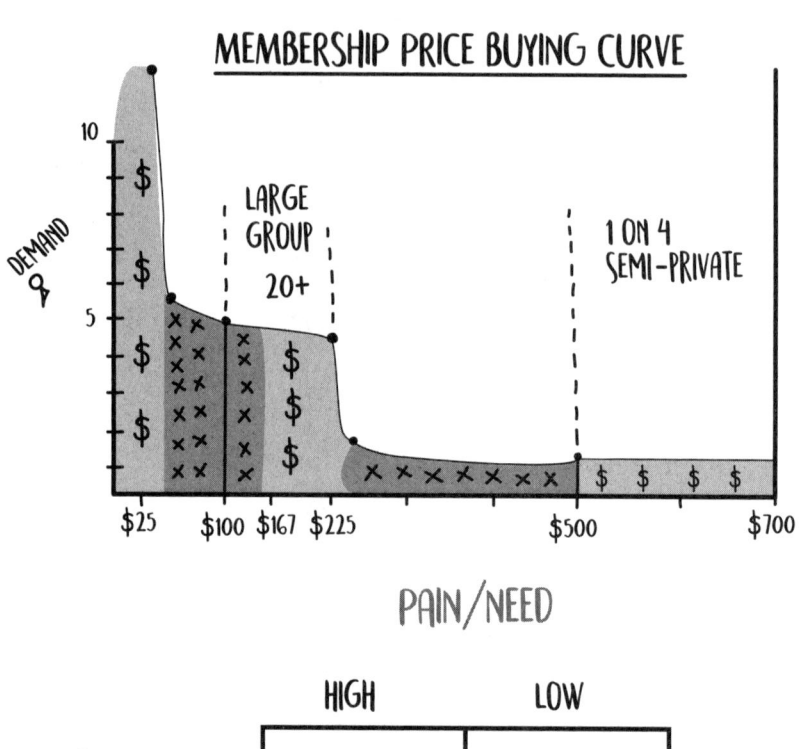

	HIGH	LOW
HIGH (Income)	$499+/MO	$199/MO
LOW (Income)	$499/MO	$199/MO

PAIN/NEED

THE "PIE" EQUATION

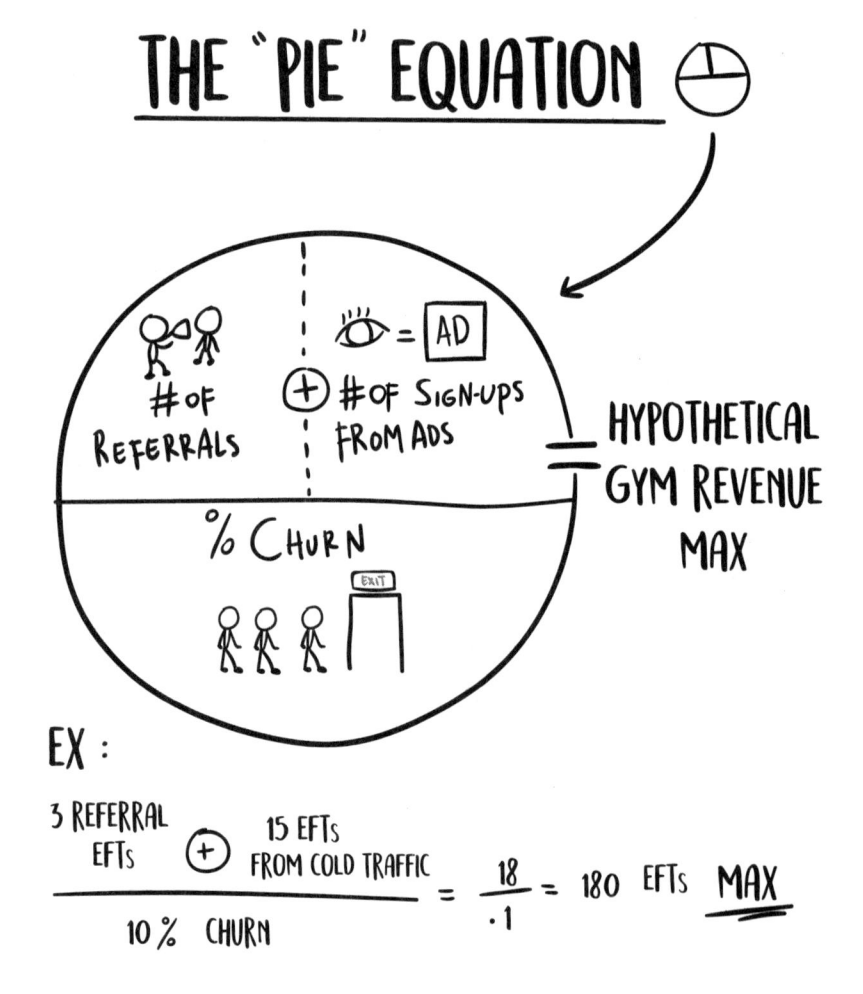

$$\frac{\text{\# of Referrals} + \text{\# of Sign-ups from Ads}}{\text{\% Churn}} = \text{HYPOTHETICAL GYM REVENUE MAX}$$

EX:

$$\frac{3 \text{ REFERRAL EFTs} + 15 \text{ EFTs FROM COLD TRAFFIC}}{10\% \text{ CHURN}} = \frac{18}{.1} = 180 \text{ EFTs } \underline{\text{MAX}}$$

DETERIORATING SERVICE DELIVERY

TIME

	BEGINNING →	NOW
SERVICE LEVEL	NEW, PERSONAL, UNDERDOG, DEALS	BROKEN-IN, HOURLY TEAMMATES, "OWNER", COMMODITIZED
CHURN BY %	SMALL	LARGE
COMMUNITY	OPEN, INVITING	OGs, CLIQUES
TYPE OF TRAFFIC	REFERRALS	LBOS, COLD TRAFFIC

ICING (FRONT END CASH) ← | → CAKE (RECURRING CASH)

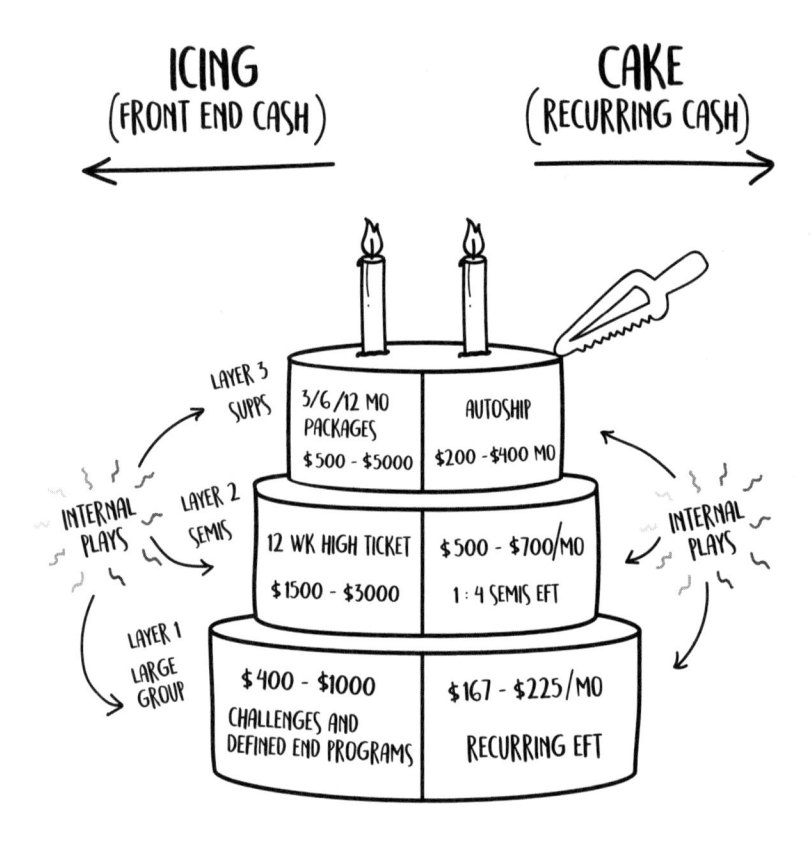

Layer 3 — Supps
- 3/6/12 MO PACKAGES — $500 - $5000
- AUTOSHIP — $200 - $400 MO

Layer 2 — Semis (Internal Plays)
- 12 WK HIGH TICKET — $1500 - $3000
- $500 - $700/MO — 1:4 SEMIS EFT

Layer 1 — Large Group
- $400 - $1000 — CHALLENGES AND DEFINED END PROGRAMS
- $167 - $225/MO — RECURRING EFT

Acknowledgements

So many people have guided me to where I am today to make this book possible. To name them all would require a book in and of itself. But in an effort to be concise...

I want to thank Dan Kennedy. I owe a debt of gratitude to this man. He taught me so much. Broke my beliefs and changed my life forever, without even meeting me. I promised myself when I read and re-read his books that when I wrote my first book, he would be thanked.

I want to thank Russell Brunson for believing in me and having a group of entrepreneurs who took this young gym owner in and gave me the conviction to break the mold. I still don't know where I would be if I hadn't joined your Inner Circle on a whim that fateful day in February. Thousands of gym owners—and, by extension, hundreds of thousands of people—would not have been impacted if it were not for your guidance and belief pattern breaking.

Thank you to Alex Charfen for your friendship. Your intense understanding of the "being" of entrepreneurs has made me more comfortable in my own skin. You helped me lean into the oddness that most would call intolerance. You helped me create tranquility through structure. The team, our clients, and my relationship wouldn't be the same without it.

Thank you, Dr. Trevor Kashey, for the uncompromising effort you put into the supplement line. Hundreds of thousands of lives have been impacted by your hard work, and gym owners can finally sell a product with conviction.

I want to thank Henry Ospitia for teaching me the value of attention.

I want to thank Travis Jones for helping me get started early on. I'll never forget it.

I want to thank Carlos Negrete and John Waite for teaching me about partnerships and for believing in me early on.

I want to thank Sam Bakhtiar for responding to my email and opening up his doors to me long ago.

And thank you to Julie Eason and her team for helping make this book a reality.

About The Author

When Alex started his first gym and realized his rent was more than what he had left in his bank account, he learned fast that he needed to figure out a way to turn leads into walk-ins into sales. And he did. Since then, he has closed over 4,000 one-on-one sales and trained a sales team of 10 to do the same. He now runs his company, Gym Launch, which specializes in high-ticket lead generation and sales with his elite sales staff for bootcamps, crosscuts, and small-group training studios. He helps gyms go from zero to capacity in 30 days or less.